To
Gervase
with love.
from Joe

KL   1st Ed 1945

£1.25

THE ROMANCE OF THE ENGLISH THEATRE

John Gielgud in *Love for Love* (from the painting by Anthony Devas)

THE ROMANCE OF THE
ENGLISH
THEATRE

by

DONALD BROOK

SALISBURY SQUARE · LONDON · E.C. 4

1945

COPYRIGHT 1945

PRINTED AT
THE BURLEIGH PRESS
LEWIN'S MEAD
BRISTOL

CONTENTS

ILLUSTRATIONS

7

INTRODUCTORY NOTE

THIS is a book for the "ordinary" playgoer who is sufficiently interested in drama to be mindful of its past and careful for its future. It tells the story of the English theatre in a way which, I hope, will interest and help the many thousands who can see in the renascence of our national culture a means of ensuring the happiness, enlightenment and general well-being of our people.

Owing to the severity of the paper rationing, I have been compelled to condense what would normally have been a book of at least five hundred pages into a volume of barely two hundred pages of text, and although I hope that the illustrations in this book will to some extent compensate for its brevity, I beg the reader's indulgence if my efforts to summarize have overloaded the story with bare facts.

I also regret that it has been impossible to include the complete history of all the provincial theatres that have played so important a part in the making of this country's theatrical history. A fairly representative number of them appear in the following pages, but I am fully aware that there is much information of importance and interest which must wait for more propitious times to be recorded.

Finally, may I thank all those who have so kindly assisted me in obtaining information and illustrations.

DONALD BROOK.

London,
January, 1945.

Chapter I

EARLY DRAMA

TO trace the origins of drama we should have to go back far into the ancient histories of Egypt, China, Greece and Rome, and even then it would be impossible to discover precisely when people began to express their emotions by acting. We may safely assume, however, that drama evolved from the primitive dancing and music that characterized the early forms of worship.

Until the twelfth century, there was little that could be called drama in England; but in those early days the folk festivals, which were responsible for the earliest forms of folk-drama, were developing rapidly. More and more dramatic action was put into the tremendously popular sword and Morris dances; more music and songs were added, until finally, with the introduction of dialogue, there emerged what was generally known as the Mummers' Play. This is really the foundation of English drama.

It seems that the Mummers did not always perform plays. They were little bands of men (and occasionally women) who ensured that their villages took part in the general gaiety of the traditional festivals by dressing up in fantastic clothes and going about indulging in varying degrees of tomfoolery. Some historians insist that women were never allowed to act as Mummers, but there is little evidence to prove this, although there is no doubt that any women who were permitted to take part were kept very much in the background.

In all parts of the country there was great enthusiasm for the Mummers' Play. The principals were St. George, Captain Slasher, the Doctor and the Turkish Knight, but they had a " full supporting cast " of plenty of minor characters ! The play itself varied considerably according to local taste and ingenuity, but the fact that one of the participants was invariably slain and then miraculously restored to life by the Doctor, suggests that the universal theme was the celebration of the death of the old year and the idea of resurrection associated with the coming of the new.

The lord of the manor frequently took a keen interest in the local Mummers' Play, and it was a common occurrence to find the village folk being invited to perform in the hall of the manor house. One can well imagine this typically English scene. On May Day, at harvest time, or on Christmas Eve, the lord of the manor with his family and friends would form the nucleus of an audience at one end of the hall, and the Mummers with blackened faces or wearing masks would perform at the other. At the end of the play the performers would take a collection to defray the cost of making their costumes, and then the lord of the manor would provide refreshments liberally for everybody.

Now let us see what other forms of drama there were in mediæval times. So few of the people could read the bible that the clergy would often act plays in the churches to bring home to their congregations the stories from the scriptures. These Mystery and Miracle plays had a most important effect upon the growth of drama in England, though they lacked the force and national character of the Mummers' Play.

Miracle plays generally depicted incidents in the lives of the saints and martyrs, and Mystery plays dealt more with the story of man's fall and redemption. Such cities as York, Coventry, Wakefield and Chester were famous for them, and in London they were a regular occurrence at Clerkenwell and Skinner's Well.

On much the same lines were the Morality plays, which were intended to illustrate the conflict between good and evil in the life of man, but in these the characters were abstract: they were personifications of vice, folly, chastity, wisdom, and so forth. The play called *Everyman* is an excellent example.

Performed originally in Latin by the priests and choir-boys, the Miracle and Mystery plays gradually gave way to the Morality plays, and became more secularized. More and more of the laity took part in them, the English language was adopted, and they became more entertaining than uplifting. In time, the religious element became decidedly threadbare, and the perfectly natural desire of the people to be amused led to a great deal of profanity, which, of course, horrified the clergy, who subsequently dropped out of the picture altogether. By this time, the plays had already grown so elaborate and irreligious that they had been moved out of the churches, and were being performed on stages erected in the open and visible from all sides.

Historical matter—often of an entirely irrelevant nature— found its way into many of these plays, and became so popular that it tended to transform them into dramas of history or fable. This explains the fact that when in the sixteenth century men began seriously to write drama, they generally turned to history for their plots or themes. Even the early dramatists were careful to give the people what they wanted!

THE FIRST PROFESSIONALS

By this time, the professional actor had already come into being. As the plays moved into the sphere of pure entertainment, experienced men with a flair for acting would visit the villages and towns in their vicinity and offer their services in return for payment. To what extent this was done is not at all certain—they were rarely employed in the Mummers' plays, which were invariably performed by the villagers themselves—but very often these " professionals " would find that they could make a livelihood by going around from town to town and would naturally prefer to do so rather than to toil upon the land.

We have to go but one stage further to see how the first troupes of actors were formed. The odd " professional " actor soon met others in the course of his work, particularly if he frequented the larger towns, and found that it paid him better to join a little company of actors that could perform without bothering with amateurs. All over the country these little troupes were forming in the sixteenth century. Generally they consisted of four, five or six men and a boy, the latter being compelled to play the feminine parts. Some of the men were quite intelligent individuals ; men who had been minstrels or entertainers in the houses of the wealthy, but it was not at all uncommon to find with them persons of the very lowest type—vagabonds who had been taken up when the little band was deficient in number.

These troupes played in the residences of the nobility, on village greens, or wherever an audience could be found. A favourite spot was the yard of the old galleried inn, not because of the proximity of stimulating refreshment, but because these taverns were like ready-made amphitheatres. Apart from the fact that a good audience was always assured, wealthy individuals and persons of high rank were frequently to be found there, and as we shall see in a moment, the players had a good reason for ingratiating themselves with the nobility.

The troupes paid very little, if anything, to the landlord for the use of his yard. In most cases he was a genial soul, fond of amusement and quite willing to allow the players to add to the amenities of his house.   Their chief difficulty was in the collection of money, because most people regarded the inn-yard as a public place, and were not always very polite when the players demanded a penny or two for services rendered.   It was rarely possible to charge for admission to the yard : the players had to be content to scramble round after the performance collecting up money wherever they could.

In London, the Cross Keys in Gracechurch Street, La Belle Sauvage on Ludgate Hill, the Bull in Bishopsgate Street, the Boar's Head in Eastcheap and the famous old Tabard Inn at Southwark were regularly used by troupes of actors.   A perfect specimen of the galleried inn beloved by the players is the New Inn at Gloucester.   Here you can still see and walk around the splendid galleries where the well-to-do patrons of the hostelry sat and watched the players in the yard below.

At inns of this type, the poorer folk would gather in the yard at the opposite end to the actors and stand while the play was in progress.   Unfortunately there is evidence that " the pit " would sometimes get very rowdy, but this can be readily understood when one considers that the ale was very much stronger than it is to-day.   The Puritans, of course, looked upon these dramatic performances with horror, for after the play the landlord would often entertain liberally, and the merry-making was apt to become riotous before the end of the evening.

It must not be imagined that these troupes had an easy life, in fact, the laws of vagrancy and the precariousness of their liveli-hood made most of them seek the protection and continual support of rich and powerful patrons.   Many of the noblemen at that time assisted by engaging them as members of their permanent household staffs, giving food and clothing in return for entertain-ment at banquets.   When they were not required by their patron, the players were permitted to entertain in the villages for the benefit of the tenants of the estates, and to visit neighbouring towns.

In 1572 this system of patronage was officially approved and made compulsory, for a statute was introduced compelling all troupes to obtain a licence from a nobleman.   Thus they became known by the name of their licensor : " The Earl of Leicester's Men," " The Lord Admiral's Servants," and so forth.   As we shall see later, some of the companies became highly skilled in dramatic art, and it was quite a common occurrence for them to visit the large cities to perform in the Guildhall at the invitation

Performance of a Mystery Play at Coventry (above)
A Play in an Inn-yard in Elizabethan times

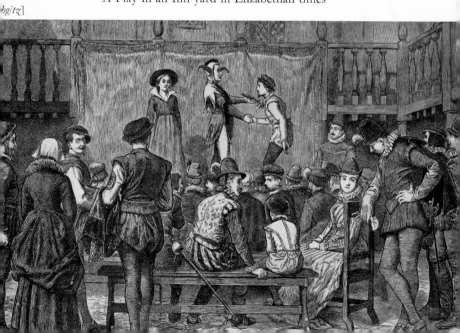

THE GLOBE THEATRE,

On the 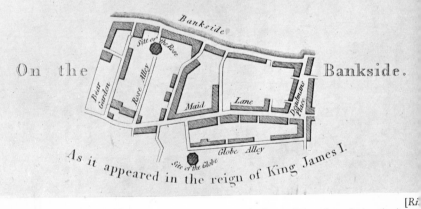 Bankside.

As it appeared in the reign of King James I.

The 2nd Globe Theatre (from an engraved view of London circa 1612)

of the Mayor. On such occasions as this they were generally paid from the Corporation funds.

COURT PERFORMANCES

There remain two other factors to be considered before we conclude this opening chapter. First, the influence of the court. By this time, various forms of entertainment, including masques and pageants, had become extremely fashionable with royalty. Before Queen Elizabeth came to the throne there was in office a Master of the Revels who was responsible for such festivities. He was in charge of all the arrangements, costumes, materials, etc., and generally employed a small band of tailors, painters, weavers, haberdashers and carpenters. It is recorded that he was expected to be competent in " skill of devise, in understandinge of historyes, in iudgement of comedyes, tragedyes and shewes, in sight of perspective and architecture," and to have " some smacke of geometrye and other thynges."

From the middle of the sixteenth century onwards, plays were far more popular at court than the traditional masques, until James I revived the latter on astonishingly elaborate lines. The Queen's preference for the plays is important, because had it not been for this royal interest, drama might have been stamped out by the Puritans just as it was approaching its most glorious years. Moreover it brought the players more into touch with court life, because whereas the ladies and gentlemen of the court had been accustomed to appear in the masques and pageants, the tendency was for the plays to be performed exclusively by professional actors.

DRAMA IN THE SCHOOLS

The schools and colleges were also making an important contribution to the development of dramatic art. At Eton and Westminster, classical plays were encouraged, and the boys of St. Paul's School had the honour of performing plays of Plautus and Terence, the great Roman dramatists, before Cardinal Wolsey. During the sixteenth century, dramatic activity spread throughout our educational establishments, in fact it was Nicholas Udall [1506–1556], headmaster first of Eton and then of Westminster, who wrote the first complete English comedy divided into acts on classical lines—*Ralph Roister Doister*.

Chapter II

THE FIRST THEATRES

DURING the reign of Queen Elizabeth, London expanded rapidly, and with the exception of the Puritans, its prosperous citizens became ardent lovers of sport and amusement. Even those who were not particularly prosperous became infected with the love of entertainment. Observing this, James Burbage, a carpenter who had become an actor and joined the " Earl of Leicester's Men," decided to build a public playhouse near the capital. It had to be *near*, and not *in* London because the Mayor and many of the city fathers were Puritans of a most vinegary variety, and made it quite clear what would happen if he dared to erect his temple of iniquity within the city boundaries.

So Burbage found a site between Shoreditch and Finsbury Fields, just outside the jurisdiction of the Mayor, and in 1576 erected a circular wooden structure at a cost of between six and seven hundred pounds. He called it simply The Theatre. It was supposed to have accommodated over a thousand people, but this, I think, is rather doubtful. Having played in many of the inn-yards, Burbage naturally built his theatre on much the same lines as the galleried inn, except that he made it circular instead of rectangular. Little is known of its structural details except that it had galleries around the yard (the pit) and that this was open to the sky. The stage had a balcony at the rear, beneath which a curtain was hung to form a small inner stage, and on either side of this there was probably a " tiring house " in which costumes and properties, such as they had, were kept.

However primitive it was, The Theatre served its purpose very well, for drama thrived in it for over twenty years, and it was only when a quarrel arose concerning its lease that Burbage's two sons pulled it down and used its timber to build The Globe, of which we shall hear more later.

It was to The Theatre that William Shakespeare came when in 1590, or thereabouts, he first appeared in London; and it is highly probable that on its stage were performed *The Comedy of Errors, Love's Labour's Lost, The Two Gentlemen of Verona, Romeo*

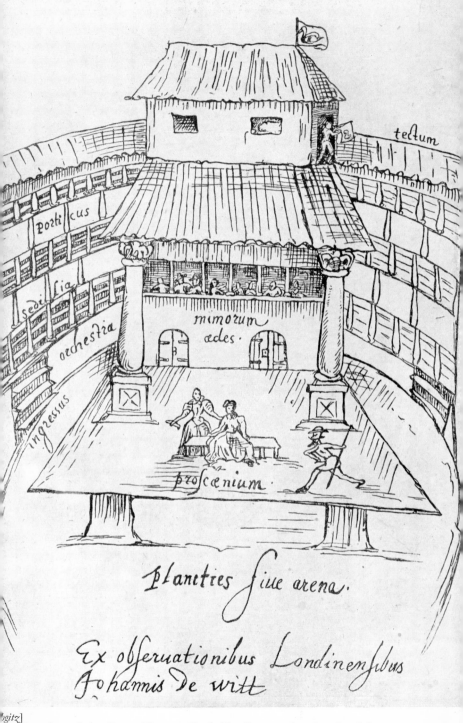

Interior of the Swan Theatre, Bankside (from a drawing by Johannes de Witt)

EDWARD ALLEYN (from the painting at Dulwich College)

and Juliet, A Midsummer Night's Dream, Richard II, King John, The Merchant of Venice and *Henry IV*. The leading actors in the company were Richard Burbage—son of James Burbage, Henry Condell and John Heminge. Augustine Phillips was the clown. It was Condell and Heminge who after Shakespeare's death undertook the publication of the first printed collection of his plays.

The year 1576 is also significant because it saw the establishment of the first Blackfriars Theatre : a small " private " playhouse adapted from six upper rooms by Richard Farrant for the use of certain of the Children of the Chapel, Windsor, who were child actors connected with the court. The so-called " private " theatres of the Shakespearean period were smaller theatres to which the more aristocratic playgoers resorted. They were little more than large halls with a stage at one end, though they probably had galleries of some sort.

No sooner had Burbage opened The Theatre than another was built in Moorfields on a piece of land called Curtayne Close. This was called The Curtain, after the name of its site, and not because its builder had a theatrical curtain in mind. It was run by Henry Laneman, who apparently sought an alliance with Burbage against the animosity of the Puritans.

In the following year, the bigoted John Northbrooke published a pamphlet called *A Treatise against Dicing, Dancing, Plays and Interludes* in which he declared that : " . . . Satan hath not a more speedie way and fitter schoole to work and teach his desire, to bring men and women into his snare of concupiscence and filthie lustes of wicked whoredom, than those places, plays and theatres are ; and therefore necessary that those places and players shoulde be forbidden, and dissolved, and put down by authoritie, as the brothell houses and stewes are . . ." This had very little effect, and even when some twenty years later the Lord Mayor succeeded in persuading the Queen to suppress the playhouses, the order was never carried out. It ran : " Her Majestie being informed that there are verie greate disorders committed at the common playhouses both by lewd matters that are handled on the stages, and by resorte and confluence of bad people, hath given direction that not onlie no playes be used within London or about the Citty, or in any other publick place, during this tyme of sommer, but that also those playhouses that are erected and built onlie for suche purposes shall be plucked downe, namelie the Curtayne and the Theatre nere to Shoreditch. . . ."

Nevertheless, the playhouses remained and prospered. The Rose was built on the Bankside in 1591 or thereabouts, and used first by "Lord Strange's Men." It was circular and had a thatched roof to its galleries, but the pit was roofless.

Larger than any before it was The Swan, a twelve-sided theatre erected in 1594. According to some historians, it was not very suitable for dramatic productions, and it was frequently used for other purposes : exhibitions and cruel sports. After 1621 it was used only for prize-fighting.

In 1598 Burbage's two sons pulled down The Theatre and took its great oak timbers to Bankside, where they made their builder erect The Globe, the most famous theatre of its time. The work was finished in the following year, and it was opened with a performance of *King Henry V*. It was for this theatre and "The Lord Chamberlain's Men" that Shakespeare wrote his most famous plays. It was almost certainly circular in shape, for in the prologue to *King Henry V* we find :

> " . . . . Can this cockpit hold
> The vasty fields of France, or may we cram
> Within this wooden O, the very casques
> That did affright the air at Agincourt ? "

Its galleries, like those of The Rose, had thatched roofs, but from all accounts it seems to have been a somewhat utilitarian structure with a bare wooden platform—" this unworthy scaffold " as Shakespeare called it. For all that, Shakespeare was very attached to this theatre. The years 1599 to 1613 were its most glorious. Here, Richard Burbage played the principal rôles in the first performances of *Julius Cæsar*, *Hamlet*, *Othello*, *King Lear*, *Macbeth*, *Timon of Athens*, *Anthony and Cleopatra*, *Coriolanus*, *Cymbeline*, *The Winter's Tale* and *The Tempest*, not to mention the plays of Ben Jonson and the other great writers of the day.

On 29th June, 1613, a rather lavish performance of *King Henry VIII* was being staged at The Globe. When in Act I scene iv the King arrived as one of a company of masquers at the house of Cardinal Wolsey, a volley of shots was fired. Alas ! the wad of one hit the thatched roof and in a few moments the whole theatre was ablaze. All the audience, it is said, escaped unhurt, though one gentleman had his breeches set on fire and had to be extinguished with a bottle of ale.

The Puritans immediately went about saying that this fire was God's judgement on the theatre, and there appeared a sonnet about the " dolefull tragedie ". However, a new Globe theatre was erected within a year ; a more substantial structure, octagonal, and with a tiled roof. But it began to decline in 1635 and was pulled down by the Puritans nine years later [April 15th, 1644].

The Hope, another octagonal theatre, was built in 1614, on much the same design as The Swan. It had brick foundations, a tiled roof, external staircases to the galleries and a moveable stage. One of its special features was its exceptional comfort in the more expensive parts : there were boxes " convenient and suitable for gentlemen to sit in ". Its company was " The Lady Elizabeth's Servants ", the leading actor being Nathaniel Field, who had previously found fame as a child actor. This theatre was later used for prize-fights and bull-baiting.

More elaborate still was The Fortune, a square theatre built north of the Thames, near Golden Lane in the parish of St. Giles, in 1600. It had brick foundations and wooden framework. There were " gentlemen's rooms " and " twopenny rooms " with ceilings, and its interior was handsomely plastered. It boasted a stage forty-three feet wide extending into the middle of the pit. This theatre opened in 1601 with a performance by " The Lord Admiral's Men," who afterwards became " The Prince's Men ". Twenty years afterwards it was destroyed by fire : everything was lost, including all the costumes and " play-books ", but a new building, circular and constructed of brick, was built within two years.

Nobody seems to know exactly when The Red Bull theatre in Clerkenwell was erected, but it probably occupied the site of an inn of the same name. It was used by " The Queen's Men," but in its later years it seems to have catered for a very vulgar type of audience. Curiously enough, it survived the Civil War and the Commonwealth, and even when Cromwell prohibited all plays, it was used occasionally for secret performances. At the Restoration, it was the first theatre to re-open, but its company was very poor. We know this because Samuel Pepys visited it on March 23, 1661, and afterwards wrote : " To the Red Bull, where I had not been since plays come up again . . . into the pitt, where I think there was not above ten more than myself, and not one hundred in the whole house. And the play, which is called *All's Lost by Lust*, poorly done ; and with so much disorder, among others, in the musique room, the boy that was to sing a song, not singing it right, his master fell about his ears and beat him so, that it put the whole house into an uproar." The Red Bull still existed in 1663, but it was in a sorry state. In D'Avenant's play *A Theatre to Let* it was said to have no other " lodgers " than the spiders.

THE PRIVATE THEATRES

It will be recalled that in 1576 Richard Farrant established a small private theatre at Blackfriars for the use of the Children of the Chapel. The six upper rooms from which it was adapted included part of the refectory of the old Priory, and it was undoubtedly these premises, not far from where Blackfriars Station stands to-day, that James Burbage acquired when in 1596 he purchased for six hundred pounds " all those seaven greate upper Romes as they are now divided, being all upon one flower and sometyme being one greate and entire rome."

On hearing of this transaction the citizens of the Blackfriars district petitioned the Privy Council : " That whereas one Burbage hath lately bought certaine roomes . . . and meaneth very shortly to convert and turne the same into a common playhouse which will grow to be a very greate annoyance and trouble . . . that therefore it would please your honors to take order that the same roomes may be converted to some other use, and that no playhouse may be used or kept there. . . ."

It was not Burbage's intention to erect a " common playhouse " at all, for he turned the premises into a private theatre which he continued to call The Blackfriars. In any case, the petition was ignored, for in 1597 he died, and his sons let the theatre to The Children of the Chapel, or rather to Henry Evans, " of Blackfriars, London ; gentleman," who was in charge of those of the choristers who formed the body of child actors.

At this time the Children of the Chapel were enjoying considerable fame, for their company included Nathaniel Field and several others who distinguished themselves on the stage in later years. The company at The Globe was evidently a trifle jealous of the boys' success : in *Hamlet* we find Shakespeare describing them through the lips of Rosencrantz as " . . . an aery of children, little eyasses, that cry out on the top of question, and are most tyrannically clapped for't ; these are now the fashion." Incidentally, their master Henry Evans let his enthusiasm run away with him, or perhaps it was just because he was lining his own pockets with the boys' earnings, for he was eventually convicted by the Star Chamber for kidnapping talented boys to fill vacancies in his company.

In 1608 the Burbage brothers took over The Blackfriars and operated it in connection with The Globe, with " The King's Men." Many famous plays were produced in it before it was destroyed in 1655.

Of the theatre at Whitefriars, which at one time also housed a company of child-actors, we have little authentic information, except that it was replaced in 1629 by a " faire new playhouse " called The Salisbury Court. This was the last theatre to be built before the Restoration. It was closed in 1644 and deteriorated to such an extent that it had to be rebuilt when it was required again in 1660. Six years later it was destroyed by fire. Part of the site on which it stood is now occupied by the Salisbury Square offices of the publishers of this book.

In the Drury Lane district was The Phœnix, known also as The Cockpit, built in 1616 and severely damaged by the riots of the apprentices on Shrove Tuesday 1617. In the " dark days " of the theatre Sir William D'Avenant produced an opera there, but that is a story which will be told in the next chapter.

A TYPICAL SHAKESPEAREAN THEATRE

It would be impossible to give an exact description of any one of the public theatres to which I have referred, but a fairly accurate impression of the type of playhouse for which Shakespeare wrote, and in which he himself played, may be gained from general details of the average theatre of that time.

In the public theatres the pits were open to the sky, so the number of performances each week depended entirely upon the weather. Flags were hoisted when a play was to be given, but if the weather suddenly changed for the worse, the flags were pulled down and the afternoon performance cancelled. The private theatres were roofed all over, so that plays could be given daily in all weathers.

The plays were well announced beforehand on handwritten or crudely printed bills displayed on posts in various parts of the city. The thoroughness with which this publicity was carried out evidently embittered the sour old John Northbrooke. He wrote : " They use to set up their billes upon posts some certaine days before, to admonish the people to make resort to their theatres, that they may thereby be the better furnished and the people to fill their purses with their treasures." It is a pity that none of these bills has been preserved, but it is fairly certain that little more than the title of the play was announced, because the practice of proclaiming the names of the actors did not start in this country until the eighteenth century.

In the public theatres most plays were given in the afternoons, starting anytime between one and three o'clock, after trumpeters had sent out a ringing call to the playgoers of the town. Enthusiastic citizens would generally send their servants two or three hours before to occupy their seats until they were ready to take them.

The pit had no seats whatever, except in The Blackfriars and one or two other private theatres, where benches were provided.

The galleries, generally three, were made comparatively comfortable, especially the boxes. The uppermost tier was thatched or tiled.

The stage was a platform extending out into the body of the theatre, taking up nearly half of the pit, and being exposed on three sides to the audience. The main action and dialogue took place at the front of it, and there was of course no front curtain. The plays in those times had few stage directions: references to properties or even doors were nothing like so common as they are to-day, so the barest stage sufficed in most cases.

At the rear of the stage was a balcony, and there can be little doubt that in all the theatres of this period it was used with a curtain beneath it to form an inner stage, just as Burbage arranged his in The Theatre. In the old plays we find repeated references to this inner stage, particularly when characters had to be discovered there: it could be a cave, bedroom or anything in which persons or things had to be concealed for a while. The balcony itself served as an upper room, the city wall, or as any other elevated place. When it was not required by the actors it was sometimes used to accommodate the musicians. Higher still was a small room or hut in the roof: " the heavens " whence gods and goddesses could conveniently descend !

It is interesting to note how our present-day stage has evolved from this inner stage of the Shakespearean theatre. When scenery was introduced, the inner stage was used more extensively for scenes specially localized; consequently, as dramatists gave more precise directions concerning locality or properties, the inner stage became infinitely more important than the outer stage. Therefore, it grew steadily in size until it absorbed the whole of the outer stage, and ultimately became the " picture frame " stage we know so well to-day.

However, to return to the Shakespearean stage: it generally

had two doors on either side of the inner stage, and above them were usually windows or tiny balconies—sometimes both. More in the centre of the outer stage were one or two trapdoors to allow the entrance and exit of devils, ghosts and suchlike.

In the open public theatres, the plays were performed by daylight, but in the private playhouses quite brilliant illumination was provided by chandeliers. There were no footlights, of course : there is evidence that these were not introduced until 1672.

The price of admission was taken at the entrance, but there were several additional " gatherers " inside the theatre whose business it was to go around claiming the extra charges from those who occupied the better seats. These collectors were invariably a dishonest lot of rascals. Dekker dedicated one of his plays to " The Queen's Men " wishing them " a full audience and one honest door-keeper." Thomas Heywood in his *Apology for Actors* wrote " So wishing you judiciall audiences, honest poets and true gatherers, I commit you all to the fulnesse of your best wishes."

In most of the theatres one could stand in the " yard," as the pit was still called, for a penny or two, but seats in the " gentlemen's boxes " could cost as much as half-a-crown—a considerable sum in those days. Prices were doubled and even trebled for first performances. As the expenses incurred by the companies were very small (the elaborate costumes were the biggest item) quite handsome profits were made.

While waiting for the play to start the audience would amuse themselves by eating apples and nuts, drinking ale, smoking, playing cards or dice. The " groundlings " (audience in the pit) were a very mixed crowd, as one would imagine. There were generally one or two pickpockets, half a dozen prostitutes, and plenty of men rather the worse for drink who were prepared to indulge in a brawl upon the slightest provocation.

Elizabethan audiences liked to see on the stage plenty of fighting, brutality, ghosts, devils and whatnot, and loved stories of horror, rape and villany. Comedies had to be decidedly vulgar, and if they were not, the actors were apt to add obscenities of their own in one way or another. Nevertheless good poetry was appreciated, particularly by the upper classes. Even the most humble people seemed to be quick witted and intelligent, and a fine oration from the pen of Shakespeare which millions of people in this so-called enlightened age would now regard as boring, would work them up into a frenzy of delight.

Few women, except those of the lowest classes, attended the public theatre in Elizabeth's time, and those who did invariably wore masks to conceal their identity.

The pleasure of exhibiting themselves to the public eye frequently induced the vain young gallants and dandies in the audience to pay extra for the privilege of sitting on little stools at the sides of the stage. Dekker refers to this odious practice in his *Gull's Hornbooke* [1609]. In Chapter VI, under the heading " How a Gallant should behave himself in a Playhouse," he writes :

" By sitting on the stage you . . . may lawfully presume to be a girder " (i.e. a witty critic) " . . . if you be a knight you may happily get you a mistress ; if a mere Fleet-street gentleman, a wife . . . you may purchase the dear acquaintance of the boys " (i.e. the boys who played the feminine parts).

Satirically, he continues :

" Present not yourself on the stage, especially at a new play, until the quaking Prologue hath by rubbing got colour into his cheeks, and is ready to give the trumpets their cue that he is upon the point to enter ; for then it is time, as though you were one of the properties, or that you dropt out of the hangings, to creep up behind the arras, with your tripos or three-footed stool in one hand and a teston . . . (a coin then worth about six pence) . . . mounted between a forefinger and a thumb in the other ; for, if you should bestow your person upon the vulgar, when the belly of the house is but half full, your apparel is quite eaten up, the fashion lost . . . avoid that as you would the bastome. It shall crown you with rich commendation, to laugh aloud in the middest of the most serious and saddest scene of the terriblest tragedy ; and to let that clapper, your tongue, be tossed so high, that all the house may ring of it ; . . . your knights are the apes of the lords, and do so too . . . all the eyes of the galleries will leave walking after the players, and only follow you . . . you mightily disrelish the audience . . . (Dekker referred previously to the presence of a ' stinkard ') . . . and disgrace the author, . . . you take up, though it be at the worst kind, a strong opinion of your own judgement."

It seems that gallants or other individuals offended by the playwrights or by one of the actors sometimes took these stage stools for the purpose of retaliation, for Dekker continues :

" . . . if the writer be a fellow that hath either epigrammed you, or hath had a flirt at your mistress . . . you shall disgrace him worse than by tossing him in a blanket . . . if, in the middle of his play, be it pastoral or comedy, moral or tragedy, you rise with a screwed and discontented face from your stool to be gone ; no matter whether the scenes be good or no ; the better they are, the worse do you distaste them ; and being on your feet sneak not away like a coward, but salute all your gentle acquaintance . . . : their poet crieth, perhaps, ' a pox go with you ', but care not for that . . ."

THE DRAMATIC COMPANIES

The theatrical profession flourished remarkably during Shakespeare's life : many actors grew wealthy and a few found fame. Moreover, they found favour at court and acquired a definite social status. Professional companies multiplied rapidly, and many toured the provinces. Such cities as Bristol, Norwich, Coventry and Leicester were visited regularly by the London players, though almost every town of any size had a company of its own.

The prosperity and favour enjoyed by the players during the early part of the seventeenth century provoked no small amount of jealousy among men in other walks of life : they could not forget that it was not so many years since the actors were considered by all respectable people to be vagabonds. In *The Return from Parnassus*, an anonymous University play dated 1601, a student complains bitterly about the players :

> " Vile world that lifts them up to high degree,
> And treads us down in grovelling misery !
> England affords these glorious vagabonds,
> That carried erst their fardels on their backs,
> Coursers to ride on through the gazing streets,
> Sweeping it in their glaring satin suits,
> And pages to attend their masterships :
> With mouthing words that better wits have framed,
> They purchase lands, and now esquires are made."

In the space available it would be impossible to sketch even briefly the lives of all the great actors of the Elizabethan and Jacobean period, and in any case, the biographical material available is scanty and not too reliable. Yet I must tell you a little about a few of the more outstanding figures.

Richard Tarlton (or Tarleton), the beloved jester, was one of the most prominent figures of his time. He was born in Shropshire, but came to London when he was quite a young man, became an inn-keeper, married a woman of doubtful reputation named Kate, wrote ballads, taught fencing, and was eventually chosen for " The Queen's Men," remaining an actor until his death in 1588. This " Lord of Mirth " as he was called, with his flat nose and squinting eyes, was as tremendously popular at court as he was in the theatre. He was a great favourite of the Queen, and was said to be about the only person in London who could get her out of a disagreeable mood. John Stow, the famous sixteenth century chronicler wrote ". . . Richard Tarlton for a wondrous plentifull pleasant extemporall wit, hee was the wonder of his time." In the theatre, his retorts to wags in the audience were an unfailing source of delight. On one occasion a wit asked him in verse how he managed to get a flat nose. He countered it immediately with an improvisation that concluded :

[1] " Though my nose be flat,
   My credit to save,
   Yet very well I can by the smell
   Scent an honest man from a knave."

Another great actor was Edward Alleyn, who was born in 1566 and rose to fame very early in life. When he was barely twenty, he was playing leading parts as a member of " The Earl of Worcester's Men." Afterwards, he joined " The Lord Admiral's Men," and later still was associated with " The Prince's Men." With Henslowe, the eminent Elizabethan theatre manager, he built The Fortune theatre, to which I have already referred, and eventually became very wealthy. He bought the manor of Dulwich from Sir Francis Calton, and founded Dulwich College, which still possesses a full length portrait of him.

There seem to be no records to tell us precisely when William Kemp, Tarlton's successor, was born ; but we know that he began his career with " The Earl of Leicester's Men." This man has gone down in theatrical history as the player who once danced the Morris all the way from London to Norwich. He made substantial bets on his ability to do this, and then set out with a taborer, a servant and a witness, on the first Monday in Lent of 1599 (some reports give 1600 as the year). He took twenty-three days, encountered bad weather, grew distressingly weary, but eventually got there, and was welcomed by the Mayor of Norwich who gave him a prize and a pension ! It is presumed

[1] *Tarlton's Jests.*

that he was for a time one of " The Lord Chamberlain's Men," but in 1602 he joined " The Earl of Worcester's Men."

We have already noted the activities of Richard Burbage [1567 ?– 1619] as a theatre manager, but on the stage this son of James Burbage rivalled the great Edward Alleyn. His earliest experiences were gained as a boy in The Theatre, and he won membership of " The Earl of Leicester's Men " when he was quite a young man. At Christmas 1594 he was summoned with William Kemp and Shakespeare to act before the Queen at Greenwich Palace. This was Burbage's first glimpse of the court. He made his name at The Globe, however, and in a very short time his services were in great demand. He excelled in tragedy, and became very highly esteemed by the dramatists of the day. A quaint but useful account of his acting is to be found in Richard Flecknoe's *Short Discourse on the English Stage* [1660] :

" . . . he was a delightful Proteus, so wholly transforming himself into his part and putting off himself with his cloathes, as he never (not so much as in the Tyring House) assum'd himself again until the Play was done. . . . He had all the parts of an excellent actor . . . his auditors being never more delighted than when he spoke, nor so sorry than when he held his peace . . ."

Curiously enough, his figure was not a striking one : it seems that he was quite short and inclined to be stout. I might add that he was regarded as a citizen of some standing, and also happened to be a good painter in oils.

Finally, a note about Nathaniel Field, born in the parish of St. Giles, Cripplegate in 1587. He was one of the Children of the Chapel, when the child actors included Salathiel Pavy, Thomas Day, John Underwood, Robert Baxter and John Frost. He had such marked ability that he was chosen for " Lady Elizabeth's Servants " as soon as he became too old to act with the Children of the Chapel. Later, he joined " The King's Men " and played leading parts with Burbage. He also distinguished himself as a dramatist, for his play *A Woman is a Weathercock* [1612] was acted before the King at Whitehall. His *Amends for Ladies* followed in 1618, and he collaborated with Massinger in *The Fatal Dowry*.

THE COURT THEATRE

In Chapter One we saw what an important influence the court had upon the early development of the theatre, and noted that a Master of the Revels was in office when Queen Elizabeth came to the throne. He acted as the official Censor of plays throughout the Elizabethan period and for some years afterwards, and therefore played an important part in the shaping of drama in the Shakespearean age, for every play had to be " licensed " by him, and he was at liberty to delete any passages that he considered to be objectionable. For doing this he was allowed to charge a fee, which in time grew alarmingly.

Sir Henry Herbert, Master of the Revels from 1623 until 1662, when the post of Censor was abolished, charged extortionately, and made a very handsome income for himself. Although he came at the end of the period we are considering, it might interest the reader if I made two short quotations from his records. Of *The Young Admiral* by James Shirley, he writes that it is free from " oaths, prophaness or obsceanes " and that it might " serve for a patterne to other poetts, not only for the bettering of maners and language, but for the improvement of the quality, which hath received some brushings of late." On the other hand, we find him recording the receipt of a fee of two pounds for reading a new play " which I burnte for the ribaldry and offense that was in it."

I have already indicated that after the middle of the sixteenth century, plays at court became more popular than the masques, and consequently the professionals, both child and adult, gradually replaced the amateurs. The Children of the Chapel and the boys of St. Paul's School appeared frequently at court, but ultimately even these popular child actors gave way to the adult companies, although some of John Lyly's best work was written exclusively for them.

When Shakespeare appeared in London, the players were taking to the court of Elizabeth the same plays that they were performing at The Theatre and The Curtain : sure proof that despite the attitude of the Puritans, the Queen and her court appreciated the drama that appealed to the masses.

The court performances were more elaborate, for it seems that scenery made of canvas on wooden framework, such as had been used in the masques, was employed. At Whitehall, Hampton Court and Greenwich, the court plays were given at night by artificial light, in the most lavish of costumes. It is recorded that for a play in 1581 over a hundred pounds was spent in constructing a hill surmounted by a castle [1] " with falling sides, tree with shields, hermitage and hermit, savages, enchanter, chariot, and incidents to these." Among other accounts we find [2] " For pro-

[1] Feuillerat: 345–6. [2] *Ibid.*, 180.

vision and carriage of trees and other things to the court for a wilderness in a play."

When James I became King, his love of the spectacular resulted in a great revival of the court masque and a rapid development of it. Largely through the work of Inigo Jones, elaborate staging became possible, and a court masque, often costing well over a thousand pounds, would include a great deal of music and dancing, a play and plenty of grand pageantry. These masques took place in the great halls of the various palaces, in which special stages would be erected.

Here we come to a significant milestone in theatrical history, for it was the lavish staging of the masques that was responsible for the introduction of the proscenium arch and front curtain. They were first used as a novelty more than anything else. Most historians agree that their first appearance was in 1610 when they were used for a performance of Daniel's *Tethys Festival*. The innovation delighted the King and his court, so it is almost certain that the proscenium arch and curtain came into regular use at court at that time; indeed there seems to have been competition in the extent to which the frame of the arch could be decorated.

Changes of scene were at this time being made with increasing ingenuity, though, strange to relate, nobody thought of lowering the curtain while this was being done! Instead, they used a device of some sort to distract the attention of the audience. In the performance of *Tethys Festival* just mentioned, it is recorded that [1]" First at the opening of the heavens appeared three circles of lights and glasses, one with another, and came down in a straight motion five foote, and then began to moove circularly : which lights and motion so occupied the eyes of the spectators, that the manner of altering the scene was scarcely discerned; for in a moment the whole face of it was changed, the Poet vanished, and Tethys with her Nymphs appeared in their several Caverns gloriously adorned."

Two or three historians have also asserted that a change of scenery was sometimes concealed by " mists made from perfumes." Incredible as this may seem, it must be remembered that in this experimental period quite extraordinary things were attempted.

For the masque *Salmacida Spolia* given at the court of King Charles in 1640, Inigo Jones perfected a system of scenes sliding in grooves. In this masque, deities ascended and descended by means of a windlass beneath the stage.

[1] Daniel: *Works* ed. Grosart III. 315.

Curiously enough, the public theatres were slow to adopt the many new ideas and improvements devised for the court performances, although properties, costumes, etc., were occasionally borrowed officially or unofficially from the court. The expense of the spectacular masques was no doubt the reason why tragedy and comedy, with the more simple settings, continued to be the mainstay of the public theatres.

The costumes in the public theatres, however, were very nearly as elaborate as at court : money was spent unstintingly to procure the most gorgeous materials of the finest quality. There are records of lavish expenditure on silk, velvet, copper lace, satin, etc. : " a doublet and a pair of hose laid thick with gold lace," " a pair of Venetians of cloth of silver wrought in red silk," and " one cloke of velvette with a cape imbrothered with gold, pearles and red stones, and one roabe of cloth of gold : £16,"—are typical of the items that appeared in the accounts of the companies in the later Elizabethan period.

DRAMATISTS OF THE ELIZABETHAN AND JACOBEAN PERIOD

The dramatists of this golden age wrote for very small payment, and many had to supplement their income by doing hackwork for the booksellers. It will never be known exactly how much Shakespeare received for his plays, because he wrote exclusively for the company to which he was attached (" The Lord Chamberlain's Men," who afterwards became " The King's Men "), and it appears that very few, if any, accounts were kept. But some idea may be gathered from the knowledge that Dekker received only five pounds for *The Triplicity of Cuckolds*, and it is thought that few playwrights received more than about seven or eight pounds for each of their plays. To make matters worse, unscrupulous persons were in the habit of attending the theatres to take down the entire text of the plays in some sort of shorthand so that they could sell " pirated " editions.

Shakespeare's fortune was made primarily out of his partnership in The Globe, though no doubt his membership of the players' company secured him better terms than outside writers. As he never played any very great parts, it is presumed that his company always desired him to work more as a writer than an actor. It is also thought that he spent some of his time as a producer, because he is almost certain to have rehearsed his own plays, and might easily have directed some of the others as well. The dramatists often produced their own plays in those times: John Aubrey wrote of Ben Jonson that he " was never a good actor, but an excellent instructor." The rehearsal of a new play in Shakespeare's time would last two or three weeks. For this, the mornings were used, and punctuality was insisted upon; in fact at The Fortune it was the custom to fine latecomers one shilling.

The fact that boys played the women's parts probably accounts for the masculinity one finds in Elizabethan drama: Shakespeare's heroines, for instance, had far less to say than his heroes. Nevertheless, the boys played their parts with great skill and charm, and were dressed for the stage with the utmost taste and care. Pepys records having seen a boy actor who " made the loveliest lady that I ever saw in my life."

Let us now look at the lives of some of the men who wrote the great plays in the times of Elizabeth, James I and Charles I. I am not going to attempt any sort of analysis of their work because that would be entirely outside the scope of this book, and besides, there are various books on the subject that can be obtained at any public library by those who are interested. Nor do I propose to include complete miniature biographies of all the dramatists of this age: the following sketches are included merely to help the reader to get a general impression of their lives, and to mention one or two of their most important works.

Most people are *au fait* with the life of William Shakespeare, but for the benefit of the few who are not, I will add a few notes, though to say that he was born at Stratford-on-Avon in 1564 is rather like declaring that London stands upon the banks of the Thames. Historians disagree about his father's profession: some say that John Shakespeare was a husbandman, others that he was a glover, butcher or wool-dealer; but we do know that the father of our greatest dramatist was an alderman and city chamberlain, and that by 1577 he had lost most of his money.

Shakespeare was educated at the Free Grammar School at Stratford, and was still in his " teens " when he became entangled with Anne Hathaway, about eight years his senior, who bore him a daughter (Susanna) six months after their marriage. Not long afterwards a pair of twins arrived, and Shakespeare found himself in the unenviable position of having a wife and three children to support on next to nothing. It is said that he left Stratford in 1585 to avoid being prosecuted for poaching. Whether that is true or not does not really matter, but he arrived in London in due course and was engaged to do minor duties at The Theatre.

He joined " The Lord Chamberlain's Men " and moved with them to The Globe. His success (more as a dramatist than an actor) enabled him to visit his native town in 1597 to buy " New Place," its largest house, to which he eventually retired in 1610.

As the Burbages gave members of their company shares in their theatres, Shakespeare acquired a partnership in both The Globe and The Blackfriars. He wrote on an average two plays a year, exclusively for his own company, who jealously withheld them from all other players. In 1627 for instance, " The King's Men " paid the Master of the Revels five pounds to forbid a performance of one of Shakespeare's plays at The Red Bull.

When he retired he was a moderately wealthy man, as he well deserved to be. Even then he paid frequent visits to London to keep in touch with the dramatists, players and poets of the day, and visited the theatres regularly until his death in 1616.

His greatness as a dramatist was of course due to his amazing comprehension of human nature, his rich, masterly depiction of character, and his genius as a poet.

Christopher Marlowe was also born in 1564, son of a shoemaker of Canterbury. He was educated at King's School in that city, and at Corpus Christi College, Cambridge. He settled in London and became attached to " The Lord Admiral's Men," who produced most of his plays. In at least three of them Edward Alleyn played the title-rôles.

Marlowe, who was on friendly terms with Shakespeare, Nashe and Sir Walter Ralegh, wrote his masterpiece *Edward II* in 1593. In the same year a warrant was issued for his arrest because of his persistent dissemination of atheistic opinions, but he was killed during a violent quarrel in a tavern at Deptford. Francis Meres in *Palladis Tamia* [1598] wrote : " . . . Christopher Marlowe was stabd to death by a bawdy serving-man, a riual of his in lewde love." William Vaughan in *Golden Grove* gives the name of his murderer as Ingram.

Closely associated with Marlowe was Thomas Kyd (or Kid), son of a London scrivener. He was born about the year 1557, and went to the Merchant Taylors' School. He became a great exponent of a somewhat bombastic type of tragedy, and his *Spanish Tragedy* [1592] is certainly of some importance. Shortly after Marlowe's death, Kyd was charged with holding " scandalous opinions regarding morality and religion." Some say that he was imprisoned and tortured before his death in 1594, but there is no definite evidence of this.

W. H. Grove]
    RICHARD BURBAGE (from the painting in Dulwich College)

MR. WILLIAM

SHAKESPEARES

COMEDIES,
HISTORIES, &
TRAGEDIES.

Published according to the True Originall Copies.

LONDON
Printed by Isaac Iaggard, and Ed. Blount. 1623.

Of an entirely different type was George Peele [1558 ?–1598 ?], one of the famous " University Wits " of the day. He was the son of a London salter, and was educated at Christ's hospital and Oxford. While he was at the University he wrote his *Tale of Troy*. When he came down, he began leading a dissipated life and was turned out of his father's house He married, thereby acquiring considerable property, and became one of the Bohemians of London. For a while he was a member of " The Lord Admiral's Men " and also of " The Queen's Men." Noteworthy among his plays are *The Arraignment of Paris*, *Edward I*, *The Old Wives' Tale*, and *David and Bethsabe*. His lyrics are particularly charming.

One of the most amazing characters of this period was Robert Greene [1560–1592]. Born at Norwich and educated at Cambridge, he went abroad as a young man and led a dissolute life for several years. Then he returned to England, married " a gentleman's daughter of good account," had a child, and then deserted his wife as soon as he had spent her dowry. He continued to live viciously in London, but died in poverty before reaching middle-age as a result of over-indulgence in pickled herrings and Rhenish wine. What is so extraordinary is that his writings are singularly free from traces of salaciousness. His best works are *The Honorable Historie of Friar Bacon and Friar Bongay* and *Menaphon*, reprinted as *Greene's Arcadia* in 1599.

Thomas Nashe [1567–1601] was born at Lowestoft, son of a minister. He was educated at St. John's College, Cambridge, and settled in London in 1588 after a tour through France and Italy. He seems to have been very poor because he confessed that he had been obliged to get money by writing bawdy songs " for gentlemen ". He detested the Puritans and all that they stood for, and flayed them mercilessly in his pamphlets, plays and novels. His political comedy *The Isle of Dogs*, in which he attacked many notorious abuses that were going on at that time, caused him to be sent to prison for several months. Unfortunately, this play has now been lost. In 1599 he published *Nashe's Lenten Stuffe : containing the Description and First Procreation and Increase of the Towne of Great Yarmouth, in Norfolke*, a burlesque panegyric of the red herring. The following year saw his *Summer's Last Will*, a satirical masque. Most important, however, is his spirited, witty *Unfortunate Traveller*, the life of Jacke Wilton, " a certaine kinde of appendix or page " at the court of Henry VIII.

Nothing is known of the early life of Thomas Middleton [1570–1627] who was probably born in London and entered Gray's

Inn as a young man. He does not appear to have become associated with the stage until 1599. Early in the seventeenth century he was writing for " The Lord Admiral's Men," and in 1613 he was commissioned to write speeches for the ceremonial opening of the New River. He also wrote a pageant to celebrate the mayoralty of Sir Thomas Myddelton, and in 1621 was appointed city chronologer. His political drama *A Game at Chesse* [1624] was extremely popular, but after a complaint from the Spanish ambassador, who strongly objected to this " very scandalous comedy acted publickly by the King's Players," Middleton and his actors were summoned before the Privy Council ; whereupon the players produced " an original and perfect copy of the play seen and allowed " by the Master of the Revels (Sir Henry Herbert) and were acquitted with only a " sound and sharp reproof." Middleton himself did not appear. Much of his work was done in collaboration with Dekker, Munday and Rowley. His most important plays are *Women Beware Women* [1612] and *The Changeling* [1621].

Quite a contrast to most of his contemporaries was Thomas Dekker [1570 ?–1641 ?], who so delightfully portrayed in his works the life of London in the Elizabethan and Jacobean period. Very little is known about his youth, but Henslowe engaged him in 1598 to write plays for his theatre, some of which were done in collaboration with Ben Jonson, Drayton and others. Dekker's most successful work is *The Shoemaker's Holiday*, one of the best Elizabethan comedies we possess. It has been revived in modern times.

He also wrote a number of pamphlets, and the amusing *Gull's Hornbooke*, to which I have already referred, has been of great value to historians of the theatre. Dekker was one of the most lovable figures in English literature : he was extremely kind and sympathetic to the poor, and was beloved by all his associates for his unfailing good humour. He was usually desperately poor, yet he lived a carefree, happy-go-lucky life. In 1613 his financial difficulties became acute, and he was sent to prison for debt. Some say that he stayed there for six or seven years. His lyric *Art thou poor, yet hast thou golden slumbers?* reflects perfectly his sunny, contented disposition. There is pure genius in all his poetry.

Ben Jonson was born in 1573 in Westminster, and was educated at Westminster School. His step-father, a bricklayer, insisted upon his entering the building trade, but after a while

Ben rebelled and joined the army.   He returned to London in 1592, married, and became associated with Henslowe's company both as an actor and playwright.   He lived a Bohemian life, and was an extremely quarrelsome character.   He fought a duel with Gabriel Spencer, a fellow actor; killed him and went to prison for a year. While he was there he became a Catholic, but twelve years later recanted.   Shakespeare played in his *Every Man in his Humour* when " The Lord Chamberlain's Men " produced it in 1598, and this was followed within a year by *Every Man out of his Humour*, in which he caricatured all that he disliked in London life.   His battle of wits with John Marston, Shakespeare and Dekker produced such comedies as *Cynthia's Revels* and *The Poetaster*.   His first tragedy *Sejanus* was performed at The Globe in 1603 with Shakespeare and Burbage in the cast.   On Twelfth Night 1605 his *Masque of Blacknesse* was given at court with scenery by Inigo Jones, and from that time he continued to write masques for the King.   James I favoured him and granted him a pension in 1616.   Jonson's greatest work was perhaps the comedy *The Alchemist* [1610], though *Bartholomew Fayre* in which he portrays a London fair, is most entertaining.   He was elected chronologer of London in 1628.

Although his quarrelsome nature must be deplored, his satiric writing had a profound effect at the time.   He showed no sympathy to the Puritans, and he was always ready to attack the corruption that was rife in those days.   He was arrogant, warm hearted, and an honest literary critic.   Towards the end of his life he lost the patronage of the court after a quarrel with Inigo Jones, but even this did not dampen his buoyant humour.   He died on August 6th, 1637, and was buried in Westminster Abbey.

John Fletcher [1579–1625] will always be associated with Francis Beaumont [1584–1616] with whom he collaborated for over ten years.   He was born at Rye, Sussex, and educated at Cambridge. It is generally acknowledged that Fletcher was responsible for part of Shakespeare's *Henry VIII*.   His comedies are rich in wit, and have a pleasant freshness, but he never achieved much success as a tragedian.

Another prominent dramatist of this period was Philip Massinger [1583–1640], who was born at Salisbury and educated at St. Alban Hall, Oxford.   He came to London seeking the acquaintance of other dramatists, and collaborated with Fletcher, Nathaniel Field, Daborne and Dekker.   His best work is the comedy *A New Way to Pay Old Debts*, in which the character

Sir Giles Overreach has always been considered to be a test of an actor's skill.

There is some doubt concerning the year in which Thomas Heywood was born. He was a Lincolnshire man, and connected first with "The Lord Admiral's Men" and then with "The Queen's Men." It is said that he wrote the majority of his plays in a tavern on the back of handbills. He was a good scholar, and translated many works of Lucian and certain Latin writers. *A Woman Kilde with Kindnesse* [*circa.* 1603] is generally considered to be his best comedy.

Little is known about the life of John Ford [1586–1639]. He was probably admitted to the Middle Temple, because his work shows a fair knowledge of the legal world. One of his most brilliant plays is the rather repulsive *'Tis a Pity She's a Whore* [1626], first staged by the "Queenes Maiesties Seruants at the Phœnix in Drury Lane." *The Broken Heart* [1633] and *The Witch of Edmonton* [1621] are also of some importance, but most of his work reflects a melancholy disposition that has been summed up in a couplet in *Choice Drollery* [1656]:

> "Deep in a dump John Forde was alone got,
> With folded arms and melancholy hat."

The recent and successful revival of *The Duchess of Malfi* has given us some idea of the power of John Webster [1580?-1625?], son of a London tailor. He collaborated with two or three of his contemporaries in comedy, but on his tragedies rests his greatness. *The White Divel* [circa. 1608] is another good specimen of his work.

Finally, we come to James Shirley [1596–1666] "the last of the Elizabethans." He was born in London, educated at The Merchant Taylors' School and both Oxford and Cambridge, and wrote something like forty dramas. His best play is *Love's Cruelty* [1640]. It is recorded that he was converted to Catholicism, and died as a result of exposure during the Great Fire of London.

THE END OF A GOLDEN AGE

From the year 1620 onwards the theatre gradually fell into disfavour. In 1642 the struggle between the King and Parliament culminated in the Civil War, and the following order was made on the second day of September in that year:[1]

"Whereas the distressed Estate of Ireland, steeped in her

---

[1] *Roscius Anglicanus.*

NATHANIEL FIELD (from the painting at Dulwich College)

[*Risc*

Thomas Betterton

own Blood, and the distracted Estate of England, threatened
with a cloud of Blood, by a Civill Warre, call for all possible
meanes to appease and avert the Wrath of God appearing in
these Judgments ; amongst which Fasting and Prayer have
been often tried to be very effectual, have been lately, and are
still enjoyned, and whereas publike Sports doe not well agree
with publike Calamaties, nor publike Stage-playes with the
Seasons of Humiliation, and the other being Spectacles of, too
commonly expressing lacivious Mirth and Levitie. It is therefore thought fit, and ordeined by the Lords and Commons in
this Parliament Assembled, that while these sad Causes and set
times of Humiliation doe continue, publike Stage-playes shall
cease, and bee forborne. Instead of which are recommended
to the people of this Land, the profitable and seasonable Con-
siderations of Repentance, Reconciliation, and peace with God,
which probably may produce outward peace and prosperity,
and bring again Times of Joy and Gladness to these Nations."

This closed the most glorious period in the history of English
drama. The brilliant theatrical splendour of the court masques
remained only as a dream in the memory.

At first there was widespread resistance to the Order, but
further orders followed in terms of the utmost severity. Actors
were threatened with imprisonment, and finally all were declared
to be " rogues and vagabonds." Players found acting in secret
were flogged, and any person witnessing a dramatic performance
was fined five shillings.

The players were almost entirely Royalists, many fought for
the King, and all were persecuted after the execution of Charles.
Many fled to the continent and continued to practise their art in
the theatres of France and Italy.

In 1647 the light of dramatic art in England was but a barely
perceptible glimmer, and it would have flickered out entirely but
for the few determined rebels who continued to play behind locked
doors. In the houses of some of the noblemen, plays were staged
in secret from time to time before select Royalist audiences, but
the only traces of public drama that remained were a few quite
negligible and stupid " drolls " at country fairs.

Chapter III

THE RESTORATION THEATRE

WE find that the years 1642–1660 are pathetically empty as we look back through the history of the English theatre. It must not be imagined that the players submitted meekly to the tyranny of Parliament however, for in 1643 there appeared a pamphlet called *The Actors' Remonstrance or Complaint for the Silencing of their Profession*. It ran:

" Oppressed with many calamaties, and languishing to death under the burthen of a long and . . . everlasting restraint, wee, the comedians, tragedians, and actors of all sorts and sizes, belonging to the famous private and publike houses within the City of London . . . in all humility present this our lamentable complaint.

" First, it is not unknowne . . . that wee have purged our stages from all obscene and scurrilous jests, that wee have endeavoured . . . to repress bawling and ranting . . . and to suit our language to the more gentle and natural garb of the times. Yet are wee, by authority, restrained from the practice of our profession . . . to the great impoverishment and utter undoings of ourselves, wives, children and dependents. Besides, which is, of all others, our greatest grievance, that playes being put down . . . other recreations of farre more harmfull consequence are permitted still to stand, viz., . . . the Bear Garden, where those demi-monsters are baited by ban dogs ; the gentlemen of Stave and Taile, namely cutting coblers, hard-handed masons, and the like rioting companions, resorting thither . . . making with their sweat and crowding, a farre worse stink than the ill-formed beastes they persecute. . . .

" Our fooles . . . are enforced to maintain themselves by virtue of their baubles. Our boyes, ere wee shall have libertie to act againe, will be grown out of use like crackt organ pipes, . . . Nay, our verie doore-keepers . . . most grievously complain that by this cessation they are robbed of the privilege of stealing from us with licence ; they cannot now seem to scratch their heads where they itch not, and drop shillings and half-

crown pieces in at their collars. Our musique, that was held
so delectable and precious that they scorned to go to a tavern
under twentie shillings salarie for two hours, now wander with
their instruments under their cloaks, I meane such as have any,
into all houses of good fellowship, saluting every roome where
there is company with 'Will you have any musique, gentlemen?' . . . our stock of cloathes, such as are not in tribulation
for generall use, being a sacrifice to moths . . .

   " The tobacco-men that used to walk up and down selling
for a penny a pipe that which was not worth twelvepence a horse-
load, are now found tapsters in inns and tipling houses. . . .
some of our ablest ordinarie poets . . . (are) being for meere
necessitie, compelled to get a living by writing contemptible
penny pamphlets, and feigning miraculous stories of unheard of
battels. Nay, it is to be feared that shortly some of them will
be incited to write ballads."

The petition concludes with an appeal that the players be reinstated,
and promises that they will admit none but reputable females into
their sixpenny rooms or boxes, permit only the best tobacco to
be sold in their theatres, and avoid ribaldry.

   Prominent among those continuing the struggle was Sir William
D'Avenant, poet, playwright and theatre-manager. Towards
the end of the Protectorate he succeeded in convincing the authorities that opera was but a revival of a branch of the ancient art of
Greece and Rome, and thus persuaded them to allow him to perform
the opera *The Siege of Rhodes* at Rutland House. This production
in 1656 was another important milestone in theatrical history,
not only because it was the first opera to be performed in this
country, but because it was the first time an Englishwoman
appeared on the stage. Her name was Mrs. Coleman. Ladies
of the Court had appeared in the masques, of course, but professional English actresses were unknown at that time. Within
two years, D'Avenant was staging other operas at the Phœnix
(the old Cockpit).

   When Charles II landed in England in 1660 three rather precarious companies had re-started, but he authorized Sir William
D'Avenant and Sir Thomas Killigrew to organize two new companies of players, for the " merry monarch " was not going to be
deprived of the amusements he had enjoyed in France.

   D'Avenant immediately gathered together a body of players
to whom was given the title " The Duke of York's Company,"
and installed them first of all at the Salisbury Court Theatre.

Killigrew assembled " The King's Company " and to provide suitable accommodation for them ordered the erection of the first Theatre Royal in Drury Lane, which was opened in 1663 with a play called *The Humorous Lieutenant* by Beaumont and Fletcher.

While the Theatre Royal was being built, Killigrew's company played at the Tennis Court Theatre in Vere Street. Pepys visited this playhouse on January 3rd, 1661, and recorded : ". . . it (the play *Beggar's Bush*) being very well done, and here for the first time that I ever saw women come upon the stage."

It should be noted, however, that boys were still being used in women's parts from time to time, because the famous old diarist tells us that a few days later he went to the same theatre and saw " Kinaston, the boy " as Epicœne in Jonson's *Silent Woman*, adding that in feminine attire the lad was " the prettiest woman in the whole house."

There was very keen competition between the King's Company and the Duke's. Cibber declares that they were both prosperous for some years, " 'till their Variety of Plays began to be exhausted : Then of course, the better Actors (which the King's seem to have been allowed) could not fail of drawing the greater Audiences. Sir William D'Avenant, therefore, Master of the Duke's Company, to make Head against their Success, was forced to add Spectacle and Music to Action ; and to introduce a new species of Plays, since call'd Dramatick Opera's, of which Kind were the *Tempest*, *Psyche*, *Circe* and others, all set off with the most expensive Decorations of Scenes and Habits, with the best Voices and Dancers."

The theatres of this period afforded ample opportunities for elaborate staging. The closed-in playhouse had triumphed over the open arena-type structure, enabling the experience gained in the lavish court masques to be put to good use. The orchestra found its place before the stage, and the theatre began to appear as we know it today.

When D'Avenant died in 1668 a new theatre for the Duke's Company was already under construction in Dorset Garden, close to the old Salisbury Court Theatre, to plans drawn by Christopher Wren. This was opened in 1671, a magnificently appointed house with decorations by Grinling Gibbons. It cost five thousand pounds, an enormous sum in those days, and caused a minor sensation in London.

THE FIRST " THEATRE ROYAL," DRURY LANE

In Killigrew's time, Drury Lane was a most aristocratic quarter of the town : the Earls of Anglesey, Craven and Clare all lived there in imposing mansions. What a contrast to its present day squalor !

The first Theatre Royal was built at a cost of fifteen hundred pounds, a structure measuring a hundred and twelve feet by fifty-nine feet. Performances were given in the afternoons, and the prices of admission were : Pit half-a-crown, Balcony one shilling and sixpence, Upper Gallery a shilling and Boxes four shillings.

The leading actors of the King's Company were Michael Mohun and Charles Hart. Mohun had served as a Major in the Civil War, fighting on the side of the King at Edgehill in 1642. Hart, a grandson of Shakespeare's sister Joan, was a tall, dignified man of exceptional ability, particularly in tragedy. The Company also included John Lacey, a famous Falstaff, who was a great favourite with the King.

It was at Drury Lane in 1665 that Nell Gwynne made her first appearance as an actress. The story of her life is really astonishing, but before telling it briefly, I must point out that historians disagree on certain incidents in her early years.

There is some doubt about her birthplace, but the city of Hereford seems to have the strongest claim. It is said that she ran away from home when she was quite a child, came to London, found lodgings in Coal Yard, near Drury Lane, and first earned her living by selling herrings in the streets. This voluptuously good-looking, impudent little wench was later employed to sell oranges in the pit at the Theatre Royal, where she soon proved that she could match the audacity of the coarsest of the beaux who tried to flirt with her. Despite the fact that she swore like a trooper, John Lacey took a benevolent interest in her, and gave her instruction in elocution, deportment, and so forth. She improved so quickly that it was but a matter of months before she won the affection of Charles Hart, who began giving her lessons in dramatic art. His patient training enabled her to take the part of Cydaria in Dryden's *Indian Emperor* when she was only fifteen years of age. She was not much of a success in this particular rôle, but as soon as they tried her out in comedy she caused a furore. She spoke well, danced perfectly, and acquired a most fascinating laugh. Crowds swarmed from all over London to see and hear her, and our old friend Pepys declared that a play without Nell was no play at all.

The King visited the theatre one afternoon in 1669 when she was playing and was completely captivated. That very evening he carried her off and made her his mistress. In the following year she bore a son Charles, and a second arrived within the next twelve months. This younger boy died at the age of nine.

One day, in the presence of the King, she addressed her son Charles using a vulgar expression referring to his illegitimacy. When reproved, she told the King that she did not know what else she could call the lad, so Charles made his illegitimate son an earl, and in due course the boy became the Duke of St. Alban's.

Doran, in *Their Majesties' Servants*, tells us that the last of Nell Gwynne's original characters was that of Almahide in Dryden's *Conquest of Granada*, and adds that she spoke the prologue in a straw hat " as broad as a cartwheel, and thereby almost killed the King with laughter."

Her outrageous extravagance became a public scandal. The King was so obsessed with her charms that he gave her a luxurious residence in Pall Mall and another at Windsor (Burford House) and in four years she extorted from him over sixty thousand pounds, which would be something like half-a-million pounds to-day. Not content with this she induced the King to secure her an income of six thousand pounds a year from the Excise, and to command that a further three thousand a year be paid to her son. The people had some justification, therefore, in making bitter complaints about the expense of the King's pleasures. It is said that Nell Gwynne lost fourteen hundred pounds in one evening at Basset (a card game). She died *heavily in debt* in November, 1687, aged thirty-seven.

The King was a keen patron of the theatre at this time, and he saw that the players enjoyed a high social status. Colley Cibber in his *Apology* informs us :

" About ten of the King's company were on the Royal Household Establishment, having each ten yards of scarlet cloth, with a proper Quantity of Lace allow'd them for Liveries ; and in their Warrants from the Lord Chamberlain were stiled ' Gentlemen of the Great Chamber ' ; Whether the like Appointments were extended to the Duke's Company, I am not certain ; but they were both in high Estimation with the Publick, and so much the Delight and Concern of the Court, that they were not only supported by its being frequently present at their publick Presentations, but by its taking Cognizance of their private Government, insomuch, that their particular Differences, Pretensions or Complaints, were generally ended by the King or Duke's Personal Command or Decision . . ."

In 1670 Parliament tried to impose a tax upon the theatres, but the Court party strongly opposed the suggestion on the grounds that the actors were the King's servants and part of his " pleasure." This caused Sir John Coventry to ask in the House whether His Majesty's pleasure was to be found among the actors or actresses. Whereupon the King hired a band of desperados to waylay Sir John and cut off his nose.

THE SECOND "THEATRE ROYAL," DRURY LANE

In January 1672 the Theatre Royal was destroyed by fire, and the Company withdrew for a while to Lincoln's Inn Fields while a new playhouse was being built. This was designed by Wren, cost four thousand pounds, and opened on March 26th, 1674. We are told by H. Barton Baker in *The London Stage* that it was built to rival the magnificence of the Duke's House. Referring to its stage, he quotes Cibber to inform us that it " projected in a semi-oval figure right forward to the front bench of the pit, with side wings for the entrances in place of stage boxes, so that the whole action of the play was carried on beyond the pillars of the proscenium." Although considerable alterations were made later, Cibber was very much in favour of the original arrangement because " the most subtle shades of facial expression could be seen, and the softest whispers and most delicate intonations of the voice could be heard and better appreciated by the spectators."

Rivalry between the two companies continued, but Hart and Mohun were getting old, and the audiences were deteriorating in both quantity and quality. For that reason, the two companies were amalgamated on November 16th, 1682, "by the King's advice." The signatories to the agreement were Charles D'Avenant, son of Sir William, William Smith and Thomas Betterton for the Duke's Company, and Charles Hart and Edward Kynaston for the King's. In the same year, Killigrew died and Hart retired.

The union of the two companies did little to improve matters. The support of the public continued to dwindle until in 1690 Charles D'Avenant sold his interests to a roguish lawyer named Christopher Rich who treated the players so badly that in 1695 they appealed to the King, William III, to intervene. His Majesty showed them great sympathy and kindness, and commanded that a licence be granted to them to re-open the old theatre in Lincoln's Inn Fields.

Two years before this happened, William Congreve, a young

law student of whom we shall hear more later, had amazed the theatre world with the success of his first comedy *The Old Bachelor*. He had been entirely in sympathy with the Theatre Royal players in all their troubles, and when they embarked upon this new venture he took an active share in the management and gave them his immortal comedy *Love for Love*, which he had written for Drury Lane. This play was staged on the opening night, April 30th, 1695, with Betterton, Dogget, Underhill, Sandford, Mrs. Barry, Mrs. Bowman and Mrs. Bracegirdle in the cast, and was a great success.

Alas! in 1697, just as some small measure of prosperity was returning, Jeremy Collier published his *Short View of the Profaneness and Immorality of the English Stage* and stirred up a strong puritanical agitation against the theatres again. Collier's attack was not entirely unjustified, but it confused the levities of men like Congreve with the vulgarities of various second-rate writers of the time. Nevertheless, Congreve replied in the following year with *Amendments of Mr. Collier's False and Imperfect Citations*, but made little impression upon public opinion.

In 1699 the King's Chamberlain felt obliged to send a warning to both Drury Lane and Lincoln's Inn Fields about the use of profane and indecent expressions in plays.

RESTORATION PLAYHOUSES

Before we go any further, let us note one or two general conditions prevailing in the playhouses in the middle and towards the end of the seventeenth century. The theatres, as in Elizabethan times, still attracted gallants and fops who went primarily to show themselves off. This was harmless enough, but some of them, following the example of certain young noblemen, were not content to indulge in badinage with the orange-girls; and instead of making themselves a nuisance by sitting on the stage, they started a much more objectionable practice: haunting the tiring-rooms of the actresses when they were dressing and undressing. Because of the rank and influence of some of the young noblemen, it was at first thought inadvisable to reprove them; but in time their behaviour caused such a scandal that Charles II had to forbid it.

It is to be regretted that the theatres still remained a hunting ground for those bent on promiscuity. The middle gallery became notorious for its genteel courtesans who wore masks and carried on flirtations incognito, and this, too, developed into a

NELL GWYNNE by Sir Peter Lely

WILLIAM CONGREVE by Sir Godfrey Kneller

highly undesirable form of amusement. Finally, in 1704, Queen Anne felt obliged to prohibit the wearing of masks by members of the audience.

The uppermost gallery was the cheapest part of the house, and was therefore the resort of the rabble. Christopher Rich, at a time when audiences were numerically poor, once started allowing the lackeys to sit in the Upper Gallery free of charge, but as they behaved so badly the practice had to be stopped.

We now enter upon another period of vicissitudes in the history of the London theatres, but as we have other matters to consider, it would be impossible to set out in detail and in sequence all these ups and downs, and in any case, they are not of any very great importance to us, for we are concerned with the general story of the theatre rather than masses of minor historical facts. So let us now turn to the lives of some of the actors, actresses and playwrights of this Restoration period.

PLAYERS AND PLAYWRIGHTS

Thomas Betterton [1635 ?–1710] was the greatest actor on the English stage in those days. He was born in Tothill Street, Westminster, son of the under-cook to Charles I. He was apprenticed to John Holden, a bookseller, and acquired a taste for reading good literature, but we have few reliable facts about his early life. He made his first appearance at The Cockpit with a company of players under John Rhodes in 1660, but Sir William D'Avenant engaged him with the rest of the company for the new theatre at Lincoln's Inn Fields in the following year. He stayed with the Duke's Company, and after D'Avenant's death took over the managership. When the two major companies were amalgamated in 1682 he went to Drury Lane, and played there until all the principals seceded in 1695. He then shone at Lincoln's Inn Fields for several years but when the theatre came into another period of disfavour, he retired from the stage. His last appearance was in 1710 as Melantius in *The Maid's Tragedy* (Beaumont and Fletcher).

Pepys regarded Betterton as "the best actor in the world" and the King, Charles II, esteemed him so highly that he sent him to Paris to make a study of French theatrical art. As Hamlet, particularly, he could command "an universal attention even from the fops and flower-girls." He was fairly tall, a dignified austere figure, possessing a voice with a remarkable range of intonation. At his benefit performance he played Valentine in

Love for Love, and made a profit of over five hundred pounds. He died on April 28th, and was buried in Westminster Abbey.

Elizabeth Barry [1658–1713] was the daughter of a barrister who fought as a Colonel on the side of the King in the Civil War. After her father's death, D'Avenant took her into his house and trained her for the stage. She was very dull at first, but the young Earl of Rochester took an interest in her (for more than one reason) and instructed her personally. In his *Dramatic Miscellanies*, Davies tells us that Rochester, having wagered that within six months he would make her into an actress, "taught her not only the proper cadence or sounding of the voice, but to seize also the passions, and adapt her whole behaviour to the situations of the character." She first appeared in 1673 at Dorset Garden as Isabella, Queen of Hungary, in *Mustapha* by the Earl of Orrery, and in a few years blossomed as one of the greatest actresses of the seventeenth century. Cibber said that she had a presence of " elevated dignity " in characters of greatness ; and that her voice was full, clear and strong " so that no violence of passion could be too much for her ": yet she could subside into " the most affecting melody and softness," and in the art of exciting pity she had a power greater than any actress he had ever seen. Her private life was notorious. She was last seen on the stage in Dryden's *Spanish Friar*, at the Haymarket in 1710, the day after Betterton retired, and she died at Acton (then a country village) in 1713.

Another famous actress in the seventeenth century was Anne Bracegirdle [1663 ?–1748], a most fascinating woman. She came from Northamptonshire as a child, and was placed in the care of Thomas Betterton and his wife. It is said that she first appeared when little more than a child at Dorset Garden as a page in *The Orphan* (Otway). She was much admired by Congreve, who wrote the parts of Araminta in *The Old Bachelor*, and Angelica in *Love for Love* specially for her. It was in these rôles that she became so famous. She retired from the stage early in life—in 1707—as soon as she saw that her supremacy was challenged, though she returned on one occasion to play in Betterton's benefit performance. She was buried in the cloisters of Westminster Abbey.

Turning to the writers of the Restoration period we come first to John Dryden [1631–1700]. He was born at Aldwinkle, Northants, educated at Westminster School and Cambridge, and came to London in 1657. He was an admirer of Cromwell, and wrote the *Heroic Stanzas* as a tribute to him, but when the Stuarts returned to the throne he adapted himself readily to the new order, celebrating their restoration by his *Astræa Redux* [1660], which was followed shortly afterwards by a *Panegyric on the Restoration*.

Deciding to seek a livelihood from the theatres, he wrote a tragedy about Henry, Duke of Guise, but this was a failure, so he turned, somewhat reluctantly, to comedy. After two more failures he wrote a comedy called *The Rival Ladies*, which was produced in 1663 and was very well received. Pepys described it as " a very innocent and most pretty, witty play." But this did not establish him very firmly as a dramatist because several of his later plays met with little success.

Dryden's first notable success was with *The Indian Queen*, a play written in collaboration with Sir Robert Howard, which was lavishly produced in 1664. In little more than a year he followed it up with *The Indian Emperor*. Then came *Secret Love* and *Sir Martin Mar-all*, which were both staged in 1667. The latter is an adaptation of Molière's *L'Étourdi*. It was at about this time that he made a contract to write regularly for the Theatre Royal, Drury Lane, but never produced the number of plays agreed upon.

He was appointed Poet Laureate in 1668 and Historiographer Royal two years later. His most important works are undoubtedly his *Tyrannic Love* [1669], *The Conquest of Granada* [1670] and *All for Love* [1678]. In the last of these, which is generally considered to be his finest play, he adopted blank verse.

Dryden was suspected of being the author of Mulgrave's *Essay on Satire* [1679], an attack on the court and the Earl of Rochester in particular, and was severely beaten in Rose Alley, Covent Garden, by a gang of ruffians in the pay of the Earl. Actually, his sympathies were entirely on the side of the court, and he wrote later as a satirist in support of these views.

He became a Catholic on the accession of James in 1685, and in consequence was deprived of his offices and pension three years later at the Revolution. He died at his house in Gerrard-street, London, on May 1st, 1700, and was buried in Westminster Abbey, in Chaucer's grave.

Thomas Otway was born at Trotten, near Midhurst, Sussex, in 1652, son of a parson. He was educated at Winchester College and Christ Church Oxford. His early work is not important, though his *Friendship in Fashion* was quite a success when it was first performed. When in 1749 it was revived at Drury Lane, it was hissed off the stage for its gross indecency.

Otway cherished an overwhelming but unrequited passion for Mrs. Elizabeth Barry, and embittered by her coquettish scorn, he enlisted in the army that was sent to Holland in 1678. Returning to London in the following year, almost penniless and in tattered clothes, he settled down to write what proved to be his best works : *The Orphan* and *Venice Preserved*. He died destitute in 1685 at the age of thirty-three, and was buried in the churchyard of St. Clement Danes.

Some mention must be made of Sir George Etherege [1634 ?– 1691 ?], though not because his work has any great literary value. He was almost unknown until his *Comical Revenge, or Love in a Tub* was produced by the Duke's Company in 1664. This play is important because it was the first English prose comedy. It was a great success and ensured the production a few years later of his *She Would if She Could*, which drew from our friend Pepys the exclamation " Lord ! how full the house and how silly the play." Etherege's most successful play was *The Man of Mode, or Sir Fopling Flutter* [1676].

Sir George can best be described as a witty, handsome seducer ; and if more were known about his private life, it would not make a very pretty story. He had a passionate affair with Mrs. Barry, who bore him a daughter, and after many years of quite ruthless wenching in London, married a fortune and got a knighthood. Some historians say that he married the fortune so that he could buy the knighthood ; others that he bought the knighthood so that he could marry the fortune. In any case, it doesn't really matter. " Gentle George," as he was called, found favour at court, secured one or two attractive appointments that enabled him to dabble in diplomacy—what little work there was he delegated to one or two personal servants—and eventually died in Paris.

Another master of polite obscenity with talent as a dramatist was William Wycherley [1640–1716]. He was born at Clive, near Shrewsbury, educated in France (because of Cromwell) and Oxford, and became a professional gentleman of the most precious variety. With his first play *Love in a Wood* he won the favour of the Duchess of Cleveland, the King's mistress. Most of his time was spent in the pursuit of pleasure, and in middle age he married the widowed Countess of Drogheda, who obligingly died after a while and left him her fortune. To his dismay, the title to the property was disputed, and after lengthy and extremely costly litigation, Wycherley found himself in prison for debt. He stayed there for

ANNE BRACEGIRDLE (from an old print)

Sir John Vanbrugh by J. Closterman

seven years, and then James II secured his release and gave him a pension of two hundred pounds a year. When finally he inherited his family property, he married, at the age of seventy-five, a young girl to spite his nephew, who was the next in succession.

Wycherley's best plays are *The Country Wife* and *The Plain Dealer*. In the latter he painted a vivid picture of the vicious life he knew so well in London : it is a masterpiece of repartee.

William Congreve [1670–1729] is generally considered to be the greatest English master of comedy. He was born of an ancient family at Bardsey, near Leeds. Because his father was sent to Ireland to command the garrison at Youghal, he was educated at Kilkenny School and Trinity College, Dublin, a fellow student of Swift at both institutions. Later, the family moved to Staffordshire, and it was probably there that Congreve wrote *The Old Bachelor*.

He entered the Middle Temple as a law student in 1691, and while he was there his comedy *The Old Bachelor* was first produced at Drury Lane, winning the generous praises of Dryden, who said he had never seen such an excellent first play. In the following year, 1694, he wrote *The Double Dealer*, which again drew the acclamation of Dryden, but which was not much of a success in the theatre because it scandalized a certain section of the ladies.

Congreve was always flattered in high society, and it was rumoured that he had been secretly married to Mrs. Bracegirdle. He was also a great favourite of the second Duchess of Marlborough. When Voltaire visited him towards the end of his life, he was disgusted to find that Congreve desired to be regarded as a *gentleman* rather than an author.

His crowning success was *Love for Love* [1695] produced at the opening of the new theatre in Lincoln's Inn Fields. Its scathing wit has again been proved in modern times, having been revived in both New York and London during the second world war.

Congreve signed a contract to supply the Lincoln's Inn theatre with a new play every year, but owing to ill health, his intention was never carried out. He attempted a tragedy *The Mourning Bride* in 1697, and it was a great success. This play contains the familiar lines ; " Music has charms to soothe a savage breast," and

" Heaven has no rage, like love to hatred turned,
Nor hell a fury, like a woman scorned."

In 1700 Congreve wrote his masterpiece, *The Way of the World*, but to his utter amazement this wonderful comedy with its truly brilliant dialogue was coldly received ; and it is said that in his disgust and anger he rushed on to the stage and vehemently up-braided the audience.   It was undoubtedly this deplorable lack of appreciation that made him decide to write no more plays.

In 1705 he associated himself with Vanbrugh in the manage-ment of the Queen's Theatre, but still retained an interest in the Lincoln's Inn house until persistent gout made him retire altogether from theatre management.   He died on January 19th, 1729, as a result of an injury sustained when his carriage was overturned on a journey to Bath ; and was buried in Westminster Abbey.

Another great dramatist of the Restoration period was George Farquhar, who was born in Londonderry in 1678, educated locally in the first instance, and then entered Trinity College, Dublin, as a sizar when he was sixteen.   It is said that he was later expelled for making a profane jest, but this cannot be proved.   He joined a company of strolling players and eventually became a favourite on the Dublin stage, where he is said to have appeared as Othello. He accidentally wounded a fellow actor during a fencing scene in *The Indian Emperor* (Dryden), and it was doubtless the ill-feeling caused by this that made him come to London.   In 1703 he married a lady who posed as an heiress, but discovered immediately after the ceremony that she possessed nothing.   He died in poverty in 1707.

One of his earliest plays, *The Constant Couple*, was made a great success by Robert Wilks as Sir Harry Wildair, and consequently he wrote a sequel, using the name of that character as its title. Wilks again played the lead with the beautiful Anne Oldfield as Lady Lurewell, but with rather less success.   Farquhar's two best plays are undoubtedly *The Recruiting Officer* (1706) and *The Beaux' Stratagem*, a rollicking comedy.

Chapter IV

THE CIBBER PERIOD

WE now come to what is often called " The Cibber Period " ; the first part of the eighteenth century. It covers roughly thirty years.

The unpleasantness caused by Christopher Rich was probably responsible for Sir John Vanbrugh's decision to build a grand new theatre in the Haymarket. According to Cibber he persuaded " thirty persons of quality " to subscribe a hundred pounds each " in consideration whereof every subscriber for his own life was to be admitted to whatever entertainments should be publicly performed there, without further payment for his entrance."

The new Queen's Theatre, as it was called, was completed in 1705, and attracted Betterton and his colleagues from Lincoln's Inn Fields. They placed themselves under the direction of Vanbrugh and Congreve, but the new playhouse was a bitter disappointment to them : it was a triumph of impressive architecture and handsome ornament, but an appalling building for acoustics. In *The London Stage*, H. B. Baker says " At the first opening, the flat ceiling, that is now over the orchestra, was then a semi-oval arch that sprang fifteen feet higher from above the cornice. The ceiling over the pit, too, was still more raised, being one level line from the highest back part of the upper gallery to the front of the stage ; the front boxes were a continual semi-circle to the bare walls of the house on each side. This extraordinary and superfluous space occasioned such an undulation from the voice of every actor that generally what they said sounded like the gabbling of so many people in the lofty aisles of a cathedral . . . the articulate sounds of a speaking voice were drowned by the hollow reverberations of one word upon another."

Congreve was quick to see the hopelessness of the situation, and retired forthwith, so Vanbrugh let the theatre to Owen Swiney, one of Rich's associates, who converted it into an opera house in which Nicolini's famous company achieved great success.

The quarrels and intrigues that centred around Rich in time brought about the closing of the Theatre Royal, but soon after

Rich had been deprived of his rights in the patent, William Collier, a member of Parliament, obtained a licence to re-open the theatre. H. B. Baker tells us " . . . as the old patentee refused to give up possession, Collier employed people to force an entrance, but only to find that Rich had previously removed everything portable in the shape of dresses and properties."

Collier's venture was not a success, but he was fortunate in finding Cibber, Dogget and Wilks ready to take it off his hands. But before we go on, let me say something about these three men.

Colley Cibber was born in Bloomsbury, London, on November 6th, 1671, son of Caius Cibber, the sculptor. He was educated at Grantham School, Lincolnshire, and came to London to find an immediate and irresistible attraction towards the stage. After a short period in the army, he haunted the Theatre Royal in the hope of obtaining membership of the united companies there. At last, when he was nineteen, he was given a very minor part in which he had to take a message to Betterton. He was overjoyed, but at the performance was suddenly stricken with stage fright and caused a general confusion. Betterton was very angry, and told the prompter afterwards to see that the young man paid a forfeit. The prompter explained that as " Master Colley " received no salary this could not be done. Betterton immediately retorted " Why then, put him down for ten shillings a week and forfeit him five shillings." That, it is said, is how Colley Cibber began his career in the theatre.

In time he rose to fifteen shillings a week, and after playing Lord Touchwood in *The Double Dealer*, he drew a word of praise from Congreve which increased his salary to a pound a week. Cibber was not a great actor, but he had some literary ability, and wrote a number of plays including *Love's Last Shift* and *The Careless Husband*. In the former, the character Sir Novelty Fashion, a caricature of a typical dandy of that time, was a source of great delight to the playgoers, and induced Sir John Vanbrugh to write a sequel called *The Relapse*.

A good-natured man, liberally endowed with commonsense, tact and business acumen, he was the ideal theatre manager, as we shall see shortly.

Robert Wilks [1655–1732] was born in Ireland of a Worcestershire family, and began his career in Dublin. As a young man he came to London, but his progress under Rich was not rapid enough to satisfy him, so he returned to Dublin to make his name. He became so highly esteemed in Ireland that when he again pro-

schgitz]

ANNE OLDFIELD (from the painting in the National Portrait Gallery)

JAMES QUIN by Hogarth

posed to move to London, the Duke of Ormond, Lord Lieutenant of Ireland, tried to prevent his leaving the country. However, Wilks and his wife slipped out and travelled to London with Farquhar, who wrote *The Constant Couple* especially to create the character of Sir Harry Wildair for Wilks. The play was a great success, chiefly through Wilks's splendid acting, and firmly established its author's reputation.

Wilks was a born actor. " To beseech gracefully, to approach respectfully, to pity, to mourn, to love, are the places wherein Wilks may be made to shine with the utmost beauty," said Steele.

Thomas Dogget was also an Irishman. Nothing is known of his early life, but he joined a travelling company and made his way to London when he was quite a young man. It appears that he first played at Drury Lane in 1691 in D'Urfey's *Love for Money*. H. B. Baker in *The London Stage* says " he chiefly shone in old men and characters of low life; he was the original of Fondlewife in Congreve's *Old Bachelor*, and Ben in the same author's *Love for Love*. He had a passion for speculating on the Stock Exchange and was so enthusiastic a Whig that in his will he left a sum of money for a coat and badge to be annually rowed for by the Thames watermen on the first of August, to celebrate the accession of the House of Hanover."

There you have the three original members of the Cibber, Wilks and Dogget partnership. Dogget being an extremely shrewd, miserly financier, became the treasurer.

It is significant that as soon as this triumvirate became the proprietors and managers, Drury Lane entered upon a period of twenty years prosperity. "In the twenty years we were our own directors," Cibber records, " we never had a creditor that had occasion to come twice for his bill; every Monday morning discharged us of all demands before we took a shilling for our own use. And from this time we neither asked any actor, nor were desired by them, to sign any agreement whatsoever. The rate of their respective salaries were only enlisted in our daily pay roll, which plain record everyone looked upon as good as city security."

At that time a great new tragedian was making his name: Barton Booth. He appeared at Drury Lane in the title rôle at the first performance of Addison's *Cato*, and created such a sensation that Lord Bolingbroke used his influence to secure him a share in the theatre's patent. This infuriated Dogget, who forthwith sold his share in the partnership and withdrew entirely. Booth was therefore taken in willingly, and, if anything, the union became stronger for the change.

Barton Booth was the youngest son of a well-connected Lancashire squire, and was educated at Westminster School under Dr. Busby. He made up his mind to become an actor, but found it impossible to make a start in London, so he went to Dublin, secured an engagement for two seasons, and then came back to London to work with Betterton. His first appearance was as Maximus in *Valentinian* at Lincoln's Inn Fields in 1700, where he remained playing secondary parts until in 1705 he went with Betterton to The Queen's in Haymarket. Later he transferred to Drury Lane where he made his reputation as a tragedian and successor to Betterton. He was inclined to be pompous and had little sense of humour, but was greatly respected in the more select circles. He died at Hampstead on May 10th, 1733.

This period of prosperity at Drury Lane was due partly to two excellent actresses who delighted every type of playgoer from the most intellectual and sophisticated downwards: Mrs. Oldfield and Mrs. Porter.

Anne Oldfield, the cleverest comedienne of her time, was born in Pall Mall in 1683, a daughter of an officer in the Guards who had squandered a small fortune and made no provision for his children. She was apprenticed to a seamstress, but caught " stage-fever " and spent all her time reading plays. With her mother she lived with an aunt who kept The Mitre Tavern in St. James's Market, and it was here that Farquhar overheard her reciting passages from *The Scornful Lady* (Beaumont and Fletcher), and spoke highly of her ability. Her mother mentioned the incident to Sir John Vanbrugh, who also frequented the tavern, and he introduced Anne to Rich at Drury Lane. In 1692 she found herself engaged at fifteen shillings a week, but she seems to have done little until 1700, when she played Aurelia in *The Perjured Husband*. Her early efforts were not always satisfactory, as we find a writer at that time concluding a criticism by referring to her as " rubbish that ought to be swept off the stage with the dust and filth." But this spiteful remark must surely have been unjustified, because in December, 1704, she triumphed gloriously in Cibber's *Careless Husband*. From that time she maintained a steady stream of successes until 1730, the year in which she died. Her last appearance was on the 28th April in that year, when she played Lady Brute in *The Provok'd Wife* (Vanbrugh). She was buried in Westminster Abbey.

Mrs. Oldfield was an unusually beautiful woman, and according to Chetwood ". . . of a superior height, but with a lovely proportion; and the dignity of her soul, equal to her force and stature, made up of benevolent charity, affable and good natur'd to all that deserv'd it." She was a great favourite in fashionable circles and generally went to the theatre attended by two footmen. She had two illegitimate sons.

The date of Mary Porter's birth is unknown. She was seen as a child by Mrs. Barry and Mrs. Bracegirdle, and recommended to Betterton, who engaged her as an attendant to Mrs. Barry. It seems that she first appeared in 1699 at Lincoln's Inn Fields as Orythia in a play called *Friendship Improved*. In time she became Mrs. Barry's successor, and was acknowledged as the leading tragédienne of her time. She was not a beautiful woman, and her voice was apt to be coarse and rough, but she had a way of carrying passionate scenes to such a height of power and ardour that her audience would sit almost entranced: hence her great popularity.

She was obliged to retire from the stage for two years owing to an unfortunate accident when travelling home one night to her house near Hendon. A robber stopped her chaise, but she threatened him with a pistol and discovered that he was not a highwayman, but a poor fellow desperate through affliction. She gave him ten shillings and then whipped her horse sharply to get on her way, but the animal bolted and overthrew the chaise. Mrs. Porter's thigh-bone was dislocated, and she was afterwards compelled to support herself with a stick when on the stage.

To conclude this section, we have to return to the man whose name designates this period of theatrical history. Colley Cibber was appointed Poet Laureate in 1730, chiefly because of the Whig principles expressed in his *Nonjuror*, which was an adaptation from Molière's *Tartruffe*. This honour caused amazement and bitter resentment in Jacobite and Catholic circles, and Cibber was fiercely attacked by a number of other writers.

The days of the Cibber triumvirate drew to a close in 1732. Booth's last performance was in 1728, Mrs. Oldfield died two years later, and Wilks died in 1732, so Cibber decided to retire from management when he received an offer of three thousand pounds for his share from a gentleman amateur named Highmore.

Cibber's appearances on the stage were rare after that time, though he was far from idle, for apart from various minor activities (chiefly literary) which need not be recorded here, he published in 1740 his famous autobiography *An Apology for the Life of Colley Cibber, Comedian*, a work which has been of great value to historians of the theatre.

At the age of seventy-four he made his final appearance (at Covent Garden) as Pandulph in his own *Papal Tyranny in the Reign of King John*, a wretched perversion of Shakespeare. He died on December 12th, 1757, and was buried at what used to be the Danish Church, Wellclose Square, Whitechapel.

Highmore's lack of experience in theatrical matters ruined him within a month : Cibber's worthless son Theophilus stirred up a revolt among the players, and they all left, declaring that they could not be bought and sold like slaves. Highmore was helpless, for the actors had no contracts, and could walk out without notice of any kind, so he sold out at a great sacrifice to Charles Fleetwood, a rich young man who succeeded in collecting an indifferent crowd of old and new players and carrying on.

Fleetwood, a dishonourable gambler, allowed the standard of dramatic art at Drury Lane to sink to an appallingly low level, and for the next eight or nine years it ceased to be of any importance in the theatrical world.

LINCOLN'S INN FIELDS

When Christopher Rich was driven from Drury Lane he at once started to rebuild the old theatre in Lincoln's Inn Fields, but did not live to see the completion of this venture, and it was his son John who opened the new house on December 8th, 1714. It was a [1] " handsome building, the interior superbly adorned with mirrors on each side, the stage furnished with new scenery and ' more extended ' than Drury Lane."

John Rich was in every way a different man from his father. He was kind-hearted and amiable, and though a poor actor was brilliant as a harlequin, and became a master of pantomime.

Here we come to another rather important milestone in theatrical history : the first English pantomime of any importance. This was staged early in 1723 by a dancing master named Dr. Thurmond at Drury Lane, and called *Harlequin Doctor Faustus*. John Rich accepted this as a challenge from his rivals, and at the following Christmas produced his celebrated *Necromancer: or Harlequin Executed*, the most spectacular public show of its kind ever seen in this country up to that time. The tremendous success of this established pantomime as a fixture in the calendar of the theatres.

[1] H. B. Baker: *The London Stage* 120.

Another important date was January 29th, 1728, when Rich produced the first performance of *The Beggar's Opera*, that famous old ballad opera that has been played down through the centuries to quite recent times. The original was written by John Gay [1685–1732] the Devonshire poet and playwright who wrote his own epitaph (which may still be seen in Westminster Abbey):

"Life is a jest, and all things show it
I thought so once, and now I know it."

The music to *The Beggar's Opera* was originally arranged by Dr. Christopher Pepusch.

Rich had already succeeded in tempting away from Drury Lane an actor who was later to save his life : James Quin. He was born either in 1692 or 1693, in King Street, Covent Garden ; educated in Dublin, and in the same city made his début at the Smock Alley Theatre. He was engaged at Drury Lane somewhere about 1714, and after playing various minor parts scored a great success as Bajazet in Nicholas Rowe's *Tamerlane*. At Lincoln's Inn Fields he distinguished himself as Falstaff, and was recognised as the leading actor of his day—until Garrick came on the scene.

Karl Mantzius said of him [1] "Like his predecessor Barton Booth, he considered imperturbable dignity, regular declamation, never interrupted by a smile or an impulsive movement, the only admissible style in tragedy. And his taste was shared by the public. . . . Outside tragedy, in comedy, and especially in private life, Quin was most jovial and humorous. Very fond of a good table and a bottle, Quin possessed the genuine, old-fashioned, broad English humour, which can neither be taught nor imitated, the same humour which renders Falstaff an incomparable and inimitable character to us ; . . . his performance of fat Sir John was, according to all *connoisseurs*, a masterpiece of natural comic art."

An illustration of the appalling manners of some of the nobility in those days is an incident which occurred in 1721 during a scene in *Macbeth*. A nobleman who had been given the privilege of sitting at the side of the stage had the audacity to get up and walk across the stage in front of the players to speak to a friend. John Rich remonstrated with him and received a slap across the face for his trouble. Rich retaliated, and a general fracas ensued. Swords were drawn, and Rich's life was saved only by Quin's prompt intervention. The nobleman and his friends retired, only to

[1] *A History of Theatrical Art* 369.

return later reinforced by a gang of hooligans who smashed the mirrors at the side of the proscenium, ripped open the upholstery of the seats, and tried to set fire to the stage with torches. Fortunately, before the fire began to spread, the military arrived and quelled the commotion. From that time a guard of soldiers was posted at both Lincoln's Inn Fields and Drury Lane during the performances.

THE FIRST THEATRE AT COVENT GARDEN

In 1732 Rich abandoned his theatre in Lincoln's Inn Fields because of its dilapidated condition, and having started a subscription list for the erection of a new theatre, built a handsome new house in Covent Garden. H. B. Baker says in *The London Stage* : " The house was gorgeously decorated by the Italian artist Amiconi, who painted a magnificent ceiling representing the gods banqueting in the clouds ; the scenery, said to have been very fine, was by the same artist assisted by George Lambert, a founder of the Beefsteak Club. It was but a small theatre ; from the stage to the back of the boxes the length was only fifty-one feet, and it would hold when full not more than two hundred pounds, although space was economized to such an extent that only twenty-one inches were allowed to each person. The prices of admission were : boxes five shillings, pit three shillings and six pence, galleries two shillings and one shilling, and seats on the stage ten shillings and six pence ; there were two entrances, one under the Piazza, and the other in Bow Street." The high price of seats on the stage was fixed by Rich " in order to prevent the wings from being overcrowded."

On the opening night [December 7th, 1732] Quin appeared as Fainall in Congreve's *Way of the World*, and there was such a tremendous demand for seats that the pit was put up to five shillings : an exceptionally high price for those days.

It was at this new and fashionable house at Covent Garden that Quin enjoyed most of his greatest years. He played there for the rest of his life, with the exception of seven years at Drury Lane from 1734–41. He was a serious rival of Garrick, of whom we shall hear a great deal later, and on one memorable occasion [November 14th, 1746] he played Horatio with Garrick as Lothario, and Mrs. Cibber as Calista, in *The Fair Penitent* (Rowe). The audience cheered so loudly that the players were quite disconcerted. Garrick himself admitted it, adding " Faith, I believe Quin was as much frightened as myself."

At the beginning of the 1747–8 season, Quin wrote to Rich from Bath :

> " I am at Bath.
>> Yours,
>>> James Quin."

By return he received the reply :

> " Stay there, and be damned.
>> Yours,
>>> John Rich."

In 1750 Garrick tried to tempt Quin away from Covent Garden, and although he had no intention of moving, Quin used Garrick's offer to extort a salary of a thousand pounds a year from Rich : the greatest salary ever paid to an actor up to this time.

Quin retired in 1751 to Bath, a city he greatly admired, but returned to London on March 16th, 1752, and again on March 19th, 1753, to play Falstaff for the benefit of his old friend and colleague, Ryan. He died at his house in Bath on Tuesday, January 21st, 1766, and was buried in Bath Abbey three days later. Garrick wrote his epitaph.

THE " LITTLE THEATRE " IN HAYMARKET

Before we leave the early part of the eighteenth century, let us look at one or two of the other theatres in London at that time.

In 1720 a carpenter named John Potter acquired the site of an old inn called The King's Head, in Haymarket and erected a small theatre on it between Little Suffolk Street and James Street, almost opposite The Queen's Theatre. The Little Theatre, as it was called, opened on December 29th with the French comedy *La Fille à la Mode, ou le Badaud de Paris*, played by a company called " The French Comedians of his Grace the Duke of Montague."

The Little Theatre had a chequered existence, and in but a few years was being used for any kind of show : acrobats and whatnot. Not until 1730 did it suddenly come into the limelight, when Henry Fielding produced in it his famous burlesque of the leading writers of the day : *Tom Thumb, A Tragedy of Tragedies*. After that the theatre was used for several more of his works, including the sensational political and social satires that caused so much irritation to Sir Robert Walpole.

Fielding took over the management of the theatre in 1734. Three years later, another of his satires, *The Historical Register*, infuriated Sir Robert and brought about the Licensing Act [1737], though the actual play that made Walpole take action was an anonymous effusion called *The Golden Rump*, which had been submitted to Giffard, who was then the manager at Lincoln's Inn Fields. There was more than a grain of truth in the rumour that this pernicious play was actually written by Walpole himself—or written under his auspices—because he was anxious to lay his hands upon a thoroughly libellous work which he could show in support of his demand for a limitation of theatrical liberty. Giffard received a thousand pounds " for his loyalty " (in taking the play to Walpole), but there have always been the gravest suspicions about this anonymous work which had never been performed or printed, and had never been known to any other person in the theatrical world.

As one would imagine, the Licensing Act was extremely unpopular with the audiences, for not only did it jeopardize the existence of The Little Theatre and another small playhouse that had been built in 1729 (Goodman's Fields), but it gave an advantage to the French companies that were trying to take possession of the London stage.

The people's feelings were displayed in no uncertain manner when in 1738 a French company was billed to appear at this small Haymarket theatre. The authorities, anticipating a disturbance, sent a detachment of soldiers with a Westminster magistrate to keep order. As soon as the curtain rose, the audience found that the military had been posted actually on the stage, and with one accord they turned on the magistrate and demanded the removal of the soldiers. The magistrate thought it best for his own safety to respect the wish of the audience, and dismissed the guard, but immediately the players began to speak, their words were drowned by hisses and cat-calls. Finally the actors were pelted with peas.

THE OPERA AT HAYMARKET

Now we go over to the other side of the Haymarket where, it will be recalled Sir John Vanbrugh built an expensive new theatre in 1705 which proved acoustically a failure. It was originally named The Queen's, but it was also known as Her Majesty's, and later The King's. I mention this because these additional names are apt to be misleading.

When Owen Swiney took it over from Vanbrugh, he arranged that it should be devoted primarily to opera, and it was here that Italian opera was first established in England, although *Arsinoë* (Motteaux) had been performed at Drury Lane in 1705. Several principals were brought over from Italy, but it was not long before

CATHERINE (KITTY) CLIVE by Hogarth

DAVID GARRICK AND HIS WIFE (from the painting by Hogarth at Windsor)

a number of English singers distinguished themselves at The Queen's.

Mrs. Katherine Tofts, for instance, might be called the first English prima donna. She was born about 1680 and took part in *Arsinoë* at Drury Lane. One of her most notable performances was in Scarlatti's *Pyrrhus and Demetrius* at Haymarket in December, 1708. Cibber in his *Apology* said of her : " The beauty of her fine-proportioned figure, the exquisitely sweet silver tone of her voice, with that peculiar rapid swiftness of her throat, were perfections not to be imitated by art or labour."

Nicolini came to England in 1708, appeared in *Pyrrhus and Demetrius*, and was acclaimed to be the first truly great singer that had ever sung in a theatre. He was engaged by Swiney for three years at a salary of eight hundred guineas a year.

Two years later an even greater musician arrived in this country, the illustrious George Frederic Handel [1685–1759], who at once set to work on his opera *Rinaldo*. He finished it in fourteen days, and it was produced lavishly by Aaron Hall at The Queen's, on February 24th, 1711. It was an enormous success, though the *Spectator* found it all very amusing :

" How would the wits of King Charles's time have laughed to have seen Nicolini exposed to a tempest in robes of ermine, and sailing in an open boat upon a sea of pasteboard. What a field of raillery would they have been let into had they been entertained with painted dragons spitting wildfire, enchanted chariots drawn by Flanders mares, and real cascades in artificial landskips. . . ."

Handel brought the famous soprano Faustina to London in 1726. She made her début on May 5th, in his *Alessandro,* and for two seasons was a rival to Cuzzoni. Francesca Cuzzoni had come to London in 1722 and first appeared as Teofane in Handel's *Ottone*. It is said that at the rehearsal she refused to sing the first air in this opera because she disliked it, but Handel was having no nonsense : he picked her up by the waist and said that unless she agreed to sing it he would throw her out of the window. She then sub-mitted, and it was that very air that established her reputation in London. She became a great favourite in the opera house. At one of her performances, a man in the gallery was so moved by her singing of a high warbling passage that he exclaimed during a moment's pause for all to hear " Damn her : she's got a nest of nightingales in her belly ! " Cuzzoni fell upon hard times in later years when her voice failed her.   She was obliged to earn money by making buttons, and she died in poverty in 1770 at Bologna.

During the reign of George I the theatre became known as The King's Theatre, and in 1720 a Royal Academy of Music was established in connection with it, chiefly to supply musicians for the opera, but a series of financial failures ensued and after a loss of about fifty thousand pounds in seven years, the Academy was closed in 1728.

Observing that the public interest in opera seemed to be waning, Handel wrote the oratorio *Esther*, which was first performed in the King's Theatre.   It should be noted that this was the first oratorio to be heard in England.   Shortly afterwards his *Acis and Galatea* was sung on the same stage with equal success.

Another sensation was caused in 1734 when Carlo Farinelli came to England.   He was a castrato soprano, and possessed the finest voice in the world at the time.   Born in Naples in 1705, he was involved in a riding accident when a boy, and this necessitated the peculiar operation which enabled him to retain his fine soprano voice.   He became one of the wonders of the world, because he possessed not only a voice that would eclipse an entire orchestra in power and beauty of tone, but exceptional musicianship as well.

At his first rehearsal in London the members of the orchestra stopped playing as soon as he began to sing, and gasped in amazement : they had never known such a voice.   He received a salary of fifteen thousand pounds a year for singing in the opera here, and some idea of the prestige he enjoyed may be gathered from a report [1] that a lady who generally occupied a box used to say : " One God and one Farinelli."

Handel retired from opera in 1741, and in the same year the Earl of Middlesex took over the management of the King's Theatre.

SADLER'S WELLS

In 1683 an ancient well was discovered by some workmen who were digging in a Clerkenwell garden owned by a man named Sadler.   While the men continued to unearth the discovery their employer made investigations and found that the well contained chalybeate water, and was none other than the long lost well that had been the property of Clerkenwell Priory, and to which the most miraculous cures had been attributed.

Sadler was quick to see the possibilities of making money out of the well, because at Tunbridge Wells and Epsom the medicinal

[1] Hogarth : *The Rake's Progress.*

waters were being made the source of a princely revenue. So he exploited the discovery to the utmost, and in but a couple of weeks people with rheumatism and allied complaints, and those with purely imaginary illnesses, were flocking in their hundreds to partake of the waters.

Fortunately, Sadler's grounds were fairly extensive, so he proceeded to enclose the gardens, to lay them out tastefully, instal a dignified marble basin into which the spring of water could run, and to provide light musical entertainment for his visitors, who now numbered something like five hundred a day. And he found that it was all very profitable.

In 1699 we find two partners upon the scene: James Miles and Francis Forcer, and a wooden "Musick House" catering for a very mixed crowd: certainly nothing like the genteel patrons of the early days. A splendid picture of this "Musick House" in 1699 is given in *The London Spy* by Ned Ward. The author and his lady were out for a walk in the fields of Clerkenwell, and decided to visit Sadler's Wells:

" We enter'd the house, were conducted upstairs,
    There lovers o'er cheesecakes were seated by pairs,
    The organs and fiddles were scraping and humming,
    The guests for more ale on the tables were drumming ;
    Whilst others, ill-bred, lolling over their mugs,
    Were laughing and toying with their fans and their jugs,
    Disdain'd to be slaves to perfections, or graces,
    Sat puffing tobacco in their mistresses' faces.
    Some 'prentices, too, who made a bold venture
    And trespass'd a little beyond their indenture,
    Were each of them treating his mistress's maid,
    For letting him in when his master's abed."

Ward goes on to describe the pit :

" Where butchers and bailiffs and such sort of fellows,
    Were mix'd with a vermin train'd up to the gallows,
    As buttocks and files, housebreakers and padders,
    With prizefighters, sweet'ners, and such sort of traders,
    Informers, thief-takers, deer-stealers and bullies ;
    Some dancing, some skipping, some ranting and tearing,
    Some drinking and smoking, some lying and swearing,
    And some with the tapsters were got in a fray,
    Who without paying reck'ning were stealing away."

Miles died in 1724 and the management passed to Forcer's son, a barrister, who provided a better type of entertainment, and succeeded in attracting a more fashionable class of patron. As a Spa, too, it continued to flourish, and in 1735 Princess Amelia went there with Princess Caroline to take the waters, so for several years thereafter the nobility made it a favourite resort.

In 1743 the gardens passed to a man called Rosoman, and once again Sadler's Wells began to decline. Referring to it in his *Memoirs of Macklin*, Kirkman says :

" I remember when the price of admission here was but three-pence, except a few places scuttled off at the sides of the stage at sixpence, and which were usually reserved for people of fashion who occasionally came to see the fun. Here we smoked and drank porter, or rum and water, as much as we could pay for ; and every man had his doxy (a common loose wench) that liked it, and so forth ; and though we had a mixture of very odd company, for I believe it was the baiting place of thieves and highwaymen, there was but little or no rioting. Some hornpipes and ballad singing, with a kind of pantomimic ballet, and some lofty tumbling. . . ."

For the next twenty years Sadler's Wells provided only the lowest types of entertainment, with the exception of pantomimes, so for the present we leave it.

EARLY EIGHTEENTH-CENTURY DRAMATISTS

Before we go further, we must consider a few of the leading dramatists of this period.

Joseph Addison [1672–1719] can scarcely be regarded as a dramatist because he wrote only two plays : *Cato* and *The Drummer, or The Haunted House*. The former is of considerable importance, but the latter, a mediocre comedy, was a failure.

Sir Richard Steele was born in Dublin in the same year as Addison, and was educated with him at Charterhouse. He proceeded to Oxford and then entered the Life Guards. His fine comedy *The Christian Hero* was produced in 1701, and was notable in that it broke away from the general licentiousness of the Restoration period, but neither this nor its two successors pleased the public. So he turned to journalism and politics, becoming M.P. for Stockbridge in 1713. In the following year he was expelled from the House on account of his Hanoverian tendencies, but with the accession of George I he came back into favour and was appointed to various offices, one of which gave him the supervision of the Drury Lane theatre. He was knighted in 1715. His last

PEG WOFFINGTON (Jones Collection: artist unknown)

[*Riscl*

The Second Drury Lane Theatre (designed by Sir Christopher Wren;
the Adam front shown here was added later)

play, *The Conscious Lovers*, based on the *Andria* of Terence, was his best work for the stage. He died at Carmarthen in 1729.

Another writer whose plays were of a high moral tone was Nicholas Rowe, who was born at Little Barford, Bedfordshire, in 1674. He was educated at a private school in Highgate and then went as a King's Scholar to Westminster in 1688. In due course he entered the Middle Temple as a law student, and although he was later called to the bar and found favour with the Lord Chief Justice, he preferred to become a dramatist. His father died in 1692 and left him an income of three hundred pounds a year, which enabled him to abandon his legal career.

Rowe made the acquaintance of Addison and Pope and soon established himself as a playwright. His poetical works include a fine translation of Lucan [1718] and one of his more important achievements was his edition of Shakespeare's plays, published in 1709. On August 1st, 1715, he was made Poet Laureate in succession to Nahum Tate. Rowe failed at comedy, but his tragedies were very well received, notably *Tamerlane* [1702], *The Fair Penitent* [1704], adapted from Massinger's *Fatal Dowry*, and *Jane Shore* [1714]. He died on December 6th, 1718 and was buried in the Poets' Corner, Westminster Abbey.

The poet James Thomson did not concern himself with writing for the stage until he was nearly thirty years of age. He was born at Ednam, on the Scottish border, in September, 1700, and went to school at Jedburgh Abbey, passing on to Edinburgh University in due course. He decided upon a literary career and came to London in 1725. He had been scarcely a day in the capital when a pickpocket stole his various letters of introduction ; but nevertheless, he was able to make valuable contacts. After several encouraging successes as a poet, he wrote his first play *Sophonisba*, and had it produced at Drury Lane. Certain revisions had to be made before long because it contained the slightly ridiculous line :

"O Sophonisba, Sophonisba O ! "

—and every wit in London wrote some sort of parody on it. Fielding could not resist the temptation, for in his *Tom Thumb* he put :

"Oh ! Huncamunca, Huncamunca, Oh ! "

For all this, Thomson was not perturbed, and continued writing with considerable success. He collaborated with David Mallet in the writing of the masque *Alfred*, which contains the famous song *Rule, Britannia*.

E

Thomson's last plays were *Tancred and Sigismunda*, produced at Drury Lane in 1745 with Garrick as Tancred; and *Coriolanus*, staged posthumously at Covent Garden in January, 1749, with Quin in the leading part. He died on August 27th, 1748, and was buried in Richmond Parish Church.

Henry Fielding, the author of the famous novel *Tom Jones*, began his literary career as a playwright. He was born at Sharpham Park, near Glastonbury, Somerset, on April 22nd, 1707, and was educated at Eton. We are told that he " threw himself recklessly into the pleasures of London life " and supported himself by writing for the stage—chiefly comedies. Then he went to Leyden to study law, but returned after a while because of " a failure of remittances." Returning to play-writing in London, he found a steady demand for his comedies, farces and burlesques, but wrote too hastily to produce anything of great literary value. I have already referred to the outcome of the production of his *Tom Thumb* at the Little Theatre. Swift greatly admired this play, remarking that he had only laughed twice in his life, and that one of the two occasions was at *Tom Thumb*.

Fielding gave up play-writing at the age of thirty, and spent the rest of his life in trying to earn a steady income to support his family, having married Charlotte Craddock in 1734. He entered the Middle Temple, and was called to the bar in 1740. Four years later his wife died, and after three years as a widower he married her maid Mary Daniel.

Political journalism appealed strongly to Fielding, and ultimately with the help of Lord Lyttelton, he was made a justice of the peace for Westminster and did a great deal to suppress robbery in the neighbourhood. His great novel *Tom Jones*, described by himself as " the labour of some years of my life " was published in 1749, and his *Amelia* followed two years later.

In 1753 he became seriously ill, and in the following year had to make a voyage to Portugal, in the hope that the warmer climate would improve his condition, but he died at Lisbon on October 8th, 1754, after a stay of about two months, and was buried in the English cemetery there.

Chapter V

DAVID GARRICK

GARRICK was born on February 19th, 1717, at the Angel Inn, Lichfield, where his father, Captain Peter Garrick, who had married the daughter of a vicar-choral of the cathedral, was conducting a recruiting campaign. He was educated first at the Lichfield Grammar School, but in the summer of 1736 was sent with his brother George to the " academy " at Edial, which had just been opened by Samuel Johnson. After about six months this school closed, and Garrick left Lichfield with Johnson (who was seven years his senior) to come to London: the latter " with twopence halfpenny in his pocket " and the former " with three-halfpence in his."

With a legacy of a thousand pounds from an uncle, Garrick went into partnership with his brother Peter in a wine merchant's business, opening a branch of the original Lichfield concern in Durham Yard, Adelphi. But residence in London turned his interest in the theatre into an overwhelming passion, and he made up his mind to become an actor. He took part in amateur performances at St. John's Gate, Clerkenwell; wrote dramatic criticisms, and in a surprisingly short time succeeded in getting a play accepted for production at Drury Lane. It was a satirical revue called *Lethe*, or *Æsop in the Shades*. Haunting the theatres, he made contact with actors and managers whenever he had the chance, but it seemed almost impossible to get a start.

Opportunity came at last. One evening he was behind the scenes at Goodman's Fields when Yates, who was taking the part of Harlequin in a pantomime called *Harlequin Student*, was taken ill suddenly and asked Garrick if he could take his place incognito. Thus Garrick's first appearance on the stage was an unofficial one in March, 1741. Then he got an opportunity to join a small company going to Ipswich, and played under the name of Lyddal, gaining sufficient experience to enable him to make his début at Goodman's Fields on the following October 9th as Richard III.

This theatre had been closed on account of the Licensing Act

[1737], but the manager had found a way of evading the law by presenting " A Concert of Vocal and Instrumental Music, divided into Two Parts " and giving a play *gratis* between the first and second half! The playbill announcing the concert on October 9th proclaimed that the part of King Richard would be played by a " Gentleman who had never appeared on any stage."

The unnamed " Gentleman " caused the biggest sensation the theatre had known for many a year. Playgoers crowded night after night into the hitherto unfashionable Goodman's Fields Theatre to see this masterly young actor whose fire and passion could hold them spellbound. The press duly reflected the wonder and delight of the audiences, and within a week all London was bubbling with excitement. Pope declared " That young man never had a rival and never will. . . ." William Pitt proclaimed that Garrick was the only actor in England, and " a dozen dukes a night," it was said, could be found in the house.

The critics, though full of praise, were puzzled; for Garrick's technique was something quite new. Quin declared that if Garrick were right, then he and all the other actors were wrong. For the theatrical profession generally, it was all very disconcerting.

Garrick, finding that he had lost five hundred pounds in the wine business, wrote to his brother without further delay asking to be released from the partnership. Then he threw himself utterly and completely into the work he loved. He played in one of Cibber's comedies, produced a farce of his own, *The Lying Valet*, played Lothario in *The Fair Penitent*, the Ghost in *Hamlet*, and Fondlewife in Congreve's *Old Bachelor*, scoring a fresh triumph every time. His versatility was phenomenal.

The extent to which people forsook Drury Lane and Covent Garden for Goodman's Fields so alarmed the managers of the larger theatres that they sought the help of Sir John Bernard to enforce the Licensing Act, and succeeded in closing their little rival theatre again on May 27th, 1742.

Garrick was then engaged by Fleetwood for Drury Lane at a salary of six hundred guineas a year, but before starting there he went on a short visit to Dublin, where his success, according to Hitchcock in his *Correct View of the Irish Stage* " exceeded all imagination." Dublin, it is said, went down *en bloc* with " Garrick fever." He played there with the fascinating Peg Woffington, who was also his mistress, and to whom, we are told, he wrote the following verses :

The Sun, first rising in the morn,
That paints the dew-bespangled Thorn,
Does not so much the day adorn,
As does my lovely Peggy.

While bees from Flowers to Flowers rove,
And Linnets warble through the Grove,
Or stately swans the waters love,
So long shall I love Peggy.

And when Death with his Pointed Dart,
Shall strike the blow that rends my heart,
My words shall be when I depart,
Adieu, my lovely Peggy.

This alluring creature had been born in Dublin to very humble parents, and had gained her first experience in a children's company. As a young woman her pretty face and voluptuous figure helped her to find employment in London, and she soon proved her ability. She lived with Garrick for several years, taking it in turn, month by month, to pay the household expenses. Garrick was decidedly parsimonious, and their guests had to become accustomed to lavish hospitality when Peg was paying, but to the most meagre victuals when it was Garrick's turn!

Peg Woffington was extremely kind-hearted and generous, but she had no moral sense whatever, and even during her years with Garrick she indulged regularly in promiscuous relations with half-a-dozen other men. For all that, she burst into a frantic rage when Garrick announced his intention of marrying somebody else. In 1757 she was playing Rosalind in *As You Like It* when she sustained a paralytic stroke and was carried screaming with terror from the stage. She died three years later and was buried at Teddington.

When Garrick returned from Dublin he was not an entire stranger at Drury Lane, for he had already made an appearance there on May 11th, 1742, as Chamont, in Otway's play *The Orphan*. Among the other players he found there were Charles Macklin, Kitty Clive and Mrs. Pritchard.

Macklin is important because it was his initiative that raised Drury Lane out of the depth of artistic decay into which it had sunk after Cibber's retirement. He was born in the north of Ireland towards the close of the seventeenth century, educated at Island Bridge, near Dublin, and became interested in amateur theatricals. He ran away from home, came to London, and at first supported himself by serving in a public house.   Then he joined a company of strolling players, gaining experience here and there until in 1725 he appeared in London playing the part of Alcander in *Œdipus* (Dryden and Lee) at Lincoln's Inn Fields.   Fleetwood engaged him for Drury Lane, and his first appearance there was on October 31st, 1733, as Brazen in *The Recruiting Officer ;* but the audiences continued to diminish, and in 1741, when business was about as bad as it could be, Macklin went to Fleetwood and suggested that as *The Merchant of Venice* had not been performed for forty years, he should revive it in its original form. (A spurious version by Lord Lansdowne entitled *The Jew of Venice* had been staged occasionally).

Macklin's proposal was received with astonishment and the gravest doubt, but believing that nothing could send the box-office receipts much lower, the management decided to make the experiment.   Its success was sensational.   Macklin, as Shylock,[1] " marked a new epoch in the conception of this character, and it was the climax of his own art."   Instead of seeing the weak, ridiculous Shylock to whom they had become accustomed, the people now saw the true character in all his vileness.   Pope summed up Macklin's triumph neatly in the couplet :

> " This is the Jew
> That Shakespeare drew."

Of the early life of Kitty Clive we know little.   She was the daughter of an impecunious Irish gentleman, but appears to have been in domestic service as a girl.   It is said that she was singing while scrubbing the steps of a house opposite the Bell Tavern in London, and attracted the attention of the members of the Beefsteak Club, who were wont to meet in the tavern.   They were so enchanted by her voice that two of them (Beard and Dunstall) mentioned her to Cibber.   In 1728 she made her début as Ismenes, in Lee's *Mithridates*, and the playgoers were delighted with this spirited girl of seventeen and her fine singing voice.   Later, she made a great hit in Charles Coffey's popular little opera *The Devil to Pay*, for in this her great talent for comic parody and caricature was given boundless scope.   Curiously enough, although she married a barrister, George Clive, and left him within a few months, she led an entirely blameless life and always supported her aged father.

Little, too, is known of the early life of Mrs. Hannah Pritchard, except that she was born in 1711 and married a poor actor.   She

---

[1] Mantzius : *History of Theatrical Art* 372.

appeared in *The Devil to Pay*, and soon became one of the most brilliant stars of the Garrick galaxy. She was acknowledged to be the greatest Lady Macbeth of this period, but was also a conspicuous success as the Queen in *Hamlet*, although she was not a very intelligent person.

Mrs. Susannah Cibber was born in London in February, 1714, daughter of a Covent Garden upholsterer. Her brother, Thomas Arne, by the way, distinguished himself as a composer. Mrs. Cibber was musical and well read, and made her first appearance as a singer at the Haymarket in 1732 in the Lumpé opera *Amelia*. Within four years she was a musical celebrity. She was first seen as an actress in Aaron Hill's version of Voltaire's tragedy *Zaire*. One cannot help wondering what induced her to marry the contemptible Theophilus Cibber, but she soon discovered what a wretched fellow he was, and left him for another man. Cibber claimed five thousand pounds in damages, but was awarded only ten, the jury being quite capable of judging his character.

The great composer Handel was very favourably impressed by Mrs. Cibber's voice and musicianship : she was the first Galatea in his *Acis and Galatea*, and he wrote the fine contralto arias in his immortal *Messiah* expressly for her. When Dr. Delaney, friend of Dean Swift, heard her sing these, he exclaimed, " Woman, for this be all thy sins forgiven thee ! " Burney remarked, " She captivated every ear by the sweetness and expression of her voice." She died in 1766 at her house in Scotland Yard, Westminster, and was buried in the cloisters of Westminster Abbey.

It did not take Garrick long to discover the innumerable deficiencies in Fleetwood's appalling management. Throughout 1743 and 1744 Drury Lane prospered solely because Macklin was able to make good some of Fleetwood's shortcomings ; but the day came when the players could tolerate the management no longer, and they went to see the Lord Chamberlain in the hope of being able to obtain a licence to open in Haymarket. Alas ! he refused, and there was nothing to do but to return to Fleetwood, who in his indignation refused to reinstate Macklin because he believed him to have been responsible for the revolt. Garrick offered to pay Macklin's salary out of his own pocket, but the offended Irishman refused it, and organized a riot in the theatre on the opening night of the season. Fleetwood promptly engaged gangs of toughs and bruisers who had to be present every night to deal with the rioters. After a number of disgraceful free fights in the pit, Fleetwood was compelled to re-engage Macklin.

In 1745 Garrick, dissatisfied with the conditions at Drury Lane, went to Dublin and became joint-manager with Thomas Sheridan at the Theatre Royal, Smock Alley, where there was a splendid company, including Spranger Barry and Miss George Anne Bellamy.

After a most successful season, Garrick returned to London and accepted an invitation from Rich to play at Covent Garden, where he rose to new heights of fame.

By this time, Fleetwood at Drury Lane had become so heavily in debt that his creditors forced him to sell out, and the theatre came into the hands of James Lacy, who invited Garrick to go into partnership with him. The agreement was that Lacy should control the business side, and that Garrick should become the artistic and administrative director. The latter's share cost him eight thousand pounds, and so England's greatest actor achieved his life's ambition.

DRURY LANE UNDER GARRICK

The new regime started on September 15th, 1746, and what a change was brought about! All the slackness and indifference disappeared overnight; punctuality at rehearsals was enforced, players were suspended if they acted their parts imperfectly, and above all, the evil practice of allowing privileged people to sit on the stage was abolished.

Garrick did a great deal to restore Shakespeare's works to their original form. *Macbeth* had been turned into a distressing form of pseudo-opera, *Romeo and Juliet* into a fatuous comedy, *The Merchant of Venice* into a cheap farce, and so forth. He changed most of this, but it is to be regretted that he failed to do so completely, and that simply to please a stupid audience, he made some deplorable alterations himself. Few can forgive, for instance, his addition of a dying speech to the text of *Macbeth*. Nevertheless, we must give him credit where it is due. Quin, who had become accustomed to the Shakespeare-D'Avenant *Macbeth*, demanded in his ignorance one day, "Don't I play *Macbeth* as Shakespeare wrote it?" Shortly afterwards he heard Garrick speaking the original lines and capped this with, "Where in the world did the fellow get that from?" So we must be fair to Garrick, and remember the ignorant times he lived in.

At least twenty-four revivals of Shakespeare took place during Garrick's regime, but even with an excellent company under good management, Drury Lane had a hard struggle against Covent Garden, where Rich was drawing vast crowds to his pantomimes.

On June 22nd, 1749, Garrick married a lovely dancer named Eva Maria Speigel, known on the stage as Mlle. Violetti, " at the church in Russell Street, Bloomsbury, and afterwards at the chapel of the Portuguese embassy in Audley Street." He had become tired of Peg Woffington's wantonness, though it is reported that he offered to marry her if she would mend her ways. The Garricks took a house for a few years in Southampton Street, Strand (now No. 27), but in 1754 purchased their famous little house at Hampton.

The marriage infuriated Peg Woffington who forsook Drury Lane forthwith, and in 1750 both Spranger Barry and Mrs. Cibber followed her, though the latter returned after a while. The loss of three principals by Drury Lane gave Covent Garden by far the stronger company, and Garrick, much against his will, was compelled to stage pantomimes in opposition to Rich in order to check the diminution of his audiences.

In 1755 the King was present at Drury Lane at a Command Performance of *The Chinese Festival* (Noverre) when a riot broke out in both the pit and the gallery on account of the foreign dancers employed by Garrick. Great damage was done to the theatre, and the rioters even attacked Garrick's town house in Southampton Street. Three days later when Garrick came on the stage he told the audience politely but firmly that if such a disturbance ever occurred again, he would leave the stage and never return.

The competition from Covent Garden continued to cause anxiety at Drury Lane, and on one never-to-be-forgotten night the takings dropped as low as five pounds. So Garrick decided to make a continental tour, and left this country with his wife in September, 1763, for Paris. They were given a wonderful reception, and made the acquaintance of Diderot in the house of Baron d'Holbach. They then proceeded to Italy, toured extensively, returned by way of Munich to Paris and eventually arrived back in London in April, 1765.

Garrick's lengthy absence and the enthusiasm with which he had been greeted on the continent made the London audiences realise the greatness of the actor they had neglected. He was by then a wealthy man, and was quite prepared to retire, but the King, George III, commanded him to return to Drury Lane, and he was received by a wildly excited audience.

On December 29th, 1775, *The Merchant of Venice* was staged at Drury Lane with an unknown actress as Portia. She was a young lady named Siddons who had come up from a travelling company in the country because Garrick thought she showed some promise, but alas ! she was a complete failure, chiefly on account of " nerves." After one or two other appearances described by the critics as " lamentable," she fled back to her actor husband in the provinces. But we shall hear more of her later.

In 1776 Garrick announced his intention of retiring, and vast audiences drawn from all parts of the country flocked to his farewell performances. On June 10th he made his last appearance on the stage in *The Wonder*, by Centlivre, and there arose a [1] " universal pæan of praise . . . from the greatest men of every variety of taste and prejudice that England, or perhaps the world, has ever known."

His retirement was short, for he died on January 20th, 1779, barely sixty-two years of age, leaving about a hundred thousand pounds. He had a magnificent funeral : [2] " The streets were crowded, and the string of carriages extended from the Strand to the Abbey. The Bishop of Rochester received the *cortège*. The pall-bearers were the Duke of Devonshire, Lords Camden, Ossory, Spencer and Palmerston, and Sir Watkin Wynne." Johnson remarked " I am disappointed by that stroke of death which has eclipsed the gaiety of nations, and impoverished the public stock of harmless pleasure." Garrick was buried at the foot of Shakespeare's statue in the Abbey.

Although Garrick excelled as an actor and manager, he made one or two serious errors of judgment : for instance, he refused to perform John Home's popular tragedy *Douglas*, in which Anne Barry scored a tremendous success as Lady Randolph ; and Goldsmith's first comedy *The Good Natur'd Man*.

In addition to those I have already mentioned, there were one or two other noteworthy players of the Garrick period. Spranger Barry, for one, was born in Skinner Row, Dublin, in 1719, son of an eminent silversmith of that city. He succeeded his father into the business, but mismanaged it and became a bankrupt, so he turned to the stage for a livelihood. He was first seen at the Smock Alley Theatre, Dublin, and in time distinguished himself there in Shakespearean rôles ; then after meeting Garrick he was engaged for Drury Lane, where he found favour very quickly. In 1750 he had a dispute with Garrick, and with Mrs. Cibber went over to Covent Garden, playing there for eight years until he went back to Dublin with Woodward to build the Crow Street Theatre, which was opened on October 23rd, 1758. He also opened a new theatre

[1] H. B. Baker: *The London Stage* v. I. 93.   [2] D.N.B.

in Cork in 1761. But after a few years of fierce competition in Dublin he returned to London to play at the Haymarket.

In 1768 Barry married Mrs. Anne Dancer, and both were engaged by Garrick at Drury Lane. Mrs. Dancer was born in Bath in 1734 and played in the provinces until she obtained an engagement at Crow Street Theatre, Dublin, where she was a regular actress for nine years.

Barry went over to Covent Garden again in 1774 and took his wife with him. He died in 1777, but Mrs. Barry did not retire from the stage until some twenty years afterwards. Of the two, she was the greater, being a superb actress in both tragedy and comedy. She was buried near her husband in the cloisters of Westminster Abbey.

Mrs. Bellamy was named George Anne in mistake for Georgina. Her mother had been Lord Tyrawley's mistress, but married a Captain Bellamy and presented the poor fellow with a daughter with such promptness that he ran away from her and was never seen again. Lord Tyrawley was, of course, the girl's father, and paid for her education in a convent at Boulogne. When quite a girl, George Anne happened to make the acquaintance of Peg Woffington and Garrick, but it was Rich who first engaged her as an actress. She made a great impression in 1744 as Monimia in *The Orphan*, and Quin, who at first had objected to playing with " such a child " admitted that she was " a divine creature." Alas ! her charms intrigued Lord Byron (not the famous poet), who abducted her. His ardour brought upon her a severe illness, and she was obliged to retire from the stage for some months. She reappeared in Dublin and enjoyed two years of triumphant success there.

Her private life by this time had become a by-word in the profession. Doran in *Their Majesties' Servants* writes " To say that she was a syren who lured men to destruction is to say little, for she went down to ruin with each victim ; but she rose from the wreck more exquisitely seductive and terribly fascinating than ever. . . . She was so beautiful, had eyes of such soft and loving blue, was so extraordinarily fair, and was altogether so irresistible a sorceress, that Mrs. Bellamy was universally loved as a charming creature. . . ."

On October 22nd, 1748, she returned to Covent Garden as Belvidera in *Venice Preserved*, and played there until she went to Drury Lane to play Juliet with Garrick in 1750. For the next thirty years she appeared regularly in London, Dublin and Scot-

land. Her last performance was at her benefit night at Drury
Lane in 1785, and she died on February 16th, 1788.

COVENT GARDEN

During the Garrick period pantomime was the chief attraction
at Covent Garden. Rich died in 1761 and left the theatre to his
son-in-law, John Beard, who shortly afterwards sold it to the elder
Colman, Harris Rutherford and Powell. The partners quarrelled
over a woman—Mrs. Lessingham—and a lawsuit took place in
1770. That, however, is not of any great importance to us. What
does concern us is that on March 15th, 1773, the Covent Garden
company gave the first performance of Goldsmith's famous comedy
She Stoops to Conquer. Curiously enough, Colman originally
refused this play, and it was only the persistence of Dr. Johnson
that made him change his mind. The players, too, disliked it,
but the first night sealed the success of this play : the audience
applauded with wild enthusiasm.

Another notable date at Covent Garden was May 7th, 1789,
when Macklin at the age of *ninety-two* made his last appearance on
the stage. He played Shylock, but broke down after the first few
speeches, and turning to the audience he begged their pardon and
asked them to allow his understudy to continue in his place. He
died at the age of 100 at No. 4 Tavistock Row, Covent Garden,
and was buried beneath the chancel of St. Paul's Parish Church
nearby. At least one historian maintains that Macklin was born
in 1690, in which case he would have been 107 when he died !

THE HAYMARKET

We have already seen how one theatre manager cleverly evaded
the Licensing Act. Samuel Foote in the middle of the eighteenth
century hit upon an even more subtle plan when he wanted to give
a performance in the Little Theatre in the Haymarket without a
licence.

In the *General Advertiser* there appeared the announcement :

"On Saturday afternoon, exactly at twelve o'clock, at the
New Theatre in the Haymarket, Mr. Foote begs the favour of
his friends to come and drink a dish of chocolate with him,
and 'tis hoped there will be a great deal of company and some
joyous spirits. He will endeavour to make the afternoon as
diverting as possible. Tickets to be had for this entertainment
at George's Coffee House, Temple Bar, without which no one
will be admitted.

N.B.—Sir Dilbury Diddle will be there, and Lady Betty Frisk has absolutely promised."

Everybody's curiosity was aroused immediately, and people flocked to the theatre for this novelty. When the curtain rose, Foote appeared on the stage, greeted his "friends," and suggested that while the chocolate was being prepared they might care to watch him training some young actors and actresses for the stage! Then the performance took place in the ordinary manner while the audience enjoyed not only their chocolate but also the knowledge that once again the Lord Chamberlain had been fooled by a clever manager.

Foote then arranged evening performances, genially inviting his "friends" to have "tea" with him! The playgoers loved these shows, and "having a dish of tea with Mr. Foote" became the most fashionable pursuit of the leisured classes.

Samuel Foote [1720–1777] was born at Truro, educated at Worcester and Oxford, and came to London as a law student. Actually he became a fashionable idler with a *flair* for mimicry, and eventually found his way on to the stage. He established himself as an actor, and wrote many amusing sketches. His best work was the comedy *The Minor* [1760], a satire directed against the Methodists. All manner of prominent people were pilloried in his caricatures.

In 1766 Foote visited Lord Mexborough at the latter's country residence. Thinking that it would amuse the other guests, his host made him ride upon a singularly intractable horse, and as one might have expected, Foote was thrown off. His leg was fractured in two places, and it had to be amputated. Mexborough, feeling that some sort of amends should be made to the actor, went to the King and persuaded His Majesty to give Foote a licence to open the Little Theatre in Haymarket officially between May 14th and September 14th of each year. It was that licence that induced Foote to rebuild the house in 1767.

OLIVER GOLDSMITH

Goldsmith, son of an Irish clergyman, was born in 1728, either at Pallasmore, Longford, or at Elphin, Roscommon. His birthplace is the subject of controversy among historians. He was educated at various grammar schools, but his schooling was interrupted by a severe attack of small-pox which left a permanent disfigurement of his features. This, and the fact that he was a small and rather delicate-looking lad, made him the butt of spiteful attacks from both masters and schoolfellows. He was even branded as a dunce and flogged.

At Trinity College, Dublin, he was a sizar (i.e., a student who paid very little and who was obliged to perform certain menial duties). He was desperately poor, and frequently had to eke out an existence by writing street-ballads which he sold for five shillings each. He graduated and offered himself for ordination, but was rejected. After trying to make a start in two or three other professions, he went to Edinburgh to study medicine, but apparently took little interest in the subject, for he worked in a desultory manner and made little progress. He proceeded to Leyden, still with the intention of qualifying as a physician, but we are told that he left this university, too, without a degree. Then for some considerable time he merely wandered about France, Switzerland and Italy earning just enough money to pay for a bed and a meal here and there by playing his flute for dancing.

Returning to London in 1756, penniless and with scarcely a friend in the world, he undertook a succession of servile jobs to keep him from starvation, for although he made vague claims to having taken a doctor's degree on the continent, he was rejected as unqualified when he sought a lowly medical appointment in a hospital.

Goldsmith then became a literary hack, and took an attic to which he had to climb a long flight of stone stairs called Breakneck Steps, in the Ludgate Hill district. He wrote poems and articles, did translations and all manner of odd literary tasks for local booksellers.

In time, his work became quite popular, and he was able to withdraw from the companionship of beggars and thieves and mix with men of letters. He became acquainted with Smollett, met Reynolds the painter, and was introduced to Edmund Burke. His new friends were not enthusiastic about his garret : the scarcity of its furniture and the inadequacy of its heating made entertaining difficult. One of them called on a bitterly cold winter's day and found Goldsmith working without a fire, so a neighbour's child had to be sent out to fetch a small quantity of coal in a humble bedroom utensil.

He moved to a more comfortable dwelling at No. 6 Wine Office Court, Fleet Street, in 1760. By this time he was contributing to various magazines and enjoying a connection with leading booksellers. He met Samuel Johnson in the following year and became one of the original members of " The Club " (the famous Literary Club).

But money matters still continued to harass him. In 1764 he was living at Islington with his rent so much in arrears that his landlady had been obliged to call in the sheriff's officer. Goldsmith sent a messenger round to Johnson asking for a loan of a guinea to pay to the landlady on account. Johnson sent the money and decided to visit Goldsmith. To his astonishment he arrived to discover that his insolvent friend had changed the guinea and was abusing the landlady over a bottle of Madeira wine. Johnson put the cork back into the bottle and demanded to know how the money was going to be found. Goldsmith then produced the manuscript of his novel *The Vicar of Wakefield*. His friend glanced through it, saw that it was readily saleable, and took it stright away to a bookseller, disposing of it for sixty pounds.

In the same year Goldsmith's famous poem *The Traveller* appeared, and the success of this, with *The Vicar of Wakefield* which was published in 1766, encouraged him to try writing for the stage. His *Good Natur'd Man* was refused by Garrick, but was produced at Covent Garden in January, 1768, and although it made no great impression it brought him about five hundred pounds.

We cannot consider his other literary works in this book, so we must pass on to his second play *She Stoops to Conquer*. This was a complete triumph, and it is regrettable that its success did not induce him to write more for the stage. He died on April 4th, 1774, at the age of forty-five, and was buried in the Temple Churchyard, though no trace of his grave can now be found.

Chapter VI

THE STROLLING PLAYERS

SO far, we have been concerned chiefly with drama in London, so before we proceed, let us see how the provinces fared during the seventeenth and eighteenth centuries. There is not a great deal of reliable information about the early history of the provincial theatres, but we do know that the majority of the plays were provided by the " strolling players," though it is true that during the summer months the greater provincial cities would sometimes be favoured by a visit from one of the London companies.

It would be quite impossible to make even a rough estimate of the number of strolling companies there were in existence, but it is almost certain that there was one attached to each of the larger towns, and that such a company would generally make short tours in the immediate neighbourhood. Incidentally, some of the better established and less mobile companies disliked the designation " strolling players."

Apart from these, there were also innumerable little bands of unlicensed players who would eke out a precarious existence by touring the smaller towns. Their life was a hard one : they were often at the mercy of an unscrupulous manager who saw that the bulk of the profits went into his own pocket. We are told that they frequently went without food, and that after a week's hard work their only share of the profit would be a stock supper "which was generally ended in a Quarrel by way of Dessert." For all that, there were plenty who loved the life, and we have evidence of their high-spirits from the travellers who used to meet them on the roads.

Travelling was difficult for the poorest companies, as each man had to carry a share of the scenery or wardrobe on his back ! Usually, however, at least one waggon was employed, and of course, it was generally the manager who claimed the privilege of riding on it so that he could keep an eye on the properties. Some of the more prosperous companies had a coach as well, but even then, accidents were not uncommon. In bad weather they would get stuck on the poor roads, and there was always the danger of being overturned.

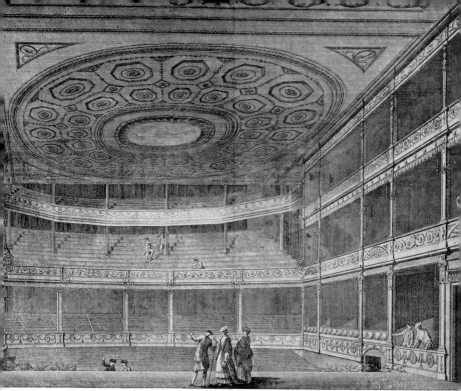

hgitz] ⸱ Interior of the Second Drury Lane Theatre (pulled down 1791). Below:
The Theatre Royal, Bristol (1766), restored by C.E.M.A. 1943
hitectural Review]

THE THEATRE ROYAL, DRURY LANE.
Built by the late   Henry Holland Esqʳ R.A.
As it appeared from the North East; Antecedent to its destruction   by Fire, on the Night of the 24ᵗʰ February, 1809. With a Plan

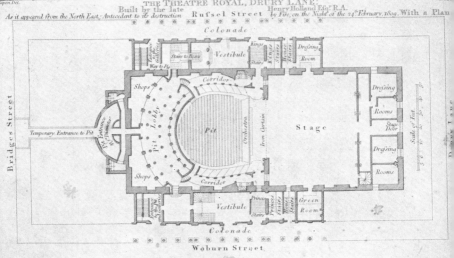

The Third Theatre Royal, Drury Lane (from the north-east)

On their arrival at a town they had first to get permission to perform from the mayor or magistrates. Sometimes one or two of the players would ride on ahead of the rest to secure this in advance. Then the players would put on their smartest clothes (generally borrowed from the company's wardrobe) and gather in the centre of the town, beat a drum and distribute playbills .

Performances had to be given wherever accommodation could be found : inn-yards, barns, town halls, and so forth. If their luck was out they would sometimes have to resort to a stable. John Bernard in his *Recollections of the Stage* says that his first experience as an actor was in a room in an inn where the manager had :

" suspended a collection of green tatters along its middle for a curtain, erected a pair of paper screens right-hand and left for wings ; arranged four candles in front of said wings to divide the stage from the orchestra (the fiddlers' chairs being legitimate division of the orchestra from the Pit), and with all the spare benches of the inn to form boxes, and a hoop suspended from the ceiling (perforated with a dozen nails to receive as many tallow candles) to suggest the idea of a chandelier; he had constructed and embellished what he denominated a Theatre."

The properties were just about as meagre as the costumes, though in *The Strollers* [Breval: 1727] a character explains proudly : " . . . we have a Second-hand Dragon, that lost a Wing and two Claws in an opera last Winter."

The larger companies would take their own little orchestra with them, but the others had to be content with engaging whatever musicians they could find in the towns they visited : generally a motley crowd whose efforts would distress even the most hardened ear. More often than not, a couple of fiddlers would represent the entire available musical talent of the town, and it would indeed be fortunate if both were found to be sufficiently capable and sober to play the music required of them.

Notwithstanding the paucity of the players and their properties, the eighteenth-century theatrical announcements in the provincial press were the most lengthy extravaganzas of verbosity and exaggeration imaginable !

Some idea of the life of the strolling players—even when they possessed a thoroughly honourable and enterprising manager —may be gained from S. W. Ryley's most interesting book *The Itinerant* [published in 1808]. He writes :

F

" The sharing plan was always my aversion; to remedy this I made a proposal to try the town of Ludlow upon small salaries of half-guinea, fifteen shillings, and a guinea, according to the merits and utility of the different performers. . . .

" . . . I was waiting at the theatre with some impatience, when the stage-keeper came running to inform me that the waggon was overturned and Mr. Long killed. In an instant I was on the spot and sure enough there lay the contents of the cart, and Bonny Long under the whole. The crowd had considerably increased: some were humanely employed in lifting off boxes in order to release the sufferer, others supported his wife, who though safe from the fall, was in fits for the fate of her husband, whilst the eight little brats in scarlet jackets ran about like dancing dogs prepared for a stage exhibition. Poor Long was at length liberated with no other inconvenience than was occasioned by the suffocating dust arising from the old scenes, which had completely preserved him from the pressure of the boxes.

" The theatre was a miserably poor place, and when filled would scarcely contain twenty pounds. We opened it the following Monday with the comedy of *The Beaux' Stratagem*. The receipts amounted to five pounds, and although the company were much reduced, I found a continuance of such receipts would disable me from paying the salaries. The second and third nights were not much better, and the third week I found myself under the unpleasant necessity of addressing the company and placing them on the old establishment.

" The houses instead of improving, went from bad to worse; dissatisfaction generally prevailed—' the sharing was not an existence.' This I very readily allowed, but surely no blame could be attached to me: in vain I urged the small receipts and heavy disbursements. One more witty than the rest chose to exercise his humour at my expense, and on the following day was seen walking down with his five shilling share in a canvas purse at the end of his stick placed over his right shoulder; jocularly informing every one who inquired that his last week's share was so heavy. This sarcasm hurt me greatly. Ludlow races now approached and great expectations were formed: overflowing houses were promised, and I vainly hoped it would be in my power to make amends for the miserable pittance they had hitherto received. But here, as in most of my undertakings, fortune dashed down the cup of hope just as I was

raising it to my lips—on the first race night, a ball opposed the
theatre, and the receipts were so trifling it was not thought
proper to perform. To make amends for this I applied to the
stewards to patronise the next night, but this could not be
effected : the grand ordinary dinner was to be that evening, and
would detain the company till a late hour. As there were only
two days' races I was now at my wits' end : the only probable
way of drawing them to the theatre was to perform in the morning. Again I waited on the stewards and obtained their consent
and promised attendance. Accordingly, the *Castle of Andalusia*
was advertised by desire of the stewards of the race, to begin at
eleven o'clock. This new and unpleasant time of performance
was particularly irksome—to shut out daylight and to substitute
candles for the glorious sun on a hot summer's morn appeared
little better than sacrilege ; but there was no alternative between
this and empty benches. The time arrived, and with this
astonishing patronage we raised eleven pounds."

The proprietors of the Wolverhampton theatre promised
Ryley that if he went there his receipts could not be less than two
hundred pounds. Here is what happened in Ryley's own words :

" We arrived without accident, and the theatre was advertised
to open on the Monday. Had I been as well acquainted as I
am now with the description of people who attend fairs,
especially merry-making fairs, I should never have undertaken
this disastrous journey. Three, four and five pounds were the
customary receipts. In a state of mind bordering on distraction
I went over to Birmingham, and, by way of *forcing* a house for
the last night, engaged Messrs. Grist, Banks and Barrymore to
perform in *Othello* and *Rosina*, for which I was to give them each
a guinea and pay the chaise-hire. The receipts of that night,
with all this *great acting*, amounted to seven pounds ! ! ! out of
which I had to pay these gentlemen three guineas, besides
travelling expenses ! ! ! I have known actors, aye and poor ones
too, who would have received the three guineas with some
appearance of regret ; nay, there are those who would not have
taken them at all : but these great people were superior to such
little prejudices. They not only received them with ease and
good-humour, but the greatest man of the three made a famous
good story of it, to the great delight of his auditors in the Birmingham green-room next day. Yet so blind was I to the
narrowness of this conduct, that the supper bill (no small one,

it may be supposed when 'tis recollected who composed the party) I discharged under the idea of gentlemanly hospitality—a prejudice which ought to have died with my shipwrecked fortune. The hour of departure arrived, and thirty pounds, the whole of the week's receipts, were all that I had to satisfy the actors, by lending each a little, and a long train of incidental expenses incurred by the journey, besides chaises to carry us back, and maintenance on the road. This was the greatest difficulty I ever experienced; to wait upon the different tradesmen with apologies instead of money was, to a man of my temperament, grating beyond all description. However, there was no alternative : when I told my story, they were gentle and kind, and would patiently wait my own time of payment. Credit for chaises to transport us back was likewise cheerfully granted, and we left Wolverhampton, after this inauspicious week, minus about fifty pounds."

Poor, generous old Ryley! One cannot help feeling sorry for this kind-hearted soul who tried so hard to improve the lot of his company. Fortunately, these losses were sometimes made good by a few successful weeks, particularly if the players had the good fortune to get a theatre in one of the larger towns. So let us now look at the theatres in a few of the provincial cities where drama prospered. It will not, of course, be possible to include in this modest volume a complete history of all the more historic provincial theatres.

BATH

Queen Anne visited Bath in 1702 to take the waters in the Pump Room, and was so charmed by this ancient city that she planned a return visit in the following year. Colley Cibber in his *Apology* tells us that during Her Majesty's second visit the Drury Lane company went down to the famous spa to entertain her, and that it was in Bath that Mrs. Oldfield made a great hit (much to his astonishment) as Leonora in *Sir Courtly Nice*.

Bath's first theatre was built in 1705 by public subscription. We are told that people of the highest rank contributed, and accordingly had their names engraved on the walls inside the auditorium. It was erected at the corner of Borough Walls and what is now Parsonage Lane, and was first used by a company known as " The Duke of Grafton's Servants," led by John Power, who had been playing in Bristol.

The Daily Courant dated September 24th, 1706, informs us that the Duke and Duchess of Beaufort and other people of quality had attended a performance of *The Recruiting Officer* at the Bath Theatre.

It seems that despite excellent patronage this playhouse deteriorated slightly in later years, because Daniel Defoe in his *Tour Through the Whole Island of Great Britain* recorded the following impression after his visit to Bath in 1725 :

" In the afternoon there is generally a Play, tho' the Decorations are mean, and the Performances accordingly ; but it answers, for the Company here (not the Actors) make the Play, to say no more."

But in 1728 John Gay visited the city to produce his famous *Beggar's Opera*, and created a great sensation. *The Bristol News* of May 11th says :

" We hear from Bath, That last Week all the Quality went to the Playhouse to hear the Rehearsal of *The Beggar's Opera*. . . And that on Monday and Wednesday last, notwithstanding the Pit and Boxes were laid together, they were so full, that they turn'd as many away as they took in : "

The Bath playhouse was closed by the Licensing Act in 1737, and was purchased by the Trustees of the Mineral Water Hospital, who demolished it forthwith. Part of this hospital now stands upon the site of this theatre. Lady Hawley then allowed the players to use the large chamber beneath the ballroom of the Assembly Rooms. Some years later they moved to The Globe Inn in Kingsmead Square for a while, and then to The George Inn. Eventually a new theatre was built in Orchard Street.

NORWICH

Immediately after the Restoration, Norwich became a popular centre for the provincial companies of players, in fact the Corporation had to ask for powers to limit the stay of strolling players because " they drain too much money from the inhabitants."

The favourite rendezvous of the players was The Red Lion (since replaced by The Cricketers' Arms), though in 1692 we find a company playing " att the Angell in St. Peter of Mancroft " as well. At the latter there was a disaster on January 27th, 1699, while a play was in progress. Dawks' *News Letter* records that " . . . the House being very full, it broke down the Gallery, which kill'd a young Woman outright, and dangerously bruised and wounded a great many people."

Early in the eighteenth century both The King's Arms and The Queen's Arms were being used for theatrical purposes, but the principal theatre was the White Swan Playhouse, which also stood near the lovely old church of St. Peter Mancroft. It was partly rebuilt in 1739 and again in 1747 when Macklin paid it a visit.

An entirely new theatre was built in Norwich in 1758. *The Norwich Gazette* of January 28th of that year declares :

" The Grand and Magnificent Theatre in this City, which is now finished, and to be open'd on Thursday the 31st of this Instant January, is allow'd by all the Connoisseurs and Judges to be the most perfect and compleat Structure of the kind in this Kingdom. It is most admirably constructed for seeing and hearing ;—the Stage is large and lofty ;—and the Scenes so highly finish'd and executed by the late ingenious Mr. Collins, that they are accounted far superior of any of the kind . . . a compleat and regular Band of Musick is provided—and the greatest Care has been taken to air the House, by keeping constant Fires, so that we can assure the Ladies, Gentlemen &c., that there is not the least Damp throughout the whole Building."

YORK

The earliest records of the players in York tell us that in 1705 the Merchant Taylors' Hall was used for theatrical performances, but there is also reliable evidence that the Market House in what is now St. Sampson's Square also provided accommodation for the production of plays. Moreover, in 1727, a " Mr. Keregan's Company of Comedians " existed, there was a " Mr. Banks' Cockpit without Bootham Bar," and yet another company in the following year playing in the Moot Hall.

In 1733 Keregan applied for permission to build a proper playhouse in York, and receiving a favourable reply from the Mayor's Court, began to erect a new theatre in Lord Irwin's Yard, on the site of the present Residentiary in the Minster Yard. It was opened in the following year, but could not have been very satisfactory because within eight years proposals were being made for the erection of " a new and commodious Theatre (to be situated in some convenient part of the city) the model of those in London." Nothing was done until 1744 when a new theatre was built on the site now occupied by the present Theatre Royal. Another building was erected in 1765 by Joseph Baker, who shortly afterwards took in Tate Wilkinson as a partner. Under Wilkinson's able management the York Theatre became famous in the annals of the English theatre.

LIVERPOOL

Taking Liverpool as another example, we find references to "The Cockpit Yard Theatre" as early as 1567. It measured fifty feet by twenty feet, had a gallery and whitewashed walls, but there is little information concerning the companies that used it. Another of Liverpool's oldest theatres, The Old Ropery, was used on one occasion, in 1742, by the players from the Smock Alley Theatre, Dublin, including the notorious Peg Woffington.

The first playhouse of any importance to be opened in Liverpool, however, was the Drury Lane Theatre, named after the famous London house. According to R. J. Broadbent's *Annals of the Liverpool Stage*, it opened either in 1749 or 1750, and was reconstructed in 1758. In 1759 it reopened as "The New Theatre in Drury Lane," and Charles Lee Lewes in his *Memoirs* noted that: "Here it was for the first time boxes were erected as a just partition for the better sort to withdraw from the near contact of drunken sailors and their female associates."

Liverpool's first Theatre Royal was erected in 1772; a commodious building of red brick in Williamson Square. It opened on June 5th with the tragedy *Mahomet*, and the farce *The Deuce is in him*, played before a large audience of the city's most wealthy residents, and from that time Liverpool has figured prominently in theatrical history. Garrick and Macklin visited the city, and Mrs. Siddons frequently played there.

RICHMOND

For centuries Richmond was a fashionable summer resort of Londoners, particularly after the opening of Richmond Wells in 1696, but we have little reliable evidence of dramatic activity there until 1718, when *Read's Weekly Journal*, dated May 31st of that year announced:

"We hear that the famous Mr. Penkethman is building a handsome Playhouse at Richmond for the Diversion of the Nobility and Quality that attend the Court of Their Royal Highnesses; and will begin to play there soon after Whitsuntide. . . ."

This theatre was opened on the following July 19th with *The Spanish Fryar* and *The Stage Coach*, after which it appears to have been in frequent use until another theatre was erected in 1730. *The Daily Journal* for June 4th, 1730, tells us:

" There is building, and almost finish'd here, a small, but very neat and regular Theatre, a little higher on the Hill than where the late Mr. Penkethman's stood. We hear it will be open'd next week by a Company of Comedians from the Theatre Royal in Lincoln's Inn Field, and that their first play will be *The Recruiting Officer*."

It came into the hands of Theophilus Cibber in 1756, and it is of some interest to note that he evaded the Licensing Act by calling the theatre a snuff warehouse, and by carrying on an academy of dramatic art in it! One of his announcements proclaimed that :

[1] " Cibber and Co., snuff merchants, sell at their warehouse at Richmond Hill most cephalic snuff, which, taken in moderate quantities . . . will not fail to raise the spirits, clear the brain, throw off ill humours . . . exhilarate the mind, give joy to the heart, and greatly invigorate and improve the understanding. Mr. Cibber has also opened at the aforesaid warehouse, late called the Theatre on the hill, an historic academy for the instruction of young persons of genius in the art of acting, and proposes, for the better improvement of such pupils, and frequently with his assistance, to give public rehearsals without hire, gain or reward."

Another theatre was built at Richmond in 1765, this time on the Green, but the old theatre on the hill continued in use for two or three years until it was converted first into a Methodist chapel and later into a granary. It was pulled down in 1826 when York Place was built.

BRISTOL

Despite the most savage air raids from the Nazi hooligans, this ancient city has been able to preserve for posterity one of the most historic theatres in the land.

At the close of the seventeenth century there was a theatrical booth in Bristol's Horsefair, and in 1704 another such booth was erected in Tucker Street, near Bristol Bridge, by John Power who, it will be recalled, appeared afterwards at the new theatre at Bath. But the Puritanical element in Bristol was very strong and in the same year we find urgent demands being made to the Mayor and Aldermen that " by regard to the ill-consequences of the introduction of lewdness and debauchery by the acting of stage-plays, players should not be allowed to act within the city.

[1] Lysons : *Environs* v. I, 469.

Later in this same year we find another effort being made to suppress the acting of plays and interludes, and a complaint about the " Great Number of Tippling Houses," both of which, it was said, " corrupt and debauch our Youth, and utterly ruin many Apprentices and Servants, already so Unruly and Licentious." Consequently, the booth in Tucker Street was sold to the Presbyterians for use as a meeting house.

Power made another attempt to produce plays in Bristol in 1706, but this was promptly suppressed by the magistrates, and provoked a stupid book by the Rev. Arthur Bedford, Vicar of Temple Church, Bristol, entitled *The Evil and Danger of Stage Plays*.

The first proper playhouse to be built in Bristol was the Jacob's Wells Theatre, erected in 1729. It opened with Congreve's *Love for Love*, played by Hippisley's company. Hippisley began his theatrical career as a candle-snuffer, but made his way to London and eventually became a comedian at Drury Lane. Macklin, by the way, frequently visited Bristol to play in the Jacob's Wells Theatre, and paid great attention to the daughter of a local gentleman.

In those days, Queen's Square and Prince's Street were Bristol's most fashionable residential quarters—the beautiful suburb of Clifton was then but a village—so when it was decided to erect a new and more worthy theatre, a site was chosen in King Street, one of the principal thoroughfares adjacent to Queen's Square. James Paty, the chosen architect, and Thomas Symons, a local solicitor who was primarily responsible for the project, came to London to inspect the metropolitan theatres, and returned with the plans of the Theatre Royal, Drury Lane, to guide them.

Bristol's Theatre Royal was erected in 1765 at a cost of five thousand pounds, and accommodated seven hundred and fifty people in the boxes, three hundred and twenty in the pit, and five hundred and thirty in the gallery. It opened on May 30th, 1766, with *The Conscious Lovers* (Steele), followed by the farce *The Miller of Mansfield;* and we are told that " when the whole was illuminated there appeared one of the finest scenes Imagination can conceive ; the rich paintings, together with the brilliancy of the ladies, formed so complete a view that Malice herself, had she been there, must (for that night at least) have put on a smile of approbation." Garrick described this theatre as " the most complete of its dimensions in England."

The " Theatre in King Street " as it was then called, had no licence, and for the next twelve years heated controversy raged in the city between the puritans and those who sought a licence. Finally, on August 27th, 1778, the patent was granted to George Daubeny, the proprietors' nominee, for a period of twenty-one years (subsequent renewals were obtained without difficulty)— and the playhouse then became known as The Theatre Royal.

This famous theatre still stands, and although considerable alterations were made during the nineteenth century, it is a building of great historic importance. It has now been cleaned and re-decorated by C.E.M.A. (The Council for the Encouragement of Music and the Arts), under whose auspices the greatest dramatic works we possess are regularly presented to the citizens of Bristol.

Chapter VII

ENTER SHERIDAN, KEMBLE AND MRS. SIDDONS

RICHARD BRINSLEY SHERIDAN was born in Dublin on October 30th, 1751, and was educated at Harrow, where he met N. B. Halhed with whom he collaborated in his earliest works. These were a metrical translation of *Aristaenetus* and a farce called *Jupiter*, written after Sheridan had left school and was living at Bath. The latter was rejected by Garrick and Foote.

While at Bath, Sheridan fell in love with Elizabeth Ann, the beautiful sixteen-year-old daughter of Thomas Linley the composer, and to protect her from the persistent attentions of the undesirable Major Mathews, he escorted her to a convent in France. While they were on their way over, he persuaded her to marry him, and some sort of a ceremony was performed at a village not far from Calais. Returning to Bath, Sheridan fought two duels with Mathews, but when Linley brought his daughter home, Sheridan was sent to Waltham Abbey to continue his studies. On April 6th, 1773, he was entered at Middle Temple, and a week later he openly married Miss Linley with her father's consent. Within a year they had taken a house in Orchard Street, Portman Square, and furnished it expensively despite the fact that Sheridan had very little money.

His first comedy *The Rivals* was produced at Covent Garden on January 17th, 1775, but made little impression at first because of indifferent playing by some of the actors. It was withdrawn, revised slightly, and put on again eleven days later with remarkable success. He followed this with his farce *St. Patrick's Day, or The Scheming Lieutenant*, and the comic opera *The Duenna*, which enjoyed seventy-five performances at Covent Garden that season—a record at that time.

When Garrick announced his intention of retiring, Sheridan, with the help of two partners, Thomas Linley (his father-in-law) and Dr. Ford, purchased his share for thirty-five thousand pounds. Two years later, Sheridan also bought Lacy's share for a similar sum, raising the money by a heavy mortgage.

Thus Drury Lane came almost entirely under Sheridan's

management. He staged *The Rivals* there early in 1777 and soon afterwards produced his adaptation of Vanbrugh's *Relapse* entitled *A Trip to Scarborough*. These paved the way for Sheridan's masterpiece *The School for Scandal*, which he produced on May 8th in the same year. It narrowly escaped suppression, and it is said that the Lord Chamberlain licensed it only because of his personal friendship with Sheridan. The plot on which this play is based had been simmering in his mind for five years. It created a furore in London, and for months drew the largest houses the profession had ever known.

His farce *The Critic* followed on October 29th, 1779, and in the same year he produced his last play *Pizarro*. Meanwhile he had become a prominent figure in society, and was elected M.P. for Stafford in the following year. The story that he paid the burgesses of that town five guineas each for their support cannot be proved, but it is significant that his first speech in the House was an eloquent defence of himself against a charge of bribery. His political career after this time need not concern us.

On October 10th, 1782, the young Mrs. Siddons (to whom I referred in a previous chapter) re-appeared at Drury Lane in Southern's *Isabella, or The Fatal Marriage* at a modest salary of five pounds a week. But what a difference now! H. B. Baker in *The London Stage* declares :

" Her beautiful face and form, the exquisite tones of her voice, her deep tenderness, seized upon every heart, and her overwhelming agony thrilled every soul as it had never been thrilled before. Men wept, women fell into hysterics, transports of applause shook the house, the excitement and enthusiasm were almost terrible in their intensity, and the curtain fell amidst such acclamations as perhaps even Garrick had never received."

On February 2nd, 1784, she first played Lady Macbeth—the rôle in which she became so famous.

Sarah Siddons—her maiden name was Kemble—was born at the Shoulder of Mutton Inn at Brecon, on July 5th, 1755, the eldest of twelve children of Roger Kemble, actor and manager of a company of strolling players. She received a desultory education, and appeared on various stages several times in minor parts as a child. A young actor from Birmingham, William Siddons, joined the company when she was little more than a girl, and the two fell in love. Her parents disapproved strongly : the young man was discharged and the beautiful Sarah sent as a lady's maid to

Guy's Cliff, Warwickshire, where she recited Shakespeare in the servants' hall and read almost every evening to her master. The young couple remained faithful to each other however, and at last Sarah obtained her parents' consent to their marriage, which took place at Trinity Church, Coventry, on November 26th, 1773.

They both accepted engagements with travelling companies, playing at Bath, Wolverhampton, Cheltenham and other centres. On December 29th, 1775, as I have already recorded, Mrs. Siddons made her first appearance at Drury Lane, failed at this and subsequent performances in town, and returned to the provinces to gain further experience.

In Manchester she scored a great triumph in 1776, and in the following year made a wonderful impression at York, Bath and Liverpool. The enterprising manager of the Bath Theatre was quick to see her worth and secured her services for over four years. It was in this lovely western city that she became famous, playing over a hundred different parts. Wildly enthusiastic reports of her acting spread to Bristol, whose wealthy merchants demanded her appearance again and again in their new theatre in King Street, and at last Sheridan had to approach her with an offer to return to Drury Lane. But Mrs. Siddons never forgot that it was the city of Bath that made her famous, and on her farewell night, amid frantic applause, she brought her three children—Henry, Sarah and Maria—on to the stage and introduced them to the audience.

Her success in London now became the talk of the town. Johnson described her as " a prodigious fine woman," Reynolds painted her as the Tragic Muse (his masterpiece), and both Gainsborough and Lawrence did portraits of her.

Soon after her return to London, her brother John Philip Kemble made his début at Drury Lane as Hamlet, after having established his reputation in the provinces. He became manager of the Theatre Royal in 1788, Sheridan being engrossed in his political work.

In 1785 Dorothea Jordan, a young actress from Yorkshire, took London by storm in the part of Peggy in *The Country Girl*. This attractive, talented young lady was born near Waterford, Ireland, in 1762, and at quite an early age established herself on the stage in " tomboy " parts in Dublin, Cork and York, before her début at Drury Lane. During her lengthy engagement in London her private life became the greatest scandal of the age. She had already had a daughter by her first manager in Ireland, but this did not prevent her from bearing four illegitimate children during an association with Sir Richard Ford, and finally she became the mistress of the Duke of Clarence (afterwards William IV) and produced another ten children, who took the name of Fitz-Clarence. The eldest was created Earl of Munster. The Duke allowed her a thousand pounds a year, but on one occasion wrote to her suggesting that this should be reduced to five hundred. For her reply she merely tore from the bottom of a playbill a strip bearing the words "No money returned after the rising of the curtain."

By 1791 the Theatre Royal had become so dilapidated that Garrick decided it would be impossible to restore Wren's structure, so on June 5th a gang of workmen arrived in Drury Lane and began the demolition of the old house.

THE HAYMARKET

Soon after Foote succeeded in getting a patent for the "Little Theatre in Haymarket," he was persuaded to sell out to George Colman for an annuity of sixteen hundred pounds a year—though the poor fellow did not live long to enjoy it. The company at Haymarket at that time was not important, though it included one or two outstanding comedians, such as Ned Shuter and Quick, a great favourite of George III. Garrick considered Shuter to be the greatest comic genius of his age. He drank heavily, and had an insatiable passion for attending prayer meetings! On one particular Sunday he went to no less than five; then he got helplessly drunk and began preaching in the streets. He was a staunch supporter of Whitefield, and contributed liberally towards the maintenance of that evangelist's "Tabernacle."

THE KING'S THEATRE, HAYMARKET

Across the road, Sir John Vanbrugh's great theatre was destroyed by fire on June 17th, 1789, and the (opera) company moved temporarily to The Pantheon in Oxford Street, a large concert hall used for all types of musical activities and balls. It was fitted out as an opera house while the new King's Theatre was being built, and appropriated the patent of the opera house. Curiously enough this, too, was burnt down in 1792.

The new King's Theatre, designed by Michael Novosielski, was opened on March 26th, 1791, but was used for three seasons by the Drury Lane company while their new Theatre Royal was being built: then it became an opera house.

SADLER'S WELLS

The wooden "Musick House" at Sadler's Wells was pulled down in 1765, and a proper stone theatre erected in its place, at a cost of £4,225, by Rosoman, the builder, who had acquired the gardens in 1743. Rosoman Street, Clerkenwell, was named after him. Prices of admission were raised accordingly to half-a-crown in the boxes, a shilling in the pit, and sixpence in the gallery; and we are told that for an extra sixpence you could have a pint of good wine that had been "four years in the wood."

The theatre was let to Thomas King, the actor, in 1772, who took in "one Serjeant, a trumpeter, and Arnold, a goldsmith" as partners. Prices were again raised, and the house was patronised by the *élite*. Pantomime was its speciality, and some spectacular effects were obtained with water displays. Between the pantomime seasons light musical shows and acrobatic performances were given.

King eventually sold his share in the theatre, and Wroughton, a Drury Lane actor, was taken into the partnership. Later Mrs. Siddons' husband became the lessee, and during his time Edmund Kean, who comes into our story later on, appeared on its stage as a boy.

OTHER METROPOLITAN THEATRES

Towards the end of the eighteenth century one or two other small theatres began to spring up elsewhere in the London area. It will be observed that whereas in Shakespeare's time the south bank of the Thames was a favourite site for the theatres, all the Restoration playhouses were built north of the river.

The first sign of activity on the Surrey side was when Philip Astley opened a circus near Westminster Bridge. One day the King was crossing the bridge when his horse reared up and showed signs of giving trouble. Astley, who had been keeping a riding school, ran to the King's assistance, and as a reward received a licence for his theatre. He then built a wooden playhouse on the site of the temporary buildings used for his circus, and eventually was able to stage pantomimes in it.

Nearby was The Surrey Playhouse, which had been built in 1782 as The Royal Circus. It was burnt down in 1803, but rebuilt a year later and converted into a theatre in 1809.

The other theatres built during the eighteenth century (as far as we are able to discover) were the Sans Souci in Leicester Square [1793], which was demolished in 1834; and the Royalty, Wellclose Square, known also as The Brunswick and The East London Theatre [1787] which was demolished in 1828.

THE THIRD DRURY LANE THEATRE

The new Theatre Royal, Drury Lane, was ready early in 1794 a fine new building by Henry Holland, R.A. " upon a much large scale than that of any other theatre in Europe," with a proscenium measuring forty-three feet wide and thirty-eight feet in height, and a stage of ninety-two feet in depth. The auditorium was fifty-six feet high from floor to ceiling. The lighting of the stage was vastl improved, being chiefly concealed from view; two handsom chandeliers were all that the audience could see.

Unique at that time was the safety-curtain : a sheet-iron affai which was the prototype of the asbestos one we know to-day The theatre accommodated 3,611 persons : 1,828 in the boxe 800 in the pit, and 983 in the galleries.

It opened on March 12th, 1794, not with drama but with grand selection from the oratorios of Handel, and the Coronatio March, performed on a stage specially arranged for the occasio to resemble a Gothic cathedral. The first dramatic productio in the new house was on the following April 21st, with Kembl and Mrs. Siddons in the leading rôles of *Macbeth*.

A special epilogue written by George Colman to allay the fea of fire was spoken by Miss Farren :

> [1] The very ravages of fire we scout
>   For we have wherewithal to put it out ;
>   In ample reservoirs our firm reliance
>   Where streams set conflagration at defiance.

The curtain was then raised disclosing a large lake of re water on the stage, with a man rowing a boat on it while a sma waterfall was cascading down at the rear. Yet within fifteen yea this theatre was again burnt to the ground !

During the last few years of the eighteenth century Sherida neglected Drury Lane and his company shamefully. Playe were obliged to ask over and over again for their salary, the trade people grew indignant because of their unpaid bills ; the war robe was utterly neglected, scenery became shabby, and th theatre's coffers were drained by his boundless private extravaganc Kemble carried on the management between 1788 and 1796 b received not a word of thanks and was once arrested for one

---

[1] H. B. Baker : *The London Stage* vol. i. 98.

SARAH SIDDONS by Gainsborough

R. B. SHERIDAN by Russell

Sheridan's debts! Then Wroughton took over for a few years, but in 1800 Kemble was again persuaded to become manager by a promise of a share in the profits. Sheridan, however, did not keep to his word, and utterly disgusted, Kemble left Drury Lane in 1802 and began negotiations for a share in Covent Garden.

Chapter VIII

THE NINETEENTH CENTURY: EDMUND KEAN

ON February 24th, 1809, Sheridan was on the floor of the House of Commons taking part in a debate on the Peninsular War, when a messenger brought the news that the Theatre Royal was in flames. The adjournment of the debate was moved immediately " in consequence of the extent of the calamity which the event just communicated to the house would bring upon a respectable individual, a member of that house." Sheridan appreciated the compliment, but insisted that his personal misfortune should not interfere with the business of the country.

When finally he was able to go across to Drury Lane, he found nothing but charred and smouldering ruins : everything had been lost, including many valuable personal possessions, and he was completely ruined. No longer could he draw large sums to maintain his reckless extravagance, but he did everything possible to hide his feelings from his friends : he would sit for hours outside the Piazza Coffee House calmly swallowing port " by the tumblerful." But the calamity seriously affected his health, and he had the unusual experience of reading his own obituary when a rumour of his death spread throughout the capital.

Sheridan's financial reputation made it impossible for him to raise money himself for the rebuilding of the theatre, but he succeeded in persuading Samuel Whitbread, an amiable brewer, to undertake the task. Everybody trusted this practical business man, and no less than four hundred thousand pounds was raised by public subscription. Of this sixty thousand went in securing the patent rights, and twenty-eight thousand was paid to Sheridan for his interest, but Whitbread firmly refused to allow him to take any part in the management.

One would have thought that Sheridan would have enjoyed a quiet and comfortable retirement on this money, but he continued his wasteful mode of living, and in a few years was arrested for debt. He died on July 7th, 1816, and was buried in Westminster Abbey. It is said that just before he was put into his coffin a stranger rushed in to the apartment in which he was lying in state, and formally arrested the dead man on behalf of a money-lender for a debt of five hundred pounds. Lord Sidmouth and George Canning paid the money between them.

The new Theatre Royal Drury Lane was built by Wyatt after the great theatre at Bordeaux, and opened on October 12th, 1812, with Samuel Arnold as manager, but Covent Garden was offering a strong opposition at that time, and a heavy loss was sustained during the first season. The audiences continued to diminish during the second season, and just as the public support was at its lowest ebb, an almost unknown, shabby strolling player named Edmund Kean appeared as Shylock. His success was instantaneous, and within twenty-four hours all London seemed to be talking of this brilliant " discovery." Arnold lost no time in showing his appreciation : fifty pounds was presented to Kean and immediate arrangements were made for him to appear as Richard III. In this rôle he scored another great success. Byron wrote in his diary " Just returned from seeing Kean in *Richard*. By Jove, he is a soul ! Life, nature, truth, without exaggeration or diminution."

Edmund Kean [1787–1833] was the illegitimate son of Anne Carey, a strolling player. She deserted him when he was a baby, and he was picked up in a doorway in Frith Street, Soho, by a couple who gave him shelter during his early years. It appears that his mother claimed him during boyhood—doubtless because he had begun to earn money as a child actor. He was still quite a lad when he ran away from his home in Southwark, walked to Portsmouth, and got a job as a cabin-boy on a ship going to Madeira. He soon found that he disliked the work, so he pretended to have some sort of paralysis, and was taken to a hospital when the ship arrived at that port. Here, the doctors could do nothing for him, and sent him back to England to the care of an uncle. He was sent to a school in Leicester Square, but after a while ran away again and found casual employment in a fair. This led to his becoming a strolling player.

Kean's success at Drury Lane had a wonderful effect upon the patronage of the theatre. His salary was raised to twenty pounds a week, and more substantial gifts were made to him from time to time. For all that, by the year 1819 the proprietors had lost eighty thousand pounds since the opening of the new theatre, so they decided to let the house to Robert Elliston, who had been managing both the Surrey Theatre and a new playhouse erected in 1806 called The Olympic. According to H. B. Baker he took over on terms that were "simply ruinous": the rent was ten thousand two hundred pounds a year, exclusive of rates, and there were six hundred and thirty-five perpetual free admissions. However, Elliston was lucky at first with several considerable financial (but not artistic) successes. In 1822 he spent twenty-two thousand pounds on internal alterations and decorations, but four years later saw him in the bankruptcy court.

Next came an American named Stephen Price, who took over the theatre at an annual rent of ten thousand six hundred pounds, but paid—nothing! Then followed a succession of lessees, most of whom lost money and allowed the artistic standard of the house to sink to any level to snatch an occasional profit. As the years dragged on, circuses ousted legitimate drama, pantomimes and spectacular extravaganzas were presented more and more frequently, and Drury Lane would have degenerated into a common music-hall but for the regular productions of opera. In 1852 its rent had dropped to three thousand five hundred pounds a year.

KEMBLE AND MRS. SIDDONS AT COVENT GARDEN

The nineteenth century started well at Covent Garden because George Frederick Cooke had established a great reputation there in Shakespeare. He might have done wonders had he not been so fond of drink. Over and over again he arrived at the theatre completely intoxicated and would excuse himself by pleading illness. At one performance he broke down helplessly drunk, and tried to fool the audience by placing his hands upon his heart and exclaiming pathetically, "My old complaint, ladies and gentlemen, my old complaint." The whole house burst into a roar of laughter.

The Covent Garden company was greatly strengthened when in 1803 John Kemble forsook Drury Lane and joined them, and again when Mrs. Siddons followed him shortly afterwards. Then London went almost crazy over a boy prodigy named Master Betty, who received fifty pounds a night. That the boy was clever cannot be denied, but the absurd craze that packed vast, suffocating crowds into the Covent Garden Theatre night after night to see him shows what stupid, capricious audiences the managers had to cater for in those difficult days. Within a couple of years this lad was entirely forgotten.

Covent Garden was destroyed by fire on September 30th, 1808 with a tremendous loss of property. Mrs. Siddons and her brother lost their entire wardrobes. But by the middle of the following year another fine theatre had been built by Smirke,

The Fourth Theatre Royal, Drury Lane and (below) the same after the erection of the portico (1819–26). The Collonade was built in 1831

Charles Kemble as Romeo, after Cowell

considerably larger than the old one, at a cost of a hundred and fifty thousand pounds. Its proscenium was forty-two feet wide and thirty-six feet high, and the stage measured sixty-eight feet by eighty-two. The auditorium was fifty-one feet by fifty-two, with four tiers; the whole house accommodating nearly three thousand people.

The heavy expenses incurred in building the new theatre necessitated an increase in the prices of admission, but on the opening night—September 18th, 1809—when Kemble addressed the audience, he was greeted with angry shouts of " Old Prices ! " This was the outbreak of the " Old Price Riots." Not a word of the play could be heard that evening: there was a continual commotion in the house, and finally the Riot Act was read from the stage and the police and military had to be called in. To Kemble's dismay, this went on night after night: everybody seemed to object to the increased charges and willingly took part in the disturbances, and after almost two months of uproar, the prices had to be reduced to the old rates.

On September 23rd, 1813, the nineteen-year-old Catherine Stephens made her début as Mandane in Arne's *Artaxerxes*. This talented singer who had been born in Park Street, Grosvenor Square, in 1794, had already thrilled the provinces with her sweet soprano voice. She excelled in opera for over twenty years, and then retired to marry the octogenarian Earl of Essex.

Mrs. Siddons announced her intention of retiring in 1812, and a farewell performance of *Macbeth* was advertised for June 29th of that year. On this occasion the audience demanded that the play should end with her sleep-walking scene, so that this last great impression of her should be left in their minds. Nevertheless, she made several incidental appearances afterwards, chiefly at benefit performances: she played ten nights in Edinburgh, for instance, for the benefit of her children. Her last appearance on the stage was on June 9th, 1819. She died at her house in Upper Baker Street on June 8th, 1831, and was buried in Paddington Churchyard.

William Charles Macready [1793–1873] made his first London appearance at Covent Garden on September 16th, 1816, having previously distinguished himself as Romeo at Birmingham.

John Kemble retired in 1817 and left his share in Covent Garden to his brother Charles, but difficulties arose, several of the leading members of the company left, and by 1829 the theatre was in very low water indeed. Disaster was averted by the sudden appearance and great popularity of Charles Kemble's daughter Fanny, although she was not a great actress.

A notable date during the next decade is March 23rd, 1833, when Edmund Kean and his son Charles played together as Othello and Iago. H. B. Baker in *The London Stage* describes the event thus :

> " The house was crammed to suffocation. Brandy had long since shattered the reputation, the genius, and the health of the great actor. He had been very ill through the winter, and was utterly unfit to sustain the fatigue and excitement of such a night ; but he went through the part, dying as he went, until he came to the ' farewell,' in which in the old days he used to stir the very souls of the spectators ; he broke down on the words ' Othello's occupation's gone.' Then, gasping for breath, he began ' Be sure thou prove . . .' but unable to proceed, he fell upon his son's shoulder moaning ' I am dying . . . speak to them for me.' And so the curtain descended upon him for ever."

During these dismal years the management of Covent Garden was constantly changing, and the prestige of the theatre was sinking as low as that of Drury Lane. The public seemed quite apathetic : Italian opera was all the rage and nobody seemed to care a jot about legitimate drama. For a couple of years, Alfred Bunn, lessee of Drury Lane, took over the Covent Garden Theatre. In the first volume of his book *The Stage* [1840] he writes :

> " The death of Mr. Kean diminished most seriously the effective force of their (the two theatres') *Dramatis Personæ ;* other members of it were about to disperse themselves in different directions—some emigrating, some retiring, some maintaining expectations too extravagant to be listened to, and such as could only be kept up through a continued rivalry of the two houses. . . . In the opinion of the most experienced men attached to the profession, there seemed to be no other means of saving them from impending annihilation, than by uniting them under one management."

This plan, however, did not give satisfaction, and after two years Covent Garden was taken over by a man named Osbaldiston, who tried to get better houses by reducing the prices of admission. But the public continued to display nothing but cold indifference. We are told in Wilson's *Noctes Ambrosianæ* that gentlemen who formerly thought it a crime not to go to the theatre would ask " Whereabouts is Covent Garden Theatre ? "

Macready took over the management on September 30th, 1837, with a good company, including an opera staff and a company of pantomimists, yet by Christmas he had lost three thousand pounds. Carrying on with revivals of Shakespeare, he attracted large audiences with splendid productions of *The Tempest* and *Henry V*, but still failed to pay his way, and in the summer of 1839 gave up the management.

Four years later we find the theatre being rented by the Anti-Corn-Law League for a bazaar, and during the years 1844 to 1846 it was used for masked balls. Its interior was then reconstructed by Albano, and it reopened as " The Royal Italian Opera House " for a " more perfect representation of the lyric drama than has yet been attained in this country," but on March 4th, 1856, it was again burnt to the ground.

BENJAMIN WEBSTER AT THE HAYMARKET

The " Little Theatre in Haymarket " had now become known simply as " The Haymarket." It was completely rebuilt in 1820 at a cost of twenty thousand pounds, and opened in July, 1821, with *The Rivals* (Sheridan). Unlike the two greater theatres, this house prospered steadily, particularly after Benjamin Webster became the lessee in 1829.

Most of the theatres at that time were abolishing the old proscenium doors and also the apron, the part of the stage that still protruded several feet into the pit—a relic of the Shakespearean stage. This was done at the Haymarket in 1843, for an advertisement at that time informs us that :

"During the recess, the theatre has undergone Extensive alterations : the Proscenium has been entirely remodelled, and the whole of the Interior decorated in the most Costly and Elegant Style. By a curtailment of the useless portion of the Stage in front of the Curtain, and advancing the Orchestra and Lights near the Actors and Scenic Effects, the Lessee has been enabled to appropriate the portion so obtained to form a certain number of Orchestra Stalls, which can be retained for the parties taking them the whole of the Evening."

One of Webster's few mistakes was made in 1844 when he offered a prize of five hundred pounds in a competition for the best comedy. The judges made the award to Mrs. Gore, the novelist, for a play called *Quid pro Quo*. It was an utter failure !

THE KING'S THEATRE: OPERA AND BALLET

The great popularity of the opera gave the rebuilt King's Theatre an advantage from the start, though the number of Italians in the company made it difficult to introduce works that were not of the Italian school. The first of Mozart's operas to be heard in London, *La Clemenza de Tito*, was produced here in 1806, but the company treated it with little sympathy, and it soon dropped out of the repertoire. *Cosi fan Tutte* was first heard here in 1811, and *The Magic Flute* followed soon after, but the latter failed at its first hearing owing to the inadequacy of the company.

Madame Catalini, the famous soprano who introduced Mozart's *Figaro* to London, first appeared here in 1806 at a fee of two thousand guineas for the season. When she increased her fee to five thousand guineas for the second season the manager objected that there would be nothing left to pay the other singers. Her husband instantly retorted, " What else do you want when you have my wife's talent ? She and four or five puppets are enough." Her demands continued to increase until in 1813 the King's Theatre could no longer bid for her. She was then clearing ten thousand pounds a season at concerts. Some idea of her husband's avarice may be gained from the fact that on one occasion she was a guest of the Marquis of Buckingham and sang seventeen songs during the evening to a few of his friends. The next day the Marquis received a bill from her husband for seventeen hundred pounds.

In 1816 another superb singer, Madame Vestris, appeared at the King's Theatre, but from the difficulties encountered by the ever-changing managers, it seems that this house, too, had ceased to show a profit. The year 1817 saw the first production of Mozart's *Don Giovanni*, and Rossini's *Barber of Seville* followed in 1818. In the same year the auditorium was reconstructed in the shape of a horse-shoe by Nash and Repton, who also added the colonnades a little later. This work cost fifty thousand pounds, but failed to bring prosperity. During his seven years as manager, Ebers, a bookseller, lost over three thousand pounds every season, but this is perhaps explained by the following quotation from a theatrical journal of that time :

" When a foreigner views the imposing exterior of the opera-house, its numerous columns, its splendid piazzas, and its colossal dimensions, he reasonably expects that the interior will exhibit corresponding attractions, and hurries to the theatre buoyant with the hope of anticipated delight. He pays his half-guinea and is introduced into this fancied temple of elegance and grandeur. The filthy condition of the corridors, where the dirt of ages reposes in undisturbed tranquility, secure from the lustrations of a scrubbing brush, soon convinces our enthusiast that no lord of the vestibule protects the flowing train of a countess from plebian pollution. He hurries on and fixes his gaze upon that venerable specimen of the antique, the drop-curtain, whose faded hues and tarnished dinginess are surpassed only by the murky sails of a coal-lighter. The indulgent spec-tator overlooks these glaring violations of common decency, and recollecting that the musical department is under the direction of a committee of noblemen of acknowledged taste and ample fortune, he makes sure that this union of talent and wealth will procure him the highest treat that a *fanatico per musica* can possibly desire. But here again he is doomed to disappointment, his high-wrought expectations terminate in a mixed feeling of scorn, contempt and indignation. . . . How long must the admirers of Italian music be subjected to the evils arising from the incapacity or misconduct of Mr. Ebers ? "

It was Ebers, however, who in 1821 succeeded in bringing to London some of the famous stars of the Parisian ballet. Lengthy negotiations had to be conducted through the British Embassy in Paris, and at last a small company, including Albert, Noblet, Coulon and Bias came over. Their phenomenal success stirred up a new, hysterical craze in the world of fashion. Noblet, the *première danseuse* was the sensation of the season : invitations from the nobility were showered upon her, and society, gossip tells us, simply worshipped at her feet! According to Ebers' accounts, the ballet cost more than the opera. Madame Camporese, the immensely popular *prima donna* received only one thousand six hundred and fifty pounds, whereas Albert drew one thousand seven hundred and eighty-five and Noblet one thousand five hundred and thirty-seven. Ballet reached a new peak of perfection when Taglioni, Carlotta Grisi and Fanny Elssler came upon the scene.

Ebers was followed by Laporte and Laurent in 1827, and at the accession of Queen Victoria in 1837, the King's Theatre was re-named " Her Majesty's." Meanwhile, opera continued to be the mainstay of this and many other London theatres. The names of many great artists catch our eyes as we turn the pages of theatrical history : Pasta, Sontag, Malibran, Lablache, Rubini, Tamburini, Persiani and Mario, to mention only a few, were all famous in their day, but the limits of this book make it impossible to enlarge upon them.

NEW LEGISLATION

So far, the story of the English theatre has centred around the two great " patent " houses, but during the first half of the nineteenth century the number of minor theatres grew steadily. At first they were allowed to open only during the summer months when Drury Lane and Covent Garden were closed, but gradually their seasons lengthened, and in time they became serious rivals of the patent theatres. A veritable feud was carried on for years, with the public and press taking sides in every dispute. Agitations against the old Licensing Act multiplied, and finally, after such men as Sir Edward Bulwer-Lytton had pressed the matter, the government appointed a committee to investigate the position of all the theatres, and this led to the passing of a Bill in 1843 abolishing the patents and placing all the theatres in London under the control of the Lord Chamberlain.

THE LYCEUM AND THE OLYMPIC

The Lyceum was built originally as an art gallery in 1765, and it was not until 1794 that its interior was reconstructed as a theatre by Dr. Arnold, the composer. Even then, it was used for non-theatrical purposes : concerts, exhibitions and the like, and it did not become a proper playhouse until 1809. It is interesting to note that Madame Tussaud used it for her waxworks when she first came to England in 1802.

When Drury Lane was burnt down in 1809, its company obtained permission to use the Lyceum while the new Theatre Royal was being built. During the summer months, of course, the theatre was vacant, so Arnold's son, Samuel James, obtained a licence to produce English opera there. Thus in 1810 the Lyceum became known as The English Opera House. It was rebuilt in 1815 with an elaborate interior including a winter-garden measuring seventy-two feet by forty feet and containing a splendid variety of flowers and shrubs. Two years later, gas-lighting was installed, first on the stage and then in the auditorium. Financial difficulties induced the management to experiment with a " twice-nightly " system, but it found no sympathy with the public, and was abandoned.

The English Opera House was burnt down on February 10th, 1830, and the company had to find a home first at the Adelphi and later at the Olympic while a new theatre was being built. It was completed in 1834 and just as the last piece of scaffolding was being removed an amazing discovery was made—the architect had forgotten to put any stairs to the gallery! A wooden staircase was hurriedly added and the house opened in July of that year with John Barnett's opera *The Mountain Sylph*.

The first Promenade Concerts ever heard in this country were given at this theatre during the winter of 1838–39. They were introduced as a novelty from Paris, but achieved nothing like the fame and popularity of the wonderful series commenced by the late Sir Henry Wood at the Queen's Hall towards the close of the century.

A gallant effort to establish truly national opera was made at the Lyceum in 1840 but failed pitifully, and in less than two years the theatre became a home for performing lions and other horrors.

The abolition of the monopoly of the patent theatres in 1843 gave the house a chance to recover, and early in the following year its name was changed from The English Opera House to " The Theatre Royal Lyceum," though most people continued to refer to it as simply " The Lyceum." A production of *Henry IV* started the new regime, but the public was in no mood for indifferent performances of Shakespeare, and it was a miserable failure. The first real success here was a dramatized version of Dickens' *Martin Chuzzlewit*, which ran for three months with Sam Emery, Alfred Wigan, Frank Matthews and Keeley in the cast.

Madame Vestris took over the management on October 18th, 1847, installed a brilliant comedy company, and secured overwhelming successes with such plays as *Box and Cox*, and Boucicault's *Used Up*. Almost overnight the Lyceum became one of the most fashionable resorts in London. James Robinson Planché, the burlesque writer and designer, made his greatest hit here with a transformation scene in *The Island of Jewels*, in 1849.

Philip Astley opened his Olympic Pavilion in 1806 with a licence for music, dancing, pantomime, burlettas and equestrian exhibitions. This crude house, known also as " Astley's Middlesex Amphitheatre," was built almost entirely of old timbers salvaged from a decrepit French warship, and was an utter failure; so he sold it in 1813 to Elliston, who renamed it " Little Drury Lane," but within a year had to revert to the original name—The Olympic Pavilion—owing to licensing difficulties. In 1815 he installed gas lighting in part of the house; a great novelty at that time. Three years later he rebuilt the theatre, but within twelve months was obliged to let it because he became the manager of Drury Lane.

The Olympic then entered upon a period of vicissitudes under various managers until Madame Vestris took it in 1830 and found favour with light comedies, burlesques, extravaganzas and so forth, cleverly staged to appeal to the more sophisticated. Charles Mathews, in his autobiography, says of her productions :

"There was introduced for the first time in England that reform in all theatrical matters which has since been adopted at every theatre in the kingdom. Drawing rooms were fitted up like drawing rooms, and fitted with care and taste. Two chairs no longer indicated that two persons were to be seated. A claret-coloured coat, salmon-coloured trousers, with a broad black stripe, a sky-blue neckcloth with a large paste brooch, and a cut-steel eye-glass with a pink ribbon, no longer marked the light-comedy gentleman ; and the public at once recognized and appreciated the changes."

Madame Vestris was born at 72 Dean Street, Soho, in 1797, and married Auguste Vestris, a dancer and ballet-master of the King's Theatre, in 1813. Four years later he deserted her. She made her first appearance in Italian opera at the King's Theatre in 1815 and rose to fame very quickly. She married Charles James Mathews [1803–1878] in 1838, and they both made an American tour before leaving the Olympic for Covent Garden. (Mathews had made his first stage appearance at the Olympic in 1835.)

Various managers tried to carry on the Olympic after Madame Vestris, but without much success, though it should be recorded that Gustavus Brooke made his début at this theatre as Othello in 1846. Three years later it was burnt down, and a new theatre was erected in 1849.

SADLER'S WELLS AQUATIC DISPLAYS

The nineteenth century at Sadler's Wells saw the development of the aquatic displays that made this theatre famous. A colossal tank, fed by the New River, was built beneath the stage, and all types of spectacular shows and nautical dramas were produced there on elaborate lines. In one of the latter, *The Siege of Gibraltar*, H. B. Baker says that :

". . . real vessels floated on real water for the bombardment of the fortress ; the heroine fell from the rocks into the sea, and her lover plunged after her ; there were a naval battle and a ship on

Covent Garden Theatre in 1809

The Old and New Haymarket Theatres, showing the relative position
of the old theatre prior to its demolition

[*Rise*

EDMUND KEAN AS BRUTUS, after Northcote

fire, from which sailors sprang into the waves to escape from the flames, and in another scene a child was cast into the water and rescued by a Newfoundland dog."

The most famous actor connected with Sadler's Wells at this time was Joseph Grimaldi, born on December 18th, 1779, at Stanhope Street, Clare Market, son of an Italian actor. At the age of three he appeared at Sadler's Wells as an infant dancer, and then got a pantomime engagement at Drury Lane. He was frequently seen on the stage as a boy, and in later years became the most famous clown of the age. Visits were made to Dublin, Bath, Bristol, Liverpool and Manchester, and in London he was often engaged at Drury Lane and Covent Garden. He died in 1837.

One of the best managers of Sadler's Wells during the first half of the nineteenth century was that famous actor of the old school of tragedy, Samuel Phelps, who took advantage of the new legislation in 1843, and began staging Shakespeare. He also put a stop to rowdiness in the gallery by instantly expelling unruly patrons.

Samuel Phelps was born at Plymouth Dock (now Devonport) on February 13th, 1804, educated locally and at Saltash, and entered the office of *The Plymouth Herald* as a " reading boy " when at the age of sixteen he was left as an orphan. In less than a year he had found a reader's job in London on the staff of *The Globe* and *The Sun*, and then began to take an interest in the theatre. He took part in amateur theatricals, and was still an amateur when he first appeared at The Olympic. Joining a Yorkshire company, he made something of a name in Sheffield, and later toured all over the north of England and Scotland before returning to play in various theatres on the south coast. This led to an engagement at Covent Garden, and to a brilliant career in the capital. He died in November, 1878, at Coopersale, near Epping.

THE SURREY AND THE " OLD VIC "

As far as we are concerned, there is little worth recording in the history of the Surrey Theatre until Elliston undertook the management in 1827 and produced Douglas Jerrold's *Black-Ey'd Susan* there on January 26th, 1829, with T. P. Cooke as William. Then, to quote *The Athenæum* :

" All London went over the water, and Cooke became a personage in society, as Garrick had been in the days of Goodman's Fields. Covent Garden borrowed the play and engaged the actor, for an after-piece. A hackney cab carried the triumphant William in his blue jacket and white trousers from the Obelisk to Bow Street, and Mayfair maidens wept over the stirring situations and laughed over the searching dialogue, which had moved, an hour before, the laughter and tears of the Borough. On the three hundredth night of representation the walls of the theatre were illuminated, and vast multitudes filled the thoroughfare . . . testimonials were got up for Elliston and Cooke on the glory of its success, but Jerrold's share of the gain was slight —about seventy pounds of the many thousands it realised for the management. With unapproachable meanness, Elliston abstained from presenting the youthful writer with the value of a toothpick. . . ."

Elliston's successor, Osbaldiston, enjoyed a similar stroke of luck with Fitzball's *Jonathan Bradford*, which ran for even longer than Jerrold's play. Unlike *Black-Ey'd Susan* it was a very poor specimen of a play.

The Surrey Theatre was destroyed by fire in 1865, and a new and pleasant theatre was erected in its place soon afterwards.

The names of Princess Charlotte and her husband Prince Leopold headed the list of subscribers who built the Royal Cobourg Theatre. It was a fine-looking building, and possessed a novelty that fascinated its patrons for years : a mirror curtain measuring thirty-six feet by thirty-two, enclosed in a gilt frame, that could be raised and lowered almost as easily as the present day asbestos curtain.

The Royal Cobourg opened in May, 1818, and for several years many of the most distinguished actors and actresses played there, but in time its patrons grew tired of its squalid surroundings, and it became a favourite haunt of the more uncouth type of audience. That, however, was not until it was renamed the Royal Victoria Theatre in 1833.

As it deteriorated the " Old Vic," as everybody called it, acquired a reputation for extravagant melodrama which was lapped up with relish by the rabble of Lambeth. Charles Mathews tells us :

"The lower orders rush there in mobs, and in shirt sleeves, applaud frantically, drink ginger beer, munch apples, crack nuts, call the actors by their Christian names, and throw them orange peel and apples by way of bouquets."

Brawls and other disorders were a frequent occurrence there, and

on one evening in 1858 sixteen persons were killed in a panic caused
by a false alarm of fire.

THE ADELPHI

The original Adelphi was a small theatre called The Sans
Pareil, erected in 1806 by a colour merchant named John Scott at
a cost of ten thousand pounds. He opened it in November of that
year for variety entertainments which generally concluded with
firework displays. Though an amateur with nothing but a shrewd
knowledge of the sort of amusement the rank and file enjoyed,
Scott prospered, and in due course was able to present some sort
of dramatic performances, most of which were written and produced by his clever and pretty daughter. Having made a small
fortune out of the theatre, he gained fifteen thousand pounds profit
in one stroke of the pen by selling the whole concern for twenty-
five thousand pounds to two partners named Jones and Rodwell,
who renamed it The Adelphi.

Advertisements at that time proclaimed that considerable
improvements had been made at The Adelphi and that " the
brilliant effect of the gas chandelier suspended from the dome is
the subject of universal admiration."

Jones and Rodwell raised the artistic standard to some extent,
and after further structural improvements and decorations in
1821, the Adelphi became one of the most fashionable theatres
in London. Its popularity was probably established by the long
and very successful run of *Life in London, or Tom and Jerry*, a
dramatized version of the extremely popular book by the journalist
Pierce Egan. Robert Keeley, an almost unknown actor at that
time, appeared in this production.

In 1825 the management of the Adelphi passed to Terry and
Yates, former members of the Drury Lane and Covent Garden
companies, who scored a great success with an adaptation of
Fenimore Cooper's famous novel *The Pilot*. The book derided
the British, but in the play it was the Americans who were ridiculed,
and Scott, in his diary, tells us that " The Americans were so much
displeased that they attempted a row, which rendered the piece
doubly attractive to the seamen of Wapping, who came up and
crowded the house night after night to support the honour of the
British flag."

The Adelphi was enlarged in 1827, and shortly afterwards
Charles Mathews paid seventeen thousand pounds for Terry's
share, but although a high standard of drama was maintained,

financial difficulties became increasingly heavy, and the theatre rarely paid its way until a man named Gladstone took it over.

It was in this theatre that John Reeve [1799–1838] won the affection of his audiences. He was born on Ludgate Hill, son of a hosier, and after several years in business became an actor, but secured only minor parts for quite a time. Then he appeared as Jerry Hawthorn in *Life in London*, and from that time enjoyed an enviable run of successes in various London theatres. He visited America in 1835 "gaining much money but little reputation," and returned to the Adelphi at a salary of forty pounds a week, but declined steadily owing to excessive drinking.

Another tremendously popular actor at the Adelphi was Edward Wright [1813–1859], who succeeded Reeve. He was born in London, but gained most of his experience in Birmingham and Bristol. Returning to London he first appeared as a comedian at the new St. James's Theatre in 1837, and secured his first engagement at the Adelphi in the following year. He had a remarkable gift of sending his audience into fits of laughter over passages that in themselves were only mildly funny.

Madame Celeste and Benjamin Webster took charge of the Adelphi in 1844, and controlled its fortunes throughout one of the best periods of its history.

Madame Celeste was born in Paris about the year 1810, made her first appearance in New York in 1827, and came to England three years later in search of ballet and pantomime engagements. After playing in various minor theatres, she went on a tour through Italy, Germany and Spain before Bunn engaged her for Covent Garden and Drury Lane. Her second visit to America in 1834 was a great success, and she returned with a fortune of forty thousand pounds. She became associated with Webster in 1843 in the management of the Theatre Royal, Liverpool, and then went with him to the Adelphi.

Benjamin Webster [1797–1882] was a native of Bath. He refused a commission in the Army, and ran away from home " to play Harlequin, small speaking parts, and second violin in the orchestra " at Warwick. After various appearances in the provinces and in Ireland he came to town and appeared at the Cobourg Theatre in 1819, from which he progressed by way of the Regency and Lyceum, to Drury Lane. H. B. Baker says in *The London Stage* :

" Webster was an actor of consummate ability, and would have been an acquisition even to the Comédie Française in its best

THEATRE ROYAL, COVENT GARDEN,

This present SATURDAY, Nov. 22, 1806, will be acted (8th time) the Tragedy of

CORIOLANUS;

Or, The ROMAN MATRON.

Caius Marcius Coriolanus by Mr. KEMBLE,
Cominius, Mr. CRESWELL, Menenius, Mr. MUNDEN,
First Officer, Mr. Jefferies, Second Officer, Mr. Field,
Tribunes, and Plebeians by
Mr. CHAPMAN, Mr. MURRAY,
Mr. SIMMONS, Mr. TAYLOR, Mr. BEVERLY, Mr. ATKINS,
Mess. Abbot, T. Blanchard, L. Bologna, Menage, W. Murray, Platt, Powers,
Rimsdyck, Sarjant, Truman, Whitmell, Wilde.
Volumnia by Mrs. SIDDONS,
The Child by Master PRICE,
Virgilia, Miss BRUNTON, Valeria, Mrs. HUMPHRIES, Servilia, Miss LOGAN.
Matrons.
Mrs. Emery, Mrs. Follett, Mrs. Whitmore.
Virgins.
Miss Cox, Miss Cranfield, Miss Searle, Miss Taylor, Miss Waddy, Mrs. Watts.
In Act II.

An OVATION.

The ODE by Mess. Denman, King, Lee, Mara, Monk, Smalley, Street, Thomas, Burden, Everard, Fairclough,
Homeyard, Linton, Meyers, Odwell, Parsons, Tett, B. Tett, Whitehorn—Mesdames Benson, Bologna,
I. Bologna, Bristow, Fawcett, Findlay, Grimaldi, Iliff, Martyr, Masters, Price, Slader.
Volscians.
Tullus Aufidius Mr. POPE,
Volusius, Mr. CLAREMONT,
Officers,
Mr. King, Mr. Treby, Mr. Fairbrother, Mr. Brown, Mr. Reeves.
The Overture and Act-Symphonies are composed by Mr. W. WARE.

To which will be added, in two acts, (third time) a New Grand Operatical Entertainment, called

The DESERTS of ARABIA.

(The SCENES, DRESSES, and DECORATIONS are entirely NEW.)
The Musick composed by Mr. G. LANZA, jun.
The principal characters by
Mr. LISTON,
Mr. INCLEDON,
Mr. CRESWELL, Mr. EMERY,
Mr. FAWCETT,
Mr. CHAPMAN, Mr. BELLAMY, Mr. DAVENPORT, Mr. TREBY.
Arabs,
Mess. Abbot, T. Blanchard, Burden, Denman, Everard, Fairclough, Homeyard, King, Lee, Linton,
Meyers, Monk, Odwell, Parsons, Street, Tett, B. Tett, C. Tett, Thomas, Whitehorn.
Persians,
Mess. L. Bologna, Brown, Goodwin, Fairbrother, Platt, Powers, Rimsdyck, Sarjant, Wilde.
Attendants, Mess. Banks, Dick, Field, Goodwin, Hoddinot W. Murray, Rye, Sturgeon, Telfer, Thurston
Mrs. C. KEMBLE.
Miss BRUNTON, Miss WADDY.
Arabians—Mesdames Benson, Bristow, Fawcett, Findlay, Grimaldi, Iliff, Leserve, Price, Whitmore.
Persians—Mesdames Bologna, I. Bologna, Cox, Cranfield, Follett, Masters, Slader, Watts.
The Piece to conclude with a representation of a

CARAVAN,

composed of Persians, Arabians, Christians, &c. with their Elephants, Camels, Palanquins, Cars,
and various Merchandize, as crossing

The DESERTS.

The SCENES designed and painted by Mess. Phillips, Whitmore, Hollogan, and their Assistants.
The Machinery and Decorations executed by Mess. Sloper, Creswell, and Goostree.
The Dresses by Mr. Dick and Mrs. Egan. Books of the Songs, Choruses, &c. to be had in the Theatre.
E. Macleish, Printer, 2, Bow-street. VIVANT REX & REGINA

The new Operatical Entertainment of The DESERTS of ARABIA, continuing to be received with
the most unbounded applause by brilliant and overflowing audiences, will be repeated every
Evening till further notice.
The new Play of ADRIAN and ORRILA; or, A MOTHER's VENGEANCE, will be
repeated for the 5th, 6th & 7th times on Monday, Wednesday & Friday next.
KING HENRY the EIGHTH—MACBETH—and CORIOLANUS,
will be acted next week on Tuesday, Thursday, and Saturday.

gitz]

THEATRE ROYAL PLAYBILL 1806

WILLIAM CHARLES MACREADY by John Jackson

days. There was greater variety in Webster than perhaps in any other actor of his generation; his range of character was very great. . . ."

Baker also declares that :

"It was by the acting, and the acting only, that the old Adelphi won its fame; little care or expense was bestowed upon mounting its pieces, its dresses were usually shabby, and its scenes and sets were little elaborated. . . ."

THE PRINCE OF WALES'S THEATRE

This theatre in Tottenham Street, Tottenham Court Road, was known by about half a dozen names—if not more. It started early in the nineteenth century as a concert hall, and was purchased by Harry Beverley for the modest sum of three hundred and fifteen pounds in December, 1814. He made various improvements and opened it shortly afterwards as The Regency Theatre of Varieties.

In 1820 we find a Mr. Brunton taking it over, renaming it The West London Theatre, and introducing a much better class of entertainment. With no licence at all, he calmly staged *She Stoops to Conquer* and *The School for Scandal* by calling them burlettas !

Other people took this theatre with varying degrees of success or failure—mostly failure—during the ensuing years. In 1829 we find it being advertised as The Tottenham Street Theatre, and in 1831 being altered and renamed The Queen's. Two years later it becomes The Fitzroy Theatre, and after another couple of years it reverts to the title The Queen's. This juggling of names goes on *ad lib.* for the next three or four years.

In 1839 a scenic artist named C. T. James took it over and began staging highly-coloured melodramas to a cut-price audience. In the profession it became known as The Dust Hole, and its reputation stank rather worse than the fried fish shops in the neighbourhood.

THE STRAND THEATRE

"Rayner's New Subscription Theatre in the Strand," as it was originally known, was fashioned out of a meeting hall in 1832. The lack of a licence never seemed to worry the manager, who specialized in burlesque, and had no qualms about attaching that appellation to anything he fancied.

This house soon became known as The New Strand Theatre, but it had a chequered career. The Lord Chamberlain closed it in

H

1834, but it was promptly re-opened by Mrs. Waylett, who admitted her patrons free of charge upon the purchase of confectionery. The Lord High Executioner closed it again in 1835, but within a year it was staging burlesques.

There is little to record apart from a succession of insignificant theatrical experiments until William Farren took the theatre in 1849 and began producing legitimate drama with a good company, including Mrs. Glover, Mrs. Stirling, Leigh Murray, Mrs. Alfred Philips, and Henry Farren.

THE ST. JAMES'S AND PRINCESS'S THEATRES

Early in the nineteenth century there was a fine tenor singer named John Braham, a Londoner born of German-Jewish parents. His voice enabled him to accumulate a considerable fortune. In his later years he became obsessed with a craze for theatrical management, and spent forty thousand pounds in buying the Colosseum in Regent's Park, and thirty thousand pounds in building a theatre on the site of an old hotel in King Street, St. James's. Both speculations were failures, but it is only with the latter that we are concerned.

He opened The St. James's Theatre, as he called it, on December 14th, 1835, with an opera by Mrs. G. A. à'Beckett, *Agnes Sorel*, but despite the fact that he was in the leading rôle himself, it failed —and so did all his other attempts to stir a thoroughly apathetic public. In the following year he let the theatre to a French company, but soon returned to the fray himself with *The Strange Gentleman*, founded on one of the *Sketches by Boz*. This ran for fifty nights or so, and induced Braham to persuade Dickens to collaborate with John Hullah in the writing of an English opera. The result was *Village Coquettes*, but it made no impression whatever. Even a farce by Dickens, *Is She His Wife?* produced at the St. James's in 1837, barely paid its way, although adaptations of his novels were generally well patronized.

By the end of 1838 Braham was ruined, but he was not beaten, and although he was well over sixty, he made a prolonged tour through America and earned enough money to provide for his old age.

The theatre continued to break the hearts of its managers. Drama was a ruinous undertaking for anyone to attempt in London, and the St. James's, like its older rivals, was used for anything that would attract a crowd: performing animals, acrobats and so forth. Everybody followed Fashion, and Fashion followed the young Queen Victoria, whose artistic propensities made her attend a circus at Drury Lane Theatre twice in one week.

At the time of the Queen's marriage, the St. James's was renamed The Prince's, and a handsome profit was made out of an execrable German opera company. They drew large crowds who knew nothing about opera, cared less, and had but one thought in their silly heads : to be fashionable, and loyal to the German prince.

In 1842 an intelligent Mr. Mitchell of Bond Street became the lessee of the theatre, changed its name back to the St. James's, and specialized for twelve years with French companies. He brought over many of the finest artists of the Parisian stage, including Déjazet, Frederick Lemaître, Ravel, Levasseur, Mademoiselle Plessy, and the renowned Rachel.

Until they got to know about her private life, the *élite* rhapsodized over Rachel : she was all the rage in London. One night she was standing in the wings talking to the Duchess of Kent and complained of the cold. In an instant, the Duchess removed her own beautiful shawl and put it around the actress. When she was ill some of the greatest physicians in the land attended her, and issued regular bulletins with great solemnity. On her return to the stage, she found the Queen and the Queen Dowager waiting to congratulate her on her recovery. Her Majesty presented her with a wonderful bracelet inscribed : " From Victoria to Mademoiselle Rachel."

The Princess's Theatre was originally an exhibition hall on the north side of Oxford Street, but in 1840 a silversmith named Hamlet converted it into a theatre during a burst of amateur enthusiasm for public entertainment. It was then used first for promenade concerts and later for opera. In 1850 it was taken over by Charles Kean and Robert Keeley who opened with *Twelfth Night*, and then embarked upon a long series of Shakespearean revivals and excellent productions of French drama. The latter created quite a stir, and had a considerable effect upon the English theatre generally at this period of its history.

DRAMATISTS OF THE EARLY NINETEENTH CENTURY

There were few professional playwrights in the first half of the nineteenth century whose work calls for any special mention in a short book of this nature.

James Sheridan Knowles [1784-1862], a native of Cork, tried the Army, and then the medical and teaching professions before he became a playwright. The great Edmund Kean played with notable success in his *Leo* in 1810, and again in his *Virginius* in 1820 at Covent Garden. Knowles's best play *The Hunchback*, was first produced at Covent Garden in 1832. Later in life he became a Baptist preacher.

We have already made the acquaintance of Douglas William Jerrold [1803–1857]. A Londoner, and son of an actor, he went to sea for two years, returned home to become a printer's apprentice, and in 1819 found a job as a compositor on the staff of the *Sunday Monitor*. Then he became a journalist and was engaged to write plays for the Cobourg Theatre at the princely salary of three pounds a week. After the success of his *Black Ey'd Susan* his remuneration was increased substantially and he began writing for other and more important theatres, making steady progress until his noteworthy play *The Bride of Ludgate* was produced at Drury Lane in 1831. In later years he distinguished himself more as a journalist.

Walter Savage Landor [1775–1864] was born at Warwick, educated at Rugby and Cambridge, and inherited a comfortable fortune in 1805. He was a headstrong, recalcitrant character who might have produced some really remarkable works had he been obliged to write for a living. His principal dramatic works are *Count Julian* [1812] and a trilogy: *Andrea of Hungary, Giovanna of Naples* and *Fra Rupert*.

The plays of such people as Henry Hart Milman, Sir Thomas Talfourd, Edward Fitzball, J. B. Buckstone, and Charles Reade seldom rise above mediocrity when we judge them by modern standards, although many of them were very popular in their day and are of some significance in theatrical history.

There were so few playwrights of real ability during this period that the greater poets and novelists were induced to attempt dramatic work, but one cannot help feeling that some of it was wasted effort.

Macready persuaded Robert Browning [1812–1889] to write for the stage. His tragedy *Strafford* was produced at Covent Garden in 1837, but neither this nor *A Blot in the 'Scutcheon*, produced six years later, found much response in the theatre. Little interest, too, was shown when his *Colombe's Birthday* was first performed in 1853.

On the other hand Edward Bulwer-Lytton [1803–1873], the famous novelist, achieved considerable success in the theatre with his romantic comedy *The Lady of Lyons*, which was produced in

1838. In the following year his *Richelieu* also found favour, and in 1840 he drew good houses again with the comedy *Money*.

The dramatic works of Lord Byron [1788–1824] commence with his *Manfred* [1817] and include the tragedy *Sardanapalus* [1821] and *The Two Foscari*, which was published in the same year. His most successful work in the theatre was his tragedy *Werner*, in which Macready made a very great impression.

Coleridge, Keats, Shelley, Lamb, Scott and Maturin all tried to write for the stage, but rarely met with any success, though Shelley's tragedy *The Cenci* and Maturin's tragedy *Bertram* were both well received.

EARLY NINETEENTH CENTURY DEVELOPMENTS

To conclude this chapter, let us see how the theatres changed during this period of roughly fifty years. At the beginning of the century the evening's performance in the average London theatre occupied between five and six hours. The curtain rose at six-thirty, and the house rarely closed before midnight. The programme generally consisted of two or even three works. Very often the evening opened with a short, light comedy; then there was a full-length drama, and finally a short farce or a light opera would conclude the performance.

Grand opera was a law unto itself, and generally commenced at eight o'clock. The length of the performance varied considerably, but the people were very insistent upon getting their money's worth.

Towards the middle of the century the London theatres began to shorten their performances considerably, though it is recorded that when in 1840 Madame Vestris began closing her theatre at eleven o'clock, the audiences were astonished. However, in less than ten years every other manager in town had followed her example.

The comfort of the audience occupied the thoughts of all the managers at this time. Great improvements were made in the seating accommodation, and around 1850 upholstered chairs began to replace the hard wooden forms. When one considers that upholstery was used in the theatres nearly a century ago, it seems all the more incredible that in many theatres today a temporary paralysis of the posterior is still considered to be part of the evening's entertainment.

Throughout this period there was steady improvement in the stage settings. More and more use was made of mechanical devices for the manipulation of scenery, and the painting of it became a highly-specialized art.

We have already noted the introduction of gas lighting in the theatres. This opened up vast possibilities in stage-lighting, though at first the people objected to the fumes that for several years retarded the development of this form of lighting. In time, however, purer gas and better burners reduced the odour to a minimum. When gas was originally installed in the theatres, naked flickering jets provided the illumination, but in a very short while they were fitted with glass chimneys, and then better control of lighting followed quickly.

Chapter IX

THE NINETEENTH CENTURY (SECOND HALF)

THE second half of the nineteenth century was a period of change and significant development. It opened with the theatre in a state of utter stagnation, and for something like twenty years the comparatively small number of theatres in existence continued to swallow up the fortunes of the majority of those who were prepared to risk their money in the promotion of drama in this country.

Then came the Bancrofts, Henry Irving and a few other enlightened individuals, and the theatre began to enter into the social life of the masses ; the great middle classes were aroused, and new theatres began to spring up everywhere. Those whose parents had regarded attendance at the theatre as one of the Seven Deadly Sins were to be seen strutting in with their wives for the " respectable " plays, or slinking in without them for the others.

When we come to the last quarter of the century the tremendous increase in the number of theatres will make it impossible for us to go on tracing with any degree of continuity the fortunes of the individual houses, though of course the more important theatres will still figure prominently in our story. To record the history of the dozens of new playhouses in London alone would be impossible in a book of this size, and a lengthy catalogue of productions during the past sixty or seventy years would only prove tedious to the reader, so we shall continue our story with facts drawn here and there to give, as far as possible, a general picture of the theatre as it has progressed right up to the present day.

DRURY LANE AND AUGUSTUS HARRIS

Just before Christmas, 1852, E. T. Smith became the lessee of Drury Lane. He opened on Boxing Night with an adaptation of *Uncle Tom's Cabin* and a pantomime by Blanchard called *Harlequin Hudibras*, and succeeded in making a profit. Then he presented Italian opera at reduced prices, Rachel in *Athalie*, circuses and various novelties ; but eventually, like so many of his predecessors, he realised that he was playing a losing game, and retired.

The usual succession of lessees followed, and all were disillusioned in their turn. Edmund Falconer and F. B. Chatterton became joint-managers in 1862 and promptly lost the thirteen thousand pounds they had made with *The Peep o'Day* at the Lyceum. Then Chatterton became the sole lessee and ruled for ten years, thereby giving an impression that he had discovered the secret of making Britain's most historic theatre pay its way. He put on Shakespeare and Byron and plenty of popular old comedies with a good company, including Helen Faucit, who always drew crowded houses, and Walter Montgomery.

In 1868 he produced *The Great City* (Halliday), in which Mrs. Madge Kendal (then Madge Robertson) made her début. Edward Stirling in a book published over fifty years ago[1] tells us that: " This realistic piece had the advantage of a real cab and living horse, thieves' dens, and burglars on house-tops escaping by telegraphic wires " and also that as a result " Money came into the treasury, the best token of popularity."

Adaptations of Scott's novels followed this inspiring example of mid-Victorian culture: we are told that Halliday's dramatization of *Ivanhoe* in 1871 with Lilian Neilson as Rebecca was a great success. But did Chatterton pay his way? He gave up, heartbroken, in February, 1879, thirty-six thousand pounds in debt.

Drury Lane was closed for eight months—nobody felt inclined to play with financial fire after Chatterton's experience—and then a very young man named Augustus Harris, son of a former manager of Covent Garden, was bold enough to open it with Shakespeare's *Henry V*. Whether he made a profit or a loss does not really matter, because a few weeks afterwards he was filling the house from top to bottom with a remarkable Christmas pantomime, *Blue Beard*, in which low comedy, shipwrecks, sea serpents, baby elephants and suchlike gladdened the hearts of all the Great Queen's loyal subjects.

With sensational drama, pantomime and other spectacular shows, Harris somehow managed to keep the wolf from the Lane, and, moreover, salved his conscience by popping in Shakespeare now and then together with such works as *She Stoops to Conquer*, *The Rivals*, and so forth,

Opera continued to be the chief attraction for many years at Drury Lane. In 1881 Harris engaged the Saxe-Meinengen Company, causing a sensation which was to be eclipsed within twelve months by Hans Richter and the German Opera Company,

[1] *Old Drury Lane.*

SIR SQUIRE BANCROFT

MARIE WILTON (LADY BANCROFT)

who gave the first production in England of Wagner's *Die Meistersinger* and *Tristan und Isolde*. The Carl Rosa Company took the theatre in 1883, and in the ensuing year several English operas were mounted. The famous de Reszke brothers appeared there in 1887, and the year 1895 is noteworthy for the interesting series of comic operas performed by the Ducal Company of Saxe-Cobourg and Gotha.

COVENT GARDEN REBUILT

Soon after the destruction of the opera house by fire in 1856, Frederick Gye decided to rebuild it at his own expense to the plans of Edward Barry, R.A. The new house—the one we know to-day—took only six months to erect, and cost seventy thousand pounds. It measured one hundred and twenty-seven feet by two hundred and ten, and had a stage ninety feet by eighty-eight.

For the opening night, May 15th, 1858, the Pyne and Harrison company gave an English version of *Les Huguenots*. Madame Patti made her début here as Amina in *La Sonnambula* in 1861, and other first appearances included those of Graziani, Tamberlik, Lucca and Albani.

In 1860, by the way, concerts were first given under Gye's auspices in the newly-built Floral Hall adjoining Covent Garden Market.

It seems incredible, but Gounod's *Faust* failed to make any impression upon Gye at that time: he repeatedly refused to produce it. Eventually, this opera was mounted at Her Majesty's and caused such a furore that he was obliged to acknowledge his mistake.

An attempt was made in 1865 to amalgamate Covent Garden and Her Majesty's, and to bring both houses under the management of a " Royal Italian Opera Company Ltd." Nothing came of the project until 1869, and then the union lasted for only two years.

For about ten years or so Covent Garden prospered : the annual profits were always over fifteen thousand pounds notwithstanding the upward trend of the artists' salaries. Wagner's *Lohengrin* was produced in 1875, *Tannhäuser* in the following year, and *Der fliegende Holländer* shortly afterwards.

On November 27th, 1878, Gye was accidentally shot while he was a guest at Dytchley Park, Oxfordshire, and the management of Covent Garden passed to his son Ernest and one of his brothers.

In 1884 the Royal Italian Opera collapsed financially. For

this, several reasons have been put forward, but the chief wa probably the attitude of the Philistine public at that time. Fashion still reigned supreme, and very few people really cared abou operatic art. They would flock to the opera house when some extravagantly paid *prima donna* was to sing; any new craze o sensation would be greeted with wild enthusiasm; but intelligent constant interest in the art of opera was beyond the powers of the majority, and the maintenance of a continual stream of costly celebrities would have strained the resources of the most affluent management.

In this country we rarely count our blessings until we lose them and therefore it is not surprising to find that the failure of the Italian Opera pricked many an artistic conscience. Consequently after a few seasons of indifferent opera mounted by an impresario named Lago, the enterprising Augustus Harris was able to secure a very large subscription to reopen in 1888 with a company he had formed at Drury Lane during the previous season, and by keeping just a little in advance of the public taste, ensured the future of the opera for many years.

Harris was knighted in 1891, not, mark you, in recognition of hi service to art, but merely because he happened to be Sheriff o London when the Emperor of Germany visited the City! However, he more than justified the honour when in the following year he was responsible for the first *entire* production in England o *Der Ring des Nibelungen*, under the baton of Gustav Mahler.

Sir Augustus Harris died at Folkestone on June 22nd, 1896 and the Grand Opera Syndicate became the lessees of Coven Garden, maintaining admirably the fine tradition that had been established.

HER MAJESTY'S

Fire, that traditional destroyer of London's theatres, consumed Her Majesty's Theatre on Friday, December 6th, 1867, and the company was obliged to move to Drury Lane. By the end o 1869 a new theatre had been built at a cost of fifty thousand pounds. but as the majority of the stalls and boxes were leased, no tenant seemed willing to be deprived of his personal fortune for the doubtful pleasure of running the new house. In 1874 Her Majesty's was put up for auction, but there was still no offer for it, so in the following year it was taken over for the revivalist mission o Messrs. Moody and Sankey!

J. H. Mapleson came to the rescue of the theatre in 1877 by

opening it as an opera house in April of that year, with Tietjens in *Norma*, under the conductorship of Costa.

Bizet's famous opera *Carmen* was first heard here on June 22nd, 1878, and in 1882 a part of *Der Ring des Nibelungen* was produced for the first time in this country. Mapleson's last Italian season was given in 1887 when Lilli Lehmann was heard in *Fidelio* and Patti in *La Traviata*. Sarah Bernhardt played here three years later.

Her Majesty's was pulled down in 1891. Five years later Beerbohm Tree built another theatre of the same name on part of the site of the old house, at a cost of seventy thousand pounds, opening it on April 28th, 1897, with *The Seats of the Mighty*. Its name was changed to His Majesty's on the accession of King Edward VII in 1901, and because of Tree's fine productions there, it is still regarded by the older playgoers as his memorial theatre.

MARIE WILTON AND THE PRINCE OF WALES'S THEATRE

Miss Marie Wilton took over the disreputable old Queen's Theatre in a fit of exuberant optimism early in 1865, but her enthusiasm was a trifle damped the first night she attended a show there. H. B. Baker quotes her own words in his book *The London Stage* :

" Some of the occupants of the stalls (the price was, I think, a shilling) were engaged between the acts in devouring oranges (their faces being *buried* in them), and drinking ginger beer. Babies were being rocked or smacked to be quiet, which proceeding in many cases had an opposite effect.

A woman looked up to our box, and seeing us staring aghast with, I suppose, an expression of horror . . . first of all ' took a sight ' at us, and then shouted ' Now then, you stuck up ones, come out of that, or I'll send this 'ere orange at your 'eads.'

Mr. Byron (H. J. Byron) went to the back of the box and laughed until we thought he would be ill. He said my face was a study. ' Oh, Byron,' I said, ' do you think the people from the West End will ever come into those seats ? ' ' No,' he replied, ' not *those* seats. . . .'

One woman in the stalls called out : ' I say, Mrs. Grove, ' ere's one for you,' at the same moment throwing a big orange ; upon which Mr. Byron remarked, ' Nice woman, Mrs. Grove . . . *orange grove*.' I think, if I could, I would at that moment have retired from my bargain, but the deed was done, and there was no going back from it."

Marie Wilton [1839–1921] was the eldest of six daughters of a provincial actor. Doncaster is believed to have been her birthplace. As a child actress she won the praise of Charles Macready and Charles Kemble, but it was Charles Dillon, manager of the Lyceum who first brought her to London. She drew high praise from Charles Dickens when he saw her play the part of Pippo in H. J. Byron's *The Maid and the Magpie*.

To start her new venture at The Queen's (which she renamed, with royal permission, The Prince of Wales's Theatre) she borrowed a thousand pounds from her brother, Francis Drake. The greater part of this sum went in cleaning and partly re-seating the house. She opened on April 15th, 1865, with only a hundred and fifty pounds in the bank, a theatre prettily decorated to her own specifications, and H. J. Byron as a partner.

The small company Miss Wilton assembled included Squire Bancroft [1841–1926] with whom she had played at Liverpool. A native of Rotherhithe, he had been educated at private schools in this country and in France, and had up to that time been playing entirely in provincial stock companies.

Bancroft made his London début on the opening night in a little comedy by J. P. Wooler called *A Winning Hazard*. Miss Wilton's speculation was a success : she concentrated first upon burlesques, but in the following June produced a new comedy by H. J. Byron, entitled *War to the Knife*. Her first outstanding production was T. W. Robertson's comedy *Society*, which every other manager in London had rejected. When it started its run on November 11th, 1865, everybody realized that a new revival in dramatic art had begun. Robertson's second comedy *Ours* made another hit in September, 1866.

In the following year Bancroft succeeded Byron as joint manager of the Prince of Wales's, and married Miss Wilton. Together they possessed practically all the qualities required for good theatrical management. They enjoyed, too, the loyal adherence of T. W. Robertson, who then wrote several more plays that did much to establish the Bancroft management : *Caste* [1867], *Play* [1868], *School* [1869] and *M.P.* [1870]. In these, Mrs. Bancroft's piquant humour and brilliant technique were the talk of the town, and her husband's Captain Hawtree in *Caste* was the best drawling " swell " the playgoers had seen for years.

Other productions by the Bancrofts while they were at this house included *The School for Scandal*, Bulwer-Lytton's *Money*, and Boucicault's *London Assurance*. But the Prince of Wales's Theatre

SIR HENRY IRVING

DAME MADGE KENDAL

soon proved to be too small for such progressive managers, and in 1879 they took The Haymarket.

Edgar Bruce was the next manager, and his greatest success was F. C. Burnand's comedy *The Colonel* in 1881. It ran for a year; then he took it around the provinces, making a handsome fortune for himself, out of which he built The Prince's Theatre in 1884. The Prince of Wales's then became a Salvation Army Hall, and its name was adopted by Bruce for his new theatre.

BUCKSTONE AND THE BANCROFTS AT THE HAYMARKET

J. B. Buckstone took the Haymarket when Webster went to the Adelphi in 1853, and collected an excellent comedy company for it. He wrote about a hundred and fifty plays himself—some of them popular at the time, but inconsequential to us—and enjoyed a great reputation as a low comedian.

He always gave good value for money: it was generally one o'clock in the morning before the Haymarket closed. His programmes usually concluded with a short farce that started at midnight, and for several years the livelier opera patrons would go across to the smaller house after leaving Her Majesty's to join in the fun. In those days, most people lived within reasonable walking distance of the theatres, and there was no scramble for the public conveyances.

For all that, Buckstone's finances grew steadily worse, and in 1861, almost in despair, he engaged Edward Sothern to play the part of Lord Dundreary in Tom Taylor's play *Our American Cousin*. The staggering reception given to this mediocre effusion is evidence of the intelligence of the average playgoer at that time: incidentally, this was the first of the " long runs " to which we have now become accustomed. Its great popularity is perhaps explained by H. B. Baker's observations in *The London Stage* :

" Sothern's success in America was one of those extraordinary instances in which greatness is thrust upon a man against his will. As the piece was originally written, Asa Trenchard, created by Jefferson, was the principal character; and Sothern, at that time the light comedian at Laura Keene's theatre, was so disgusted with the part of the silly lord that only the threat of dismissal induced him to play it. Thus coerced, he resolved in revenge to turn it into ridicule, and make it perfectly unendurable to the audience. He gagged, he hopped, he lisped, fully expecting to evoke a storm of disapprobation. To his astonishment, the audience laughed and applauded, and professional instinct told him that he had made a hit instead of a fiasco. Night after night he added some new gags, some new absurdity, until the once despised part over-shadowed every other, and was *the* thing of the comedy."

Sothern assisted Buckstone for some time in the management of the Haymarket, and his popularity in the more stupid circles of high society no doubt helped to stave off the management's creditors.

The Haymarket was entirely reconstructed in 1879 and reopened by the Bancrofts on January 31st, 1880, with Bulwer-Lytton's play *Money*. It was then the most splendid and luxurious theatre in London, but in his zeal to make it a playhouse *de luxe*, Bancroft had abolished the pit—one of the most ancient institutions in the English theatre—and the disapproval of the audience was unmistakably indicated by the disturbances which took place on the opening night.

Many of the plays that had been successful in the old Prince of Wales's Theatre were transferred here, but in their spacious new setting they failed to draw the audiences anticipated by the Bancrofts. However, when the able manager and his wife retired in 1885 they were given a great ovation.

Herbert Beerbohm Tree became the lessee in 1887 and for ten years produced and personally played in a succession of splendid plays, including works of Shakespeare, Ibsen, Wilde and Maeterlinck.

THE OLYMPIC AND THE LYCEUM

For a few years during the eighteen fifties the old Olympic was one of the most fashionable theatres in London. Frederick Robson was all the rage there in a silly farce called *The Wandering Minstrel* by H. Mayhew, and great crowds went to see the burlesques and domestic dramas that were then in vogue. Tom Taylor's *Ticket-of-Leave Man* had an extraordinarily long run, and was repeatedly revived at the same house until the late eighties, when the Olympic ceased to be of any importance in the world of drama.

Charles Dillon was the manager at the Lyceum in 1856, and delighted his patrons as D'Artagnan in *The Three Musketeers*. He was a great favourite in the sixties, " an actor of great emotional gifts, but very deficient in intellectual ones," said Westland Marston. He had risen from the very lowest ranks of the profession, and made no attempt to conceal his pathetic lack of education. Still, he knew good acting when he saw it, and must be given the credit for having introduced Miss Marie Wilton to the London stage, for she played with him in Charles Webb's *Belphegor*, in 1856.

Charles Fechter, who took over the Lyceum in 1863, was one of the few who were responsible for the initiation of the revival of the theatre. He revolutionized scenic art and the mechanics used in the theatre, improved the lighting, and attended fastidiously to details of costume. In 1865 he invited Henry Irving to join the Lyceum company, but the offer was declined.

HENRY IRVING AT THE LYCEUM

Henry Irving, whose original name was John Henry Brodribb, was born at Keinton Mandeville, Somerset, on February 6th, 1838, son of a poor and narrow-minded shopkeeper. He was educated at Dr. Pinches' City Commercial School in George Yard, Lombard Street; became a solicitor's office boy and then a junior clerk with a firm of East India merchants. He joined an elocution class and spent most of his time and money in seeing Samuel Phelps at Sadler's Wells. When he was sixteen he made the acquaintance of a member of the Sadler's Wells company, William Hoskins, who helped him in his desire to learn the art of acting. When he was eighteen, Hoskins introduced him to E. D. Davies, manager of the Lyceum Theatre, Sunderland, who engaged him. His first appearance was made on this northern stage as Henry Irving on September 18th, 1856, in the part of Gaston, Duke of Orleans, in Lytton's *Richelieu*. He received no salary for the first month, but twenty-five shillings thereafter, out of which he sent money home to help his parents. In 1857 he went to Edinburgh, played there two and a half years, and then came to London to play a small part in Oxenford's *Ivy Hall* on September 24th, 1859, at The Princess's Theatre. Disliking the insignificant part assigned to him, he asked to be relieved of his contract.

He played in Dublin for a few weeks in March, 1860, and then proceeded by way of Glasgow and Greenock to Manchester, where he stayed enjoying the esteem of the Lancashire people for nearly five years. It was at the Theatre Royal in that city that he first appeared as Hamlet.

After a tour of Edinburgh, Bury, Oxford, Birmingham and Liverpool, he returned to London in October, 1866, to play at the St. James's Theatre, having successfully appeared at The Prince's, Manchester, in Boucicault's *Two Lives of Mary Leigh*. He was then only twenty-eight, yet he had played nearly six hundred parts in the provinces. In the following February he went to Paris to play in *Our American Cousin* at the Théâtre des Italiens. Returning to England, he played at the St. James's again, the new Queen's Theatre, the Haymarket and Drury Lane, until he went to the Vaudeville in April, 1870 and scored his first real success in London as Digby Grant in Albery's *Two Roses*.

In 1871, H. L. Bateman, an American, took the Lyceum and succeeded in getting Irving to join the company, which included Bateman's two daughters, Kate and Isabel. After a few months of financially unsuccessful plays, Irving persuaded Bateman to put on *The Bells*, a dramatic version of Erckmann-Chatrian's *Le Juif Polonais*. It ran for six months with Irving playing the part of the conscience-haunted burgomaster, and did much to establish the reputation of this great actor.

Irving's next triumph was in the title-rôle of W. G. Wills's *Charles I.* The pathos and dignity of his portrayal of the King was a favourite topic in theatrical circles for years afterwards. *Eugene Aram*, another play by Wills, followed in 1873, with another superb interpretation of the title-rôle by Irving, and then the great actor appeared as the Cardinal in Lytton's *Richelieu.* His Hamlet [1874] took him to the very apex of his fame—Tennyson preferred his portrayal to that of Macready. The play ran for two hundred nights. His Othello and Macbeth were not so satisfactory, and he provoked some sharp criticism.

His finest effort in Shakespeare was in *Richard III*, which was revived in 1877, but some of the critics considered that his conception of the character, though scholarly, lacked the vitality of Garrick and Kean.

Bateman died in 1875, and for a while the Lyceum was managed by his widow, but in 1878 Irving became the sole lessee. He was then just over forty. Various alterations and improvements were made to the house, and he reopened it on December 30th with *Hamlet :* a memorable evening, with Miss Ellen Terry making her first appearance at this theatre as Ophelia.

Thus, this famous theatre entered upon the most glorious period of its history. For years, great drama really thrived there : Irving presented superb productions of *The Merchant of Venice*, *Romeo and Juliet*, *Much Ado about Nothing*, *Macbeth*, and a most lovely mounting of Tennyson's tragedy *The Cup*, to mention only a few.

In May, 1885, there was a disturbance in the house when he

started to permit the booking of seats in the pit and gallery, hitherto unreserved. Wisely, he abandoned the new practice.

The following December saw one of the greatest triumphs of his career: the production of Goethe's masterpiece *Faust* (adapted by Wills), in which his Mephistopheles was one of his most vivid and striking impersonations. An inspiration, too, was Ellen Terry's Marguerite. The theatre was literally beseiged: people started to queue for the unreserved seats soon after dawn, and it is said that thousands came from Germany to see this remarkable presentation.

The most splendid and elaborate production of Irving's career was his *Henry VIII* with music by Edward German, in January, 1892. Although it ran for over six months, the heavy cost of production—considerably over eleven thousand pounds—swallowed all the profits.

Later in the same year Irving reconsidered Tennyson's *Becket*, which he had refused in 1879. He obtained the great poet's approval for several cuts in the text, and persuaded him to write a new speech for Becket for the end of Act I scene iii. Four months after Tennyson's death—February 6th, 1893, to be exact—this tragedy was received with great enthusiasm, and a Command Performance was given before the Queen at Windsor. It ran for five months, and was frequently revived. Moreover, it proved to be Irving's most popular play when he made his fourth tour of America in the autumn of that year. His receipts during the six months he was in the United States amounted to over a hundred and twenty-three thousand pounds.

Nevertheless, towards the close of the century his good fortune wavered. The year 1897 showed a financial loss, and 1898 was even worse. *Peter the Great*, a tragedy by Irving's son Laurence, and *The Medicine Man*, by H. D. Traill and Robert Hitchens were both utter failures, and then a fire destroyed nine-tenths of his huge and costly stock of scenery.

The autumn of 1898 found him dangerously ill with pleurisy at Glasgow, and by the following February his finances were in such a precarious state that he was obliged to put his extensive library up for auction. In the same year, 1899, his interest in the Lyceum was transferred to a company.

Returning to the stage after his illness, he produced his son's translation of *Robespierre*, which Victorien Sardou [1831–1908] had written expressly for him. This was one of the plays he took on his sixth American tour which lasted from October, 1899, to May, 1900.

I

THE ADELPHI REBUILT

In 1858 the old Adelphi was completely rebuilt: an attractive and commodious theatre arising from the dust of the old play-house. Its first great hit was the domestic drama by Dion Boucicault called *The Colleen Bawn*, based on the novel *The Collegians*. It commenced on September 10th, 1860, and was the first drama on the English stage in which mechanical effects outshone the acting. The cavern scene caught the imagination of the childish public at that time, and for the best part of a year the house was packed every night. The author raked in money hand over fist, but the inventor of the effects that so intrigued the people—an old stage carpenter—received next to nothing.

Another " sensational " drama by the same author, *The Octoroon*, followed in November, 1861, and four years later his *Rip Van Winkle* (based on Washington Irving's story) with Joseph Jefferson in the title-rôle, had a six months' run. Jefferson's great artistry in his interpretation of the vagabond hero surpassed anything else the Adelphi could offer in the 'sixties. In fact, there is little more of interest to record in the history of this house during the remainder of the nineteenth century, except perhaps a fine production of *Monte Cristo*, adapted from the romance by Dumas, in 1868 ; and remarkably long runs of such plays as *In the Ranks* by Sims and Pettitt [1883] ; and F. C. Burnand's *Proof* [1878].

MARIE WILTON AT THE STRAND

The little playhouse did not emerge from the gloom of public apathy and financial instability until W. H. Swanborough took it over in 1858, and had the good fortune to enlist the help of Marie Wilton and H. J. Byron. It was while she was at this house, by the way, that Miss Wilton made so favourable an impression upon Charles Dickens. In a letter to a friend he wrote :

" I really wish you would go between this and next Thursday to see *The Maid and the Magpie* burlesque. There is the strangest thing in it that ever I have seen on the stage—the boy Pippo, by Miss Wilton. While it is astonishingly impudent (must be, or it couldn't be done at all), it is so stupendously like a boy, and unlike a woman, that it is perfectly free from offence. I never have seen such a thing. She does an imitation of the dancing Christy Minstrels—wonderfully clever—which, in the audacity of its thorough-going, is surprising. A thing that you cannot imagine a woman doing at all ; and yet the manner, the appearance, the levity, impulse, and spirit of it are so exactly like a boy that you cannot think of anything like her sex in association with it. It begins at eight, and is over by quarter-past nine. . . . I call her the cleverest girl I have ever seen on the stage in my time, and the most singularly original."

The eminent American actor, J. S. Clarke, played his famous part Major de Boots here in 1868, and afterwards became one of the theatre's most regular visitors. Edward Terry [1844–1912] was the leading comedian at this theatre from 1869–75.

The Strand Theatre [1] was reconstructed and enlarged in 1882, and reopened with *The Comedy of Errors* : an elaborate production, but financially unsuccessful. From that time its existence was precarious. For several years it was on the verge of disaster, in fact a bonus was offered to any manager who could run it rent free to save it from the ravages of mildew and moth. One of its few successes was a run of over a thousand performances of *A Chinese Honeymoon* [1901], a musical play by George Dance (music by Howard Talbot) which, according to H. G. Hibbert, a leading critic of that time, was " an ingenious attempt to get the glamour of *Aladdin* in musical comedy."

CHARLEY'S AUNT AT THE ROYALTY

Miss Kelly's little theatre was completely reconstructed in 1861 and reopened on November 12th by Mrs. Charles Selby, with a play called *Atar Gull*, but the theatre appears to have been more of a school for young players than a public playhouse. Adelaide Neilson made her début there as Juliet in 1865. From 1870 to 1883 it was in the hands of Miss Henrietta Hodson, who became noted for her ambitious productions. A noteworthy date during her reign is March 25th, 1875, when *Trial by Jury*, the first of the Gilbert and Sullivan operas, was produced at the Royalty. Then this tiny house was reconstructed again, enlarged and tastefully decorated by Miss Kate Santley. During the 'eighties it acquired a reputation for French drama.

In December, 1892, that amusing farcical comedy by Brandon Thomas, *Charley's Aunt*, took London by storm. It was backed by a city man named Hartmont, and it is said that during the rehearsals he lost confidence in it and began to moan about his rashness in putting money into such a show. The manager, who was certain of its success, offered to buy Hartmont's share (a thousand pounds), but the shrewd city man detected the eagerness with

[1] The existing Strand Theatre began its life as the Waldorf in May, 1905.

which the offer was made, and declined it. Eventually, he made over sixty thousand pounds on his original investment!—and remember, there was no ten-shillings-in-the-pound income tax to take the gilt off in those days.

It seems that by this time the Royalty had again become somewhat dilapidated, for H. G. Hibbert records in his *Playgoer's Memories* that when the old Duke of Cambridge went to see *Charley's Aunt* he sat down heavily in his stall, which collapsed forthwith and deposited him on the floor. Hibbert says " Characteristically, he swore like a trooper, then burst into hearty laughter."

THE ST. JAMES'S AND THE KENDALS

Augustus Braham, son of the founder of this house, took charge in 1859, and opened with *Raymond and Agnes*, a melodramatic ballet by Charles Farley, adapted from M. G. Lewis's work *The Monk*. It played for five nights to yawning rows of empty seats, and then Braham retired hastily.

After that there was a dismal succession of managers, of whom little need be recorded, though it is interesting to note that Richard Mansell, who was there in the 'seventies, got into serious trouble with the Lord Chamberlain when he produced *Vert-Vert*, an opera-bouffe. The scanty attire of several of the girls in it and a thoroughly indecent dance cost him his licence. He then roundly abused the Lord Chamberlain, who promptly added a note to his records to prevent the removal of the ban on Mansell in later years. The Royalty continued to ruin its lessees until the Kendals, with John Hare as a partner, took over in 1879.

William Hunter Kendal [1843–1917], a Londoner whose surname was originally Grimston, first appeared at the Royalty in 1861. He played in Birmingham and Glasgow for some time, and was then engaged by Buckstone at The Haymarket. In 1869 he married Margaret (Madge) Robertson, sister of T. W. Robertson the dramatist, and after engagements at the Opera Comique and the Gaiety, he entered into a " silent " partnership with John Hare at the Court Theatre [1875]. One of his greatest triumphs was as Dr. Thornton in *Peril* at the Prince of Wales's Theatre.

His wife was one of the finest all-round actresses of the day, and between them they were responsible for many notable productions at the St. James's. To them must be given the credit for having produced Sir Arthur Pinero's first notable play *The*

Sir Charles Hawtrey

SIR JOHNSTON FORBES-ROBERTSON

Money Spinner in 1881. They relinquished the St. James's in 1888 when the lease expired.

THE CAN-CAN AT THE PRINCESS'S THEATRE

It should be recorded that Charles Kean (son of Edmund Kean) made his farewell here in 1866, though his final appearance on the stage was made in Liverpool during the following year. After a long and painful illness he died at Queensborough Terrace, Chelsea, on January 22nd, 1868, and was buried at Catherington, Hants.

It was at the Princess's Theatre that the notorious *can-can* dance made its first appearance in London in connection with a melodrama called *The Huguenot Captain*. It ran for several months and made the *can-can* the rage of London. H. G. Hibbert in his *Playgoer's Memories* says of this dance :

" Its most remarkable exponents were Finette, Colonna, . . . and the ' celebrated ' Esther Austin. The Payne family, one of whom became the famous clown, also danced the *can-can*, which was destined to lose the Alhambra its licence . . . though it was allowed its fling elsewhere, and patronized by Royalty."

Drink, Charles Reade's adaptation of *L'Assommoir*, with Charles Warner as Coupeau, made a small fortune for Walter Gooch, who was running the Princess's in 1879.

Fire destroyed the theatre in 1880, and when it was rebuilt, it opened with a string of failures. Then Wilson Barrett ran it from 1881–86, scoring a great hit with *The Lights o' London* (George R. Sims). It ran for two hundred and twenty-eight performances, and then travelled all round the world.

When Barrett was negotiating with Sims for this play, the author was only a clerk in the city, and would gladly have sold it outright for a couple of hundred pounds. However, Barrett insisted on paying by results, and almost overnight, as it were, Sims found himself with an income of fourteen thousand pounds a year. For all that, *The Lights o' London* was not a brilliant play, but its vivid character studies caught the public in a sympathetic mood and filled the house night after night.

THE 'OLD VIC'

The Victoria closed on September 9th, 1871, but after some seven or eight years its lease was acquired by Emma Cons, a social reformer, and it was re-opened as the Royal Victoria Coffee Hall on Boxing Day, 1880, to provide " refined entertainment *without drink* " ! Ballad concerts and operatic excerpts made up most of the programmes, and although some sort of a chorus was employed in 1895 and various operatic productions were given in the following year, the theatre did not regain its status until 1914.

THE HOLBORN AND THE QUEEN'S

Having dealt with the more historic houses, let us review briefly a few of the many theatres erected during the second half of the nineteenth century. The first to be built after the theatrical " slump " in the middle of the century was the Holborn, erected in 1866 by Sefton Parry. It was renamed the Mirror in 1875, when Horace Wigan took it over, and later still became known as the Duke's Theatre. It was burnt down in 1880.

The greatest success here was *New Babylon*, a play by Paul Meritt and G. F. Rowe. Its advertisements described this extravagant inanity as :

" The most attractive drama ever written. Suits all classes. The Collision on the Atlantic. Tattersalls with its sales of horses. Cremorne, with its dancing platform and Ten Thousand Lights. Goodwood on Grand Race Day. The Thames Embankment with its electric Witness, and Seven Dials by night are pictures that must attract."

Because of the appearance on its boards of several famous actors during its short life, I must mention the Queen's Theatre, which existed from 1867–1878.[1] It was also known as The National Theatre for some time. One of the largest houses in London, it had an extensive, well-equipped stage which enabled spectacular productions to be staged lavishly. After its last failure in 1878, it became some sort of a co-operative store.

THE GAIETY AND ITS QUARTET

This theatre was originally the Strand Music Hall, but it was reconstructed in 1868 and reopened as a playhouse under the management of John Hollingshead. Almost every great player of the day appeared on its boards at some time.

It is interesting to note that a burlesque produced here in 1871 bore the names of W. S. Gilbert and Arthur Sullivan. One cannot help wondering how many people at that time realised what those two names would become in the annals of the English theatre within twenty years ! Incidentally, another of Gilbert's earliest

[1] The twentieth-century Queen's Theatre was opened in 1907.

works, a comedy-drama called *An Old Score* was produced at the Gaiety in 1869.

The famous " Gaiety Quartet " (Edward Terry, Edward Royce, Nellie Farren and Kate Vaughan) was one of the great attractions at this theatre for many years. French companies were to be found there every season from 1874, and the year 1879 stands out prominently in its history as the year in which Sarah Bernhardt made her first appearance in England with the company of the Comédie Française.

THE GLOBE, CHARING CROSS AND THE VAUDEVILLE

Another theatre to open in 1868 was The Globe, erected on part of the site of the old Lyon's Inn by Sefton Parry, but after a single success—H. J. Byron's *Cyril's Success*—it began to change hands with depressing frequency. All types of entertainment were given in it : Sir Charles Hawtrey had a wonderful reception there with *The Private Secretary* in 1884, and *Charley's Aunt* broke all records in 1893.[1]

Of the Charing Cross Theatre I have little to record except that it was converted from the Polygraphic Hall in 1869, and was taken over by Alexander Henderson in 1876 and renamed The Folly. *Les Cloches de Corneville*, an opera-bouffe by H. B. Farnie and R. Reece, with music by R. Planquette, was a great hit there in 1878. In 1882 the house was enlarged and renamed Toole's Theatre after its manager, J. L. Toole.

The Vaudeville Theatre was built in 1870 by Wybrow Robertson on the site of the former offices of *The Glow-worm*, and was opened by three partners, David James, H. J. Montague and Thomas Thorne, with Andrew Halliday's comedy *Love or Money* and a burlesque called *Don Carlos*. The three managers, by the way, were known in the profession as " The Jew, the Gent and the Gentile."

In its first year the Vaudeville scored a great success with the delightful comedy *The Two Roses*, by James Albery : the first of the long runs that have made this house famous. Always an ably-managed theatre, it seemed to have little difficulty in making good drama pay its way : *The School for Scandal* and *The Rivals*, for instance, were revived many times without causing any embarrassment in the box-office. William Farren's Sir Anthony Absolute always drew huge crowds, despite his extremely irritating habit of playing the last act with half of his make-up removed,

[1] The present-day Globe opened in 1906 as Hicks' Theatre.

so that he could dash off immediately after the show to catch a suburban train at Charing Cross, thereby saving the cost of a cab! His stinginess was the subject of many little stories, which cannot, unfortunately, be recorded here.

Another staggering Vaudeville triumph was H. J. Byron's comedy *Our Boys*, with David James as Perkyn Middlewick, in 1875. Although Byron made a handsome sum out of this play, he foolishly sold the provincial rights to a Mr. William Duck, whose profits on the transaction exceeded the author's royalties by many thousands. Duck, an illiterate creature, met Byron in Plymouth one day and exclaimed, " I've been for a walk round the 'oe." Byron immediately retorted, " Try one round the aitch for a change."

THE COURT AND THE OPERA COMIQUE

The Court Theatre in Chelsea began its career as a nonconformist chapel. In the late 'sixties it was converted into the New Chelsea Theatre, but accomplished nothing of importance. Shortly afterwards it was renamed The Belgravia, but continued to be of little consequence until late in 1870, when Miss Marie Litton reconstructed it, personally supervised the decorations, and re-opened it in January, 1871, as the Royal Court Theatre, with W. S. Gilbert's comedy *Randall's Thumb*.

In 1873 the Royal Court Theatre became the talk of the town. *The Happy Land*, a mischievous but highly amusing burlesque bristling with political satire, pilloried several leading cabinet ministers of the day, much to the delight of dozens of members of Parliament. Eventually, Mr. Gladstone intervened and the Lord Chamberlain insisted on drastic modifications in the make-up of three of the principals. Lottie Venne played in this as a prospective cabinet minister. After convincing everybody that she couldn't tell the difference between a barge and a battleship, she was solemnly presented with a portfolio marked " First Lord of the Admiralty."

John Hare took over in 1875 and ran the house for five years with a brilliant company, including the Kendals.

The next big success at the Court was in 1885 when Arthur Cecil and John Clayton were running it jointly : Pinero's farcical comedy *The Magistrate* which made all London rock with laughter. Three years later Mrs. John Wood and Arthur Chudleigh became the lessees, opening with *Mamma*, a comedy by Sydney Grundy which reflected none of the qualities associated with the author's surname.

Sɪʀ Hᴇʀʙᴇʀᴛ Bᴇᴇʀʙᴏʜᴍ Tʀᴇᴇ ᴀs Kɪɴɢ Jᴏʜɴ by Charles Buchel

Interior of the English Opera House (Lyceum Theatre) in 1817. (Below):
The Lyceum Theatre in 1860

Just near the old Globe another theatre was built in 1871 and became known as The Opera Comique. The Comédie Française played there for a while, and Madame Ristori made a sensational appearance on its boards in 1873.

Several of the Gilbert and Sullivan operas were first performed at this house : *The Sorcerer* [1877], *H.M.S. Pinafore* [1878], *The Pirates of Penzance* [1880], and *Patience* [1881]. After a very satis-factory run of F. C. Grove's *As in a Looking-Glass* in 1887, the Opera Comique declined rapidly.

THE ALHAMBRA AND THE CRITERION

The original Alhambra was built in 1854 as The Panopticon of Science and Art. In 1858 E. T. Smith leased it as an athletic and musical entertainment hall, calling it The Alhambra because of the Moorish style of its architecture. Shortly afterwards a proper stage was installed, and many beautiful ballets were to be seen there. At that time it was notorious as a rendezvous for young people bent on promiscuity.

During the Franco-German War [1870–71] it acquired a new reputation when its vast numbers of French and German patrons would gather every night in its promenade and indulge in glorious free fights. Apparently everybody enjoyed them immensely. Alas ! this and the *Can-can* brought the wrath of officialdom down upon the manager's head, and he lost his licence.

Not long afterwards, the Alhambra Company was formed, and John Baum obtained a theatrical licence for it. Comic operas and exquisite ballets were the chief attraction here for years, and the house was noted for its large and splendid orchestra. One of its best productions was Offenbach's *Le Roi Carotte*. Its old music hall licence was regained in 1884.

The Criterion in Piccadilly Circus was built in 1874 by Spiers and Pond as an appendage to their restaurant, and was something of a novelty because being underground air had to be pumped in to prevent the suffocation of the audience. Old ladies were often very nervous about patronising it, and frequently badgered the attendants asking them if they were *quite sure* that the fans were in proper working order. H. J. Byron, the first manager, opened it with his new comedy *An American Lady*, but its finances were very precarious until Alexander Henderson took it over in 1877 and specialized in adaptations of French comedies. A mild scandal was caused in March of that year when Albery's *Pink Dominoes* gave the respectable suburban matrons something to think about in the shape of a foretaste of the naughty nineties. Charles Wyndham, who was a popular light comedian in this theatre for several years, soon succeeded Henderson as manager, and made it his London stage until 1899, when he built Wyndham's Theatre.

In 1883 the Board of Works began being difficult, so the Criterion was reconstructed and considerably enlarged. Luxuriously appointed, and equipped with electric lighting, it reopened in April, 1884.

GILBERT AND SULLIVAN AT THE SAVOY

From its foundation in 1881 the Savoy was for years famous for its productions of Gilbert and Sullivan. *Patience* was chosen for the opening night, and then *Iolanthe* was given its first performance here in 1882, *Princess Ida* in 1884, the tremendously popular *Mikado* in 1885, *Ruddigore* in 1887, *The Yeomen of the Guard* in 1888, *The Gondoliers* in 1889; and after the unfortunate dispute between the famous collaborators, *Utopia Limited* in 1893 and *The Grand Duke* in 1896.

By the way, their famous quarrel is said to have arisen over the question of a new carpet for the Savoy during the run of *The Gondoliers* in 1890. I need scarcely enlarge upon the amazingly widespread popularity of these light operas, and even if for the present they are heard less frequently than in the past, I think it not at all unlikely that they will be revived and readily appreciated when the nation settles down to a life of peace.

THE COMEDY, AVENUE AND THE PRINCE'S

The Comedy Theatre we know to-day in Panton Street, Haymarket, was built in 1881 for the surprisingly small sum of twenty thousand pounds, and opened with an English version of *La Mascotte*. For several years it was devoted to comic opera, Fred Leslie making a wonderful hit in *Rip Van Winkle*, by H. B. Farnie, with Planquette's music, and W. S. Penley outshining everybody else as Brother Pelican in *Falka* (Farnie, from the French, with music by Chassaigne).

Sir Charles Hawtrey was the lessee from 1887–1893, and again from 1896–1898. It was here in 1894 that J. M. Barrie had one of his earliest successes : *The Professor's Love Story*. (The first of Barrie's plays to be produced in London was *Walker, London*, at Toole's in 1892.)

Sefton Parry built the Avenue Theatre in 1882 in the hope that the old South Eastern Railway would buy it from him at a fancy price when they embarked upon their improvement scheme in connection with Charing Cross Station. They didn't; and it afterwards became The Playhouse. At this time there was a great deal of ugly talk about speculation in property, so Parry published a curious Apology for building another theatre, drawing attention to the need for new playhouses.

One of The Avenue's most notable successes was Offenbach's *La Vie Parisienne* in 1883.

I have already mentioned that Edgar Bruce built The Prince's, one of the most pleasant houses in London at the time, in 1884, and renamed it The Prince of Wales's when the little Tottenham Street theatre of that name closed down. He opened with W. S. Gilbert's *Palace of Truth*, but his first real success was with *Called Back* (Hugh Conway and J. Comyns Carr), in May of the same year.

Some of the long runs here in the 'eighties and 'nineties were *Paul Jones* [1889], *Marjorie* [1890], *L'Enfant Prodigue* [1891], *In Town* [1892], *A Gaiety Girl* [1893], *Gentleman Joe* [1895] and *La Poupée* [1897].

THE EMPIRE, TERRY'S AND THE SHAFTESBURY

The Empire was erected in Leicester Square on the site of Saville House and what used to be the London residence of the Earl of Leicester, and opened in 1884 with the comic opera *Chilperic* (R. Reece, F. A. Marshall and R. Mansell; with music by Hervé), said to have been the most spectacular show Londoners had ever seen up to that time. Financially, it was a failure, and in three years the Empire became a music hall. The programmes in those days generally consisted of a couple of magnificent ballets supported by a splendid variety show, to which must be added the attraction of its world-famous promenade. In the naughty 'nineties this promenade shared with that of the Alhambra a reputation of being a smart hunting ground for rakes in search of young ladies of easy virtue. It was also frequented in those days by gentlemen who indulged in what were politely called " unnatural love-affairs." Needless to say, it has been a highly respectable theatre since the beginning of the present century. At one time the Empire was paying a dividend of nearly sixty per cent., yet there were many lean years in its history. Early in the nineteen-twenties it became a cinema.

As I am not mentioning *all* the theatres of this period, there is little to justify a reference to Terry's, except that Edward Terry built it on the site of the famous old Occidental Tavern in the

Strand, in 1887. Terry had a passion for church and social work, and appropriately, he opened it with a play of his own, called *The Churchwarden*. This theatre was not very prosperous, and it might have got into difficulties had not Sir Arthur Pinero come to the rescue with *Sweet Lavender*, which enjoyed a run of no less than six hundred and seventy performances.

According to H. G. Hibbert in his *Playgoer's Memories*, the Shaftesbury Theatre, built in Shaftesbury Avenue in 1888, was " run up for twenty thousand pounds by a Lancashire merchant, John Lancaster, for the exploitation of his wife, Miss Ellen Wallis, as a Shakespearean actress." Hibbert continues: " . . . on the first night the iron curtain refused to go up on *As You Like It*, and the audience sadly dispersed through the dank passages."

It was at the Shaftesbury that the famous American musical play *The Belle of New York* first delighted the London playgoers in 1898. It ran for six hundred and ninety-seven performances, making a small profit of a hundred thousand pounds. The late George Musgrove, the manager responsible for bringing the American company over here, found some difficulty in making them see eye to eye with him on the question of remuneration. He offered Dan Daly, the principal, fifty pounds a week with an air of magnanimous generosity. Daly merely stared and replied bluntly " Go to hell." So Musgrove had to think again.

THE GARRICK AND THE PALACE

The Garrick in Charing Cross Road was built for Sir John Hare by W. S. Gilbert. He opened it on April 24th, 1889, with *The Profligate* (Pinero), in which he played the part of Lord Dangars. Hare stayed there until 1895, when he first visited America, and was responsible for the original production of many plays, including *The Notorious Mrs. Ebbsmith* (Pinero) and *A Pair of Spectacles* (Sydney Grundy).

Notable long runs here in the 'nineties were *Dream Faces* [1890], *A Fool's Paradise* [1892], *Diplomacy* [1893], and *The Gay Lord Quex* [1899].

The Palace we know so well to-day in Cambridge Circus was opened by Richard D'Oyly Carte on January 31st, 1891, as The Royal English Opera House, with Sir Arthur Sullivan's *Ivanhoe*, (libretto by Julian Sturgess, based on Scott's famous novel). D'Oyly Carte's idea was to establish the Royal English Opera House as the permanent home of grand English opera, but although *Ivanhoe* was superbly mounted and had the advantage of the best

DAME ELLEN TERRY

SIR NIGEL PLAYFAIR

SIR FRANK BENSON

SIR ARTHUR PINERO

JAMES BRIDIE

singers and a splendid orchestra, it was a failure financially, despite the fact that it ran for six months.

Disappointed, but determined to persevere, he put on an English version of Messager's *La Basoche* in the following November, but after a couple of months it failed. Sarah Bernhardt played in Moreau's *Cleopatra* there during the summer months of 1892, but by that time D'Oyly Carte had become convinced that it would be impossible to run the theatre as an opera house, and towards the end of that year he sold it to Sir Augustus Harris's syndicate, who reopened it on December 10th as The Palace of Varieties.

THE LYRIC, DALY'S AND OTHERS

The Lyric Theatre in Shaftesbury Avenue was opened in December, 1888, by H. J. Leslie with *Dorothy*. It was a particularly successful house from the start, for after two long runs in 1889 (*Doris* and *The Red Hussar*), each of the following ran for many months during the next decade: *La Cigale* [1890], *The Mountebanks* [1892], *Incognita* [1892], *Little Christopher Columbus* [1893], *His Excellency* [1894], *The Sign of the Cross* [1896], *Dandy Dan the Lifeguardsman* [1897], *Little Miss Nobody* [1898], *El Capitan* [1899] and *Florodora* [1899].

A brief mention should be made of Daly's because of one or two notable productions in it during the 'nineties. It was opened in 1893 by Augustin Daly with *The Taming of the Shrew*, but its reputation was established chiefly by musical comedy. A musical show called *An Artist's Model* was given four hundred and five performances in 1895, and in the following year the first production of the popular Japanese musical play *The Geisha*, caused great delight. It ran for no less than seven hundred and sixty performances: an unusually long duration in those days. Reverting to Shakespeare: the year 1894 was memorable for a hundred and twelve performances of *Twelfth Night*, and in the same year Humperdinck's charming fairy opera *Hansel and Gretel* continued for several months. The musical comedy *A Greek Slave* ran to three hundred and fifty-two performances in 1898.

Other theatres built in the 'nineties include The Coronet [1898], Trafalgar Square, afterwards known as The Duke of York's, [1892], The Shakespeare [1896], Wyndham's [1899] and a number of East London and suburban theatres—notably The Lyric, Hammersmith, which opened in November, 1890—but lack of space precludes further details.

PHYSICAL IMPROVEMENTS IN THE THEATRE

As one would imagine, considerable improvements were made in the mechanism of stage devices during the latter half of the nineteenth century, but most important, I think, was the progress made in lighting.

The lime-light was introduced somewhere around 1860 when it was discovered that a brilliant white light could be obtained by playing a burning mixture of oxygen and hydrogen on to a small block of lime, so that it became incandescent. The gases were stored in cylinders, which, of course, were apt to be inconvenient, and although the expression " the limes " is still in use in the theatre, this form of lighting has been superseded by the electric arc-lamp. The old limes enabled colour-lighting to be developed rapidly later in the century by the use of silks placed in the front of the lantern. Henry Irving was the first producer to exploit colour-lighting to its fullest extent.

The first complete system of electric lighting to be installed in a theatre was at the Paris Opéra in 1880, and the first to be seen in this country was at the Savoy Theatre, London, in 1882. Most of the other theatres followed the Savoy's example very quickly, and the introduction of rheostats (resistances which enable electric lights to be " dimmed ") made possible the most delicate gradations of light when special effects were required.

Chapter X

PLAYERS AND DRAMATISTS

MANY of the actors, actresses and dramatists of the later Victorian period carried on their work well into the twentieth century, so in this chapter I am going to review, briefly, some of the more outstanding personalities from 1850 to the present day.

The last we heard of Henry Irving was his sixth American tour which ended in May, 1900. After producing *Coriolanus* at the Lyceum in 1901, he went back to the United States again, returning in March, 1902, to revive *Faust* at the Lyceum. This was followed by *The Merchant of Venice* : his last appearance at this theatre because his company was financially unable to carry out various structural alterations insisted upon by the London County Council. So the Lyceum closed and was later converted into a music hall.

At Drury Lane in 1903 he incurred fabulous expenses in his production of *Dante* (Sardou ; translated by Laurence Irving) but its reception was bitterly disappointing. It failed, too, in America when he made his last tour from October, 1903, to March, 1904.

He revived *Becket* at Drury Lane for his last London season [1905] and once more had the pleasure of playing to large and really enthusiastic audiences. This was the play in which he appeared at Bradford on the fateful night of October 13th, 1905, when on returning to his hotel he collapsed and died. He was buried in Westminster Abbey on October 20th.

Henry Irving was the first actor to be knighted for his services to dramatic art. Curiously enough, he refused the honour when it was suggested to him in 1883, but in 1895 he accepted it because he felt that his profession needed " official recognition."

Sir Henry was a tall, thin and aristocratic-looking figure with a dominant personality which was apt to colour the parts he played ; but his superb artistry was a sheer joy to all who appreciated his intellectual approach to his art.

I have already recorded the retirement of Squire Bancroft and his delightful wife, Marie Wilton, in 1885, but there remain a few facts still to be noted. He returned to the stage twice after his retirement : to play with Irving in *The Dead Heart* at The Lyceum in 1889, and to appear at the Garrick in 1893 for Sir John Hare.

Squire Bancroft was knighted in the Jubilee honours of 1897, and died in London on April 19th, 1926. His wife died at Folkestone on May 22nd, 1921.

We left the Kendals when they gave up the St. James's Theatre in 1888. They visited America in 1889 and appeared at the Fifth Avenue Theatre, New York, in *A Scrap of Paper*. William Kendal's last notable success was in *The Elder Miss Blossom* at the St. James's in 1898, although he did not retire for another ten years. He died in London on November 6th, 1917.

BEERBOHM TREE AND HIS CONTEMPORARIES

Sir Herbert Beerbohm Tree was born in London on December 17th, 1853, and made his first appearance on the stage as an amateur in 1876. He was still an amateur when he played the part of Grimaldi in *The Life of an Actress* at The Globe in February, 1878. This, however, secured him his first professional engagement for a tour in the provinces, after which Henry Neville booked him for the Olympic Theatre. The first time he gained really warm approval from the critics was when he took the part of the Marquis de Pontsable in the comic opera *Madame Favart* at the Strand in 1879.

On April 20th, 1887, he became his own manager and had good luck immediately at the Comedy Theatre with the Russian play *The Red Lamp* (W. Outram Tristram), in which he distinguished himself as Paul Demetrius. In the autumn of that year he made his first big speculation—the leasing of the Haymarket, to which he transferred *The Red Lamp*, having made a hundred and eighty-five appearances in it at the Comedy. Good fortune continued to favour him, and he stayed at the Haymarket for nearly ten years.

I have already referred to Her Majesty's Theatre, which he built in 1897 and made his theatrical home until the end of his career. In 1904 he founded the Academy of Dramatic Art, and in the following year started his famous series of Shakespearean Festivals. King Edward knighted him in 1909. He spent most of 1915 and 1916 in America, and returned to England only to die in the following year.

Sir John Hare, whose original name was John Fairs, was born on May 16th, 1844 at Giggleswick, Yorkshire. His first school was in London, and he was always getting into trouble for absenting himself in order to attend matinées. When his parents died he was sent to the local grammar school at Giggleswick, and by distinguishing himself in amateur theatricals he managed to persuade his guardians that he was more fitted to enter the theatrical profession than the Civil Service. On leaving school he studied for a while with Henry Leigh Murray in London, and then made his first professional appearance at the Prince of Wales's Theatre, Liverpool, on September 28th, 1864, making the acquaintance of the Bancrofts at the same time.

His début in London was made at the age of twenty-one at the Prince of Wales's Theatre in *Naval Engagement* [1865], and shortly afterwards he made a considerable impression as Lord Ptarmigan in T. W. Robertson's comedy *Society*. He stayed there with the Bancrofts for nine years, always excelling in anything from Robertson's pen.

In 1874 we find him as actor-manager at the Court Theatre, with W. H. Kendal as a " silent " partner. Then, after four quite prosperous years, he joined Kendal at the St. James's in 1879, as I have recorded elsewhere. I have also referred previously to his career at the Garrick. He was knighted in 1907 when he played in a Command Performance of *A Quiet Rubber* (Charles Coghlan), at Sandringham, and shortly afterwards took part in another such performance at Windsor, when the royal audience saw *A Pair of Spectacles* (Sydney Grundy). The latter play was billed for Hare's farewell at Wyndham's in September, 1917. He died on December 28th, 1921, in London. Sir John Hare was famous for his extraordinary ability in portraying character by facial expression, yet his acting bore not the slightest trace of exaggeration.

Sir Charles Hawtrey was born at Eton on December 21st, 1858, son of a housemaster at the College. He was educated at St. Michael's, Slough, Eton and Rugby, and in 1881 matriculated at Pembroke College, Oxford, but then changed his mind and instead of entering the University he secured an engagement to play the part of Edward Langton in *The Colonel* (Burnand) at The Prince of Wales's, London, in the same year. He played under the name of Charles Bankes, by the way.

After a tour in the provinces he made his first great achievement in London at The Prince's Theatre on March 29th, 1884, with *The Private Secretary*, his own adaptation of the farce *Der Bibliothekar*, by Gustav von Moser. Herbert Beerbohm Tree played the title rôle. Hawtrey transferred it to the Globe in May (when W. S. Penley succeeded Tree), and using his own name, played

K

Douglas Cattermole. It is said that the first pit and gallery queues ever seen in London gathered outside the Globe for this play, which ran for two years.

Hawtrey was as good a producer as an actor, and excelled in staging light comedy and farce. He visited America several times, and was knighted in 1922. Cricket, golf and horse-racing were his favourite recreations, and in 1885 he staggered his many friends by winning fourteen thousand pounds in one race. He died on July 30th, 1923.

Another prominent actor-manager was William S. Penley [1852–1912] who was born near Broadstairs of a family well rooted in theatrical history. He became one of the Children of the Chapel Royal (St. James's) and subsequently a chorister at Westminster Abbey. He served an apprenticeship with a firm of milliners in the City, but abandoned the trade in 1871 to accept an engagement at thirty shillings a week at the Court Theatre. He was first seen here on December 26th of that year in a play called *My Wife's Second Floor*, and within a few years was playing principal parts in various London houses, specializing in burlesque. His first outstanding accomplishment was at the Comedy in 1883 as Brother Pelican in the comic opera *Falka* (music by Chassaigne), though he soon eclipsed this at the Globe when he played with Hawtrey in *The Private Secretary* in the following year.

It was *Charley's Aunt*, however, that put Penley's name on everybody's lips in London: his Lord Fancourt Babberley was an impersonation not easily forgotten. When this play was transferred to the Globe in 1893 it broke all records with a run of fourteen hundred and sixty-six performances—four years! There must surely be few of the older generation of playgoers who do not remember the famous poster of the old " lady " fleeing for her life over the caption " Charley's Aunt—still running."

Penley retired to Woking in 1901, and died at St. Leonards-on-Sea on November 11th, 1912.

William Terriss [1847–1897], whose surname was originally Lewin, was a Londoner who after trying the merchant navy, medicine, farming and tea-planting, went on the stage in 1867. He soon became very popular, and joined Irving at the Lyceum in 1880. As he was entering the theatre on December 16th, 1897, a madman sprang upon him and stabbed him to death. His daughter, Ellaline, who was also on the stage, married Edward Seymour Hicks.

Dame Ellen Terry [1847–1928] was a native of Coventry, and

was first seen on the stage at the age of nine, when she played the part of the boy Mamillius in *The Winter's Tale* at the Princess's Theatre on April 28th, 1856.   In subsequent years she frequently appeared with Charles Kean in Shakespearean productions, and as a fairy in pantomime.

When she was fifteen she joined J. H. Chute's company at The Theatre Royal, Bristol, but in 1863, after an appearance at Bath for the opening of that city's Theatre Royal, she joined Buckstone at the Haymarket.   Early in the following year, however, she married George Frederick Watts, the painter, who being twenty years her senior, treated her like a child, and worse still, permitted his friends to do likewise.   In less than eighteen months a separation was arranged, and she returned to the stage, joining A. S. Wigan at the new Queen's Theatre, Long Acre, in October, 1867, to play the part of Mrs. Mildmay in *Still Waters Run Deep*.   During the following December she appeared for the first time with Henry Irving in *Katherine and Petruchio* (Garrick's adaptation of *The Taming of the Shrew*).

However, she was not really happy on the stage, and in 1868 abandoned her career to live with Edward Godwin, the architect, in Hertfordshire, and had two children, Edith Craig and Edward Gordon Craig.   It was her anxiety about the children's future that made her return to the stage again in 1874; and her Portia in *The Merchant of Venice* during the ensuing year at the Prince of Wales's Theatre made the critics realize that a brilliant young actress had " arrived."

Towards the end of 1876 she went to John Hare at the Court Theatre, and it was here that some eighteen months later she made a great impression in W. G. Wills's version of Goldsmith's *Vicar of Wakefield*.   Her penetrating conception of Olivia brought tears to the eyes of the audience.

She had by that time been divorced by Watts and had contracted another disastrous marriage, this time to Charles Kelly (Charles Wardell) the actor.   They were separated in 1881.

When Irving took charge at the Lyceum in December, 1878, he engaged her to play Ophelia in *Hamlet*, and from that time she enjoyed a succession of triumphs in leading female parts in most of his productions until 1902.   Her outstanding ability may be summed up in the words of Sir Johnston Forbes Robertson: " Everything she did was invested with great charm.   I do not suppose there ever was such an Ophelia : nor do I think there ever will be again.   In the theatre she was adored.   In the public estimation she became a fetish. Take her for all in all, she was one of the most remarkable figures in the history of the stage."

Ellen Terry's last appearance at the Lyceum was as Portia on July 19th, 1902. In less than twelve months she took the Imperial Theatre, Westminster, and produced *The Vikings*, an English version of Ibsen's play *The Vikings at Helgeland*, with herself as Hiordis. Although the critics were highly enthusiastic about it, the average playgoer had not at that time learnt to appreciate Ibsen, and the heavy expenses made it necessary to withdraw the play. No more successful was *Much Ado About Nothing* which followed, so she decided to close the theatre.

She continued to have faith in modern drama, however, and found favour as Alice Grey in J. M. Barrie's *Alice Sit-by-the-Fire* at the Duke of York's in 1905, and as Lady Cecily Waynflete in *Captain Brassbound's Conversion* (Bernard Shaw) at the Court Theatre in the following year.

Her stage-jubilee in 1906 was celebrated by London playgoers with the greatest enthusiasm. On June 12th she played Beatrice at Drury Lane in *Much Ado about Nothing* with no less than twenty-two of her relations in the cast. The subscription for her amounted to nearly ten thousand pounds.

The next year she took *Captain Brassband's Conversion* and *The Good Hope* (H. Heijermans) to America, and while she was at Pittsburg, Pennsylvania, she married James Carew (James Ussel-man), a young American actor. They separated in 1910.

Ellen Terry's last appearance on the stage was at the Lyric, Hammersmith, in *Crossings* (Walter de la Mare), in 1925, though for several years she had done very little acting because she had been lecturing extensively. In the same year she received the Grand Cross of the Order of the British Empire.

Dame Ellen died aged eighty on July 21st, 1928, at Small Hythe, Tenterden, Kent, and her ashes were placed in a casket on the wall of St. Paul's Church, Covent Garden. Her house at Small Hythe was purchased by public subscription, and made into a memorial museum.

Charles Wyndham's surname was originally Culverwell. He was born at Liverpool on March 23rd, 1837, educated at King's College, London, and at Dublin, and qualified as a surgeon; but drama appealed to him more strongly than medicine, and after some experience on the amateur stage he came to London in 1862. Later in that year, however, he went to America to serve as a surgeon in the federal army, and during the Civil War he played several

DAME MARIE TEMPEST

SIR JAMES BARRIE

times in the New York theatres. After his return to England in 1865 he appeared in various provincial theatres before he got his first London engagement at the Royalty. Considerable success in town enabled him to embark upon a three-years' tour of America, after which he came back to London to take over the Criterion in 1876.

During his twenty-three years' tenure, the Criterion acquired a great reputation for modern comedy, and Wyndham himself was tremendously popular in such parts as Bob Sackett in the farce *Brighton*, in Albery's *Pink Dominoes*, and in the title-rôle of T. W. Robertson's *David Garrick*.

Wyndham built two of our most popular theatres of the present day : the one that bears his name in Charing Cross Road was opened in November, 1899, with *David Garrick ;* and the New, which opened on March 12th, 1903, with *Rosemary* (L. N. Parker and Murray Carson). He was knighted in 1902 at the time of the coronation of Edward VII, and died on January 12th, 1919, leaving two hundred thousand pounds.

Sir George Alexander [1858–1918] excelled more as a manager than an actor, for his mannerisms were apt to spoil his work on the stage. He took over the St. James's Theatre in January, 1891, and for twenty-seven years maintained an exceptionally high standard of drama there with a brilliant company that included such talented players as Mrs. Patrick Campbell, Irene Vanbrugh, Henry Ainley and Marie Tempest. He gave two Command performances, *Liberty Hall* (R. C. Carton) and Alfred Sutro's play *The Builder of Bridges*. Alexander was knighted in 1911, and was last seen on the stage in *The Aristocrat* (L. N. Parker) at the St. James's in July, 1917. He died on March 16th, 1918, at Chorley Wood, Hertfordshire.

Nellie (Ellen) Farren was born in Liverpool in 1848 and is said to have taken a small part at the Theatre Royal, Exeter, when she was only five years of age. At nine she was singing the popular song *In 'Ninety-five* at the Old Vic, and after playing various juvenile parts, appeared at Sadler's Wells at the age of fourteen in a Christmas show called *The Rose of Blarney*. Four years' experience in light comedy and burlesque at the Olympic enabled her to join Hollingshead at the Gaiety in 1868 and to win tremendous popularity in old English comedy, farce and comic opera, while maintaining at the same time a high reputation in Shakespeare. She visited America and Australia with Fred Leslie and the Gaiety company, but lost all the money she earned in a catastrophic attempt to run the Opera Comique Theatre when she returned to London in 1895. However, a benefit performance at Drury Lane brought her the handsome sum of seven thousand two hundred pounds, and she was able to retire comfortably after all. She died in West Kensington on April 28th, 1904.

Intending to make music her profession, Marie Tempest, who was born in London on July 15th, 1864, studied for several years at the Royal Academy of Music and in Paris before she took to the stage. She made her début at the Comedy Theatre on May 30th, 1885, as Fiametta in *Boccaccio*, and then for the next fifteen years specialized in light opera, scoring her greatest success in the name-part of *Dorothy*, which ran to nine hundred and thirty-one consecutive performances—the longest run for comic opera ever known at that time. She toured America and Canada with the J. C. Duff Comic Opera Company, and became a great favourite, but in 1900 she abandoned musical plays and concentrated instead upon "straight" comedy. She found immediate success at the Prince of Wales's Theatre as Nell Gwyn in *English Nell*, but her greatest triumph was perhaps in *Hay Fever*, which Noel Coward wrote expressly for her.

Marie Tempest was made a Dame Commander of the Order of the British Empire in 1937. Her home was destroyed during the aerial attacks upon London during the early part of the Second World War, and she died on October 15th, 1942.

Sir John Martin-Harvey was born at Wyvenhoe, Essex, on June 22nd, 1863, and educated at King's College School. His parents wanted him to become a naval architect, but his love of the theatre prevailed, and he was allowed to study dramatic art under John Ryder. A tour with F. C. Burnand's *Betsy* followed his first appearance in *To Parents and Guardians* at the Court Theatre on September 24th, 1881, and then he joined Irving's company at the Lyceum, making his first appearance on September 2nd, 1882, in *Romeo and Juliet*. He stayed at the Lyceum for fourteen years, but his greatest success did not come until 1899 when as Sydney Carton in *The Only Way* (the romantic play adapted from *A Tale of Two Cities*) he reached the summit of a brilliant career. He was knighted in 1921, and died in 1944.

Sir Johnston Forbes-Robertson originally intended to become an artist and took no more than an amateur interest in the theatre until he was nearly twenty. He was born in London on January 16th, 1853, educated at Charterhouse, and admitted as a student at the Royal Academy in 1870. Elocution lessons with Samuel Phelps made him change his mind, and he went on the professional stage for the first time on March 5th, 1874, as Chastelard in *Mary Queen of Scots* at the Princess's Theatre. His first great hit was in *The Profligate* (Pinero) at the Garrick in 1889. Six years later he ventured into theatrical management when he took over the Lyceum to produce *Romeo and Juliet* with Mrs. Patrick Campbell and himself in the leading parts. In 1902 he played Mark Embury in the twelve months' run of *Mice and Men* (M. L. Ryley) at the Lyric —one of his most successful impersonations—and then spent the best part of two years in touring America. Older playgoers will probably associate him chiefly with Jerome K. Jerome's play *The Passing of the Third Floor Back*, which he revived over and over again with great success. He was created a knight at the conclusion of his farewell season at Drury Lane in 1913, and died in 1937.

Sir Frank Benson's influence on modern drama is highly significant, for many prominent actors and actresses of to-day owe their success to the wonderful experience they gained when working under his guidance. He was born at Alresford, Hampshire, in 1858, educated at Winchester and New College, Oxford, and distinguished himself in the O.U.D.S. by producing, among other works, the Greek play *Agamemnon*. He made his début as Paris in *Romeo and Juliet* at the Lyceum under Irving in 1882, and within a year was touring the country with a company of his own. By his masterly playing of such parts as Hamlet, Coriolanus, Lear, Richard II and Petruchio he won the esteem of everybody in the profession. For twenty-six years he organized the annual Shakespearean Festivals at Stratford-on-Avon, and at the conclusion of the Tercentenary Performance of *Julius Cæsar*, at Drury Lane on May 2nd, 1916, he was knighted by King George V. Sir Frank Benson died in 1939.

Sir Nigel Playfair was a barrister for a few years before he entered the theatrical profession. He was born in London on July 1st, 1874, educated at Winchester, Harrow and Oxford, and gained valuable experience in the O.U.D.S. and other amateur societies. He was first seen on the professional stage at the Garrick on July 30th, 1902, as Mr. Melrose in *A Pair of Knickerbockers*. His great popularity induced him to assume the management of the Lyric, Hammersmith, in 1919, and it was largely due to his splendid work and influence that this suburban theatre has risen to such a proud position in London's theatrical life. Playfair was knighted in 1928 and died in 1934.

Before we come to the players of to-day I must mention such names as Wilson Barrett [1846–1904] whose great triumph in *The Sign of the Cross* at the Lyric was an ever-recurring topic in theatrical circles for many years; Eleonora Duse [1859–1924], the famous Italian actress who made such a great impression in London; Lionel Brough [1836–1909], one of the greatest actors of his day; Edwin Booth [1833–1893] the most brilliant American actor of the nineteenth century; and Joseph Jefferson [1829–1905] the famous American comedian who was at one time all the rage in London. Tommaso Salvini [1830–1915] the celebrated Italian tragedian still lingers in the memory of the older generation, and there are many thousands who have vivid recollections of Lillie Langtry [1852–1929].

The death of Mrs. Patrick Campbell in April, 1940, robbed the world of one of the greatest actresses of the twentieth century; and if only by a passing mention, tribute must be paid to that distinguished actor-manager Sir Gerald du Maurier [1873–1934], and to the magnificent educational work done by his illustrious contemporary, Sir (Philip) Ben Greet [1857–1936].

SOME NOTABLE PLAYERS OF TO-DAY

In the very small amount of space I have available I shall attempt to do no more than mention a few representative actors and actresses whose talent demands special reference.

John Gielgud, who comes of the celebrated Terry family, is generally acknowledged to be the greatest actor on the English stage to-day. He was born in London on April 14th, 1904, educated at Westminster School, and studied for the stage at Lady Benson's school and at the Royal Academy of Dramatic Art, gaining scholarships at both. He was first seen at the Old Vic on November 7th, 1921, as the Herald in *Henry V*. During 1922 he toured with J. B. Fagan's play *The Wheel*, understudying and acting as stage manager; then he gained further experience here and there, so that when his first great opportunity came in May, 1924, he was able to convince the critics that he was well on the way to fame. This was when he played Romeo in Sir Barry Jackson's revival of *Romeo and Juliet* at the Regent. Another occasion on which he won everybody's admiration was when he played Ferdinand in *The Tempest* at the Savoy in 1926. The next year saw him in New York as Grand Duke Alexander in *The Patriot* at the Majestic; then he returned to London to score another success as Oswald in Ibsen's *Ghosts ;* but it was his Hamlet at the Old Vic in 1929,

W. Somerset Maugham

SIR BARRY JACKSON

and at the Queen's in the ensuing year, that established him. He maintained his high standard as Richard in Daviot's *Richard of Bordeaux* at the New Theatre in 1932 and 1933, and then at the same theatre made another great hit as Hamlet in 1934–5.

It was undoubtedly Gielgud's Romeo at the New Theatre in 1935–6 that was primarily responsible for the longest run of *Romeo and Juliet* ever known : a hundred and eighty-six performances. His next visit to New York enabled the American audiences to share the English playgoers' enthusiasm for him as Hamlet.

In 1937 Gielgud took over the management of the Queen's Theatre, London, and stayed there until May, 1938, appearing in the name-part of *Richard II*, as Joseph Surface in *The School for Scandal*, and Shylock in *The Merchant of Venice*. His company included Michael Redgrave, Peggy Ashcroft, Alec Guinness and Glen Byam Shaw.

Early in 1939 he produced a revival of *The Importance of Being Earnest* (Oscar Wilde), playing the part of John Worthing himself. In June of that year he appeared as Hamlet in the last performance at the Lyceum before it was finally closed. Gielgud's activities in wartime will be dealt with later.

Dame Sybil Thorndike was born in 1882, at Gainsborough, Lincolnshire, and received her education at Rochester High School and at the Guildhall School of Music, London. She studied for the stage at Ben Greet's Academy, and distinguished herself in Shakespearean rôles early in her career. Two of her greatest accomplishments were seen soon after the Great War when she played Hecuba in *The Trojan Women* (Gilbert Murray's translation of the tragedy by Euripides) and the title-rôle of Bernard Shaw's *Candida*. Sybil Thorndike also found favour as Jane Clegg in St. John Ervine's play of that name, and as Joan of Arc in Shaw's *St. Joan*.

Miss Thorndike married Lewis Casson, the well-known actor, in 1908, and received appropriate recognition of her work in 1931 when she was made a Dame Commander of the Order of the British Empire.

Born in London in 1888 and educated at St. Michael's School, Chester Square, Edith Evans first appeared as Cressida in *Troilus and Cressida* when it was revived by the Elizabethan Stage Society at King's Hall, Covent Garden, in 1912. Her outstanding ability and exceptional versatility attracted the attention of the critics, and she was soon winning laurels in almost anything from Shakespeare to Shaw. One of her greatest hits was as Gwenny in

The Late Christopher Bean (René Frauchois, adapted by Emlyn Williams).

Another actress of truly remarkable ability is Flora Robson, who was born at South Shields in 1902, and made her début at the Shaftesbury on November 17th, 1921, as Queen Margaret in *Will Shakespeare* (Clemence Dane), and then gained valuable experience with Ben Greet in Shakespearean repertory. A most successful period at the Festival Theatre, Cambridge, enabled her to make her first great hit as Mary Paterson in *The Anatomist* (James Bridie) at the Westminster Theatre in 1931.

Equally fine is Beatrix Lehmann, " discovered " by the Lyric, Hammersmith, in 1924. *Desire under the Elms* provided her with a wonderful opportunity to shine, and she made the most of it.

Still in his " thirties " is Laurence Olivier, whose rise to fame in recent years has been so rapid that unless the British film companies succeed in retaining him in this country, he will undoubtedly be snatched by Hollywood. Born at Dorking, Surrey, in 1907, and educated at St. Edmund's School, Oxford, Olivier studied with Elsie Fogerty and made his first appearance on the stage at the Shakespeare Festival Theatre, Stratford-on-Avon in 1922, when he played Katherine in a special boys' performance of *The Taming of the Shrew*. He was one of the principal players in the Birmingham Repertory Company for two years, and then made his début on the London stage as the Minstrel in *The Marvellous History of St. Bernard* at the Kingsway in 1926. At the Court Theatre in 1928 he played Malcolm in *Macbeth* and Martellus in *Back to Methuselah*, and then enjoyed many notable London successes. He made several visits to America between 1929 and 1933, and in 1935 he played Richard Harben in *Golden Arrow* under his own management at the Whitehall Theatre. Real distinction came when he proved his remarkable ability in Shakespearean rôles during those memorable productions which started at the Old Vic in January, 1937. His Hamlet, Sir Toby Belch, Henry V and Macbeth firmly established the great reputation he has enjoyed ever since. He has appeared in various films since 1930, and as this book goes to press [1945] the theatrical world has something to talk about in his conception of Richard III.

No less brilliant is Ralph Richardson, born in 1902, whose superb artistry was well employed in such plays as *Johnson over Jordan*, *Cornelius* and *Peer Gynt*. He has the qualities of a great actor.

Another young British actor showing exceptional promise at

the present time is Wilfrid Lawson, who comes from Bradford, Yorkshire. He was first seen on the stage at the Pier Theatre, Brighton in 1916 ; then he served as a pilot in the R.F.C. during the latter part of the Great War, and after several years in provincial repertory made his début in London at the Elephant and Castle Theatre in 1928, in *Sweeney Todd*. One of his greatest London successes was as John Brown in *Gallows Glorious* at the Shaftesbury in 1933. He has appeared in quite a number of films.

Considerably younger, but quite as promising is Stephen Murray, who first appeared at the Memorial Theatre, Stratford-on-Avon, in *Much Ado About Nothing* in 1933. Later in the same year he played Captain Odderedi in *Cabbages and Kings* at the Ambassadors' Theatre, London. Two years with the Birmingham Repertory Company eventually led to a string of London successes, notably in *Abraham Lincoln*, *Dangerous Corner* and *The Doctor's Dilemma*.

Diana Wynyard has been one of the greatest favourites in recent years. She did remarkably well in *Watch on the Rhine* and *The Wind of Heaven*, and should have a brilliant future.

Another splendid actress who must be kept on this side of the Atlantic if possible is Vivien Leigh. Born in India in 1913, educated in a convent, and trained for the stage by Mlle. Antoine at the Comédie Française as well as at the R.A.D.A., she first won the playgoers' hearts as Mrs. Dubedat in *The Doctor's Dilemma*. Her most recent success has been as Sabina in *The Skin of our Teeth*.

It was the Old Vic that first brought Michael Redgrave to London in 1936 to play Ferdinand in *Love's Labour's Lost*. He was born in Bristol in 1908, educated at Clifton College and at Cambridge, and worked as a schoolmaster before he went upon the stage. His first appearance on the professional stage, however, had taken place many years before : he had been seen as a baby in arms during a production in Australia ! As a boy he played at the Festival Theatre, Stratford-on-Avon, in 1921. Two years with the Liverpool Repertory Company prepared him for his London successes (notably Andrew Aguecheek in *Twelfth Night* and in the title rôle of *Uncle Harry*).

While we are considering the younger players of to-day some mention must be made of such people as the brilliant Donald Wolfit, who is doing valuable work with his tours of Shakespearean plays and other classics ; and Margaret Rawlings (born in Osaka, daughter of an English missionary in Japan), who has continued to distinguish herself ever since her memorable tour of Canada and

America with Maurice Colbourne and Barry Jones with the plays of Bernard Shaw.

Before we pass on to consider the dramatists of this period, a reference must be made to some of the other great figures in the modern English theatre, whose work I have been unable to describe in detail owing to the very small amount of space available. This book would not be complete without mention of the influence of such people as Sir Edward Seymour Hicks, Dame Lilian Braithwaite (who was honoured in 1943), Madge Titheradge, Sir Cedric Hardwicke, Fay Compton and Godfrey Tearle. Dame Irene Vanbrugh received appropriate recognition in 1941, and we must also include in this category Lillah McCarthy (Mrs. Granville-Barker) who will for years be remembered for her Shavian rôles. All these have played a most significant part in twentieth-century drama, even though some of them have not associated themselves with any of the progressive " movements."

Among the younger players exerting an important influence we find, apart from those already mentioned, such talented players as Jean Forbes-Robertson, Peggy Ashcroft and Leslie Banks, to mention only three whose careers will be worth watching.

TOM TAYLOR TO JAMES BRIDIE

We now have to go back to the middle of the nineteenth century to resume our brief survey of British dramatists. One of the most prolific and popular playwrights of the nineteenth century was Tom Taylor, but although his plays were invariably well constructed, they have little literary merit. He was born at Sunderland in 1817, educated at Glasgow and Trinity College, Cambridge, called to the bar in 1845, and subsequently held various official appointments. Of his hundred or more plays, *Our American Cousin*, *Still Waters Run Deep* and *Ticket-of-Leave Man* are the best.

The plays of Algernon Charles Swinburne [1837–1909], though rich in poetry, are not considered suitable for stage production, and as far as I am aware, have never been seen in the commercial theatre. They include *Rosamond* [1860], *The Queen Mother* [1860], *Atalanta in Calydon* [1865], *Bothwell* [1874] and *Mary Stuart* [1881].

As my space is so restricted, I need scarcely include biographical details concerning Tennyson [1809–1892]. On the whole, his plays were not very well received, though it will be recalled that his *Becket* was successfully produced by Irving after the great poet's death. Irving also staged his *Queen Mary* [1875] and *The Cup* [1881], and the Kendals produced *The Falcon* in 1879. His rustic drama

EDITH EVANS

John Gielgud

The Promise of May was seen at The Globe in 1882, and his poetic drama *The Foresters* was produced by Augustin Daly at Daly's Theatre in 1893. As far as I am aware, *Harold* was not staged until 1928, when it was seen at the Court Theatre.

Son of a puritanical farmer, Henry Arthur Jones did not go inside a theatre until he was eighteen. He was born at Grandborough, Buckinghamshire, in 1851, and on leaving school at the age of twelve entered his uncle's drapery at Ramsgate. Later, he became a commercial traveller, and spent all his leisure hours in reading diligently. He began to write, but all his early efforts were rejected. Eventually, he got a play called *It's Only Round the Corner* accepted for production at the Theatre Royal, Exeter, and although it did not exactly set the Exe afire, it was sufficiently well received to make him decide to become a professional playwright. His first London production was a little comedy called *A Clerical Error*, staged at the Court Theatre in 1879. Three years later, his melodrama *The Silver King* (written in collaboration with Henry Herman) ran for two hundred and eighty-nine performances at the Princess's, and firmly established him. Other successes included *Saints and Sinners* [1884], *The Middleman* [1889], and *Judah* [1890], but his best work was *The Liars*, performed by Charles Wyndham and Mary Moore at The Criterion in 1897. His powerful *Michael and His Lost Angel*, which he considered to be his best play, failed at the Lyceum and does not appear to have been revived. Jones died at Hampstead on January 7th, 1929.

Tremendously popular was the work of Sir Arthur Pinero [1855–1934]. Son of a London solicitor, he intended to enter his father's profession, but at the age of nineteen took to the stage and ultimately became a dramatist. His dramatic writings vary considerably, but he excelled in the problem play. His first production in London was £200 *a Year* at The Globe in 1877, yet it was at the Theatre Royal, Manchester, that he scored his first success. This was in 1880 with *The Money Spinner*. His comedy *The Magistrate* (recently revived) ran for over a year at the Court Theatre in the middle 'eighties, and real fame arrived with the production of *The Second Mrs. Tanqueray* at the St. James's in 1893, with Mrs. Patrick Campbell in the title rôle. This play still stands revival, and is a favourite with repertory companies. His best work was *Mid-Channel*, which was put on at the St. James's in 1909 and revived successfully at the Royalty in 1922.

Oscar Wilde was born in Dublin on October 15th, 1856. At Magdalen College, Oxford, he had his furniture and ornaments

smashed up by " hearties " who disliked his " Art for Art's sake "
pose, and he was ducked in the Cherwell for preferring cultural
activities to the more boisterous forms of athletics. Early efforts
which appealed only to a small minority led to *Lady Windermere's
Fan*, which was produced at the St. James's in 1892 and found
favour with the fashionable West-end audiences. His brilliant
wit was relished in all the more sophisticated circles. Considered by most people to be his greatest achievement, the clever
comedy, *The Importance of Being Earnest* first saw the footlights at
the St. James's Theatre on February 14th, 1895, and has been
revived again and again with unfailing success.

Sir Herbert Beerbohm Tree produced Wilde's *Woman of No
Importance* at the Haymarket in 1893, making the most of its epigram-
matic dialogue, but when it was proposed to stage his *Salomé* the
Lord Chamberlain refused a licence, and consequently it was first
produced in Paris under the direction of Sarah Bernhardt in the
following year. The first performance in this country was at the
little Bijou Theatre in Bayswater in 1905.

An Ideal Husband was first seen at the Haymarket just about a
month before *The Importance of Being Earnest* took London by storm,
and these two plays might have carried Wilde to the very height of
fame if his libel action against the Marquis of Queensberry had not
revealed facts which sent the brilliant dramatist to prison for
homosexual practices. He died in Paris on November 30th, 1900.

Sir James Matthew Barrie established himself as a novelist
before he turned his attention to the stage. He was born at
Kirriemuir, Scotland, in 1860, and was writing novels before he
left Edinburgh University. The success of his first play *Walker,
London*, which was produced in 1893 with J. L. Toole in the lead,
encouraged him to continue writing for the theatre, and by 1903
he had three plays running simultaneously in London : *Quality
Street*, *The Admirable Crichton* and *Little Mary*. All these considerably enhanced the reputation he had established by the
dramatization of his novel *The Little Minister* at the Haymarket
in 1897 ; then in 1904 he won the hearts of thousands of youngsters
with his pretty little fairy play *Peter Pan*, at the Duke of York's.
This of course has had dozens of revivals.

At the same theatre over a year's run rewarded his attempt to
ridicule the self-sufficient male in *What Every Woman Knows*, yet
one of his best plays, *The Twelve Pound Look*, was decidedly less
successful, although he used much the same theme in 1913 for
The Will. Perhaps the most successful of his later plays were

Dear Brutus (Wyndham's, 1917–18), *Mary Rose* (Haymarket, 1920–21), and *Shall We Join the Ladies?*, which was given its *première* at the Palace on December 19th, 1921, in a memorable performance in aid of King George's Actors' Pension Fund, and then ran for well over a year at the St. Martin's from 1922–23. Barrie received a baronetcy in 1913 and the Order of Merit in 1922. He died on June 19th, 1937.

Having provided all my readers with an excellent opportunity of making the acquaintance of Bernard Shaw in a previous work,[1] the only biographical details I intend to mention here are that he was born in Dublin in 1856, received instruction in " lying, dishonourable submission to tyranny, dirty stories, cowardice " and so forth at local schools, came to London when he was twenty to tread heavily upon the corns of almost everybody in the world of music and drama, and then became the Shakespeare of the twentieth century.

His first play, *Widowers' Houses*, was produced at the Royalty in 1892 and had a mixed reception, but its exposure of the slum landlords won him great favour in Liberal circles. *Mrs. Warren's Profession*, an indictment of the conditions that promote prostitution, was suppressed by the Lord Chamberlain to the satisfaction of prude and pimp alike. The first production of *Arms and the Man* at the Avenue in 1894 was not a financial success, but subsequent revivals were fully justified. The honour of first producing *Candida* (generally considered to be his best comedy) must go to a touring company in the provinces, and their success with it was responsible for the Stage Society's production at the Strand Theatre in 1900, with Janet Achurch in the title rôle (the wife of a clergyman who is tempted to run away with a young poet) and Granville Barker as Marchbanks. This play was a riotous success in America.

It seems that Shaw adopted the popular practice of writing with one eye upon the box-office when he produced *You Never Can Tell* (Royalty, 1899) for this is more of a " commercial-type " play. It is a popular stand-by with some of the impecunious " reps " when they want to stage something Shavian without breaking open the gas-meter. Such plays as *Captain Brassbound's Conversion* (Strand, 1900), *The Philanderer* (Court, 1907), *The Man of Destiny* (Comedy, 1901), *The Devil's Disciple* (Kensington, 1899; Savoy, 1907), *The Admirable Bashville*, an adaptation from his novel *Cashel Byron's Profession* (Imperial, 1903), *Cæsar and Cleopatra* (Savoy, 1907), *Getting Married* (Haymarket, 1908), and *Too True to be Good*

[1] *Writers' Gallery* : 1944.

(New, 1932) have all been revived several times with full satisfaction both in the auditorium and in the box-office.

Shaw's best works are *Man and Superman* (Court, 1905, many revivals, and a run of nearly two hundred performances at the Criterion in 1911); *John Bull's Other Island*, written at the request of W. B. Yeats for the Abbey Theatre, Dublin (Court, 1904); *Major Barbara*, his delightful play about the Salvation Army (Court, 1905); *The Doctor's Dilemma* (Court, 1906, and many revivals); *Pygmalion*, which of course was made into one of the finest films we have ever seen (His Majesty's, 1914); *Heartbreak House* (Court, 1921); *Back to Methuselah*, the five-part play cycle (Court, 1924); and his masterly *St. Joan* (New, 1924).

In recent years we have seen the film world slowly waking up to the value of Shaw's plays. We now hear of great plans for their use in a tremendous effort to establish the British film industry in its proper place in movieland's sunshine. Splendid! But we have also one or two other dramatists in this country whose excellent works have yet to be tested on the screen.

Ireland also gave us W. B. Yeats, who was born at Sandymount, near Dublin, in 1865, and who was one of the founders of the Irish National Theatre (the Abbey Theatre). His best-known plays are *The Land of Heart's Desire* [1894], *Kathleen ni Houlihan* [1902], *The Pot of Broth* [1902], and *The Hour Glass* [1903], but much of his work is considered to be unsuitable for the " commercial " theatre. Yeats received the Nobel prize for literature in 1924, and died in January, 1939.

Laurence Housman, born in 1865, will be remembered in the theatre chiefly for his masterpiece *Victoria Regina*, which was produced at the Lyric Theatre on the hundredth anniversary of Queen Victoria's Accession, June 21st, 1937, and ran for about a year.

Turning again to poetic drama, Stephen Phillips [1868–1915] must be mentioned for his first play *Paolo and Francesca*, which was commissioned by George Alexander and achieved a considerable success at the St. James's in 1901. Phillips was born at Somertown, near Oxford, son of the Precentor of Peterborough Cathedral. He left Cambridge during his first term to join Sir Frank Benson's company, but it was as a poet that he distinguished himself. Shortly before his first play was produced, Sir Herbert Beerbohm Tree staged his second, *Herod: a Tragedy*, at Her Majesty's, but neither this nor its successors, *Ulysses*, *The Sin of David*, and *Nero*, found much favour with the general public.

It was Granville Barker who persuaded John Galsworthy

FLORA ROBSON

Michael Redgrave and Leslie Banks in *The Duke in Darkness* (Patrick
Hamilton)

[1867–1933] to start writing for the stage. He was born at Coombe, Surrey, educated at Harrow and Oxford, called to the bar in 1890 but detested his profession and within a few years became a professional novelist. His first play, *The Silver Box*, was originally produced at the Court Theatre in 1906, but it was revived on several occasions and ran for over three months at the Fortune in 1931. Then followed *Joy* at the Savoy in 1907, *Strife* at the Duke of York's in 1909, and *Justice* at the same theatre in the following year. His first outstanding success in the theatre was *The Skin Game* which, despite its unpleasant title, ran for about a year when it was first produced at the St. Martin's Theatre in 1920, and *Escape* fully justified its long run at the Ambassadors' in 1926. His best play is undoubtedly *Loyalties* (St. Martin's, 1922).

Galsworthy's scrupulous care to avoid exaggeration when depicting social problems in his plays tends to rob them of some of their dramatic value, and his dialogue is sometimes too natural to be really effective on the stage, unless spoken by a most accomplished player.

Arnold Bennett [1867–1931] was also successful in the theatre. He was born in Staffordshire and was engaged in the legal profession before he secured the assistant-editorship that started him on a literary career in 1893. Among his more popular plays we find the comedies *The Great Adventure* (nearly two years' run at the Kingsway in 1913) and *The Honeymoon* (Royalty, 1911). Collaborating with Edward Knoblaugh he wrote *Milestones*, of which over six hundred performances were given at the Royalty in 1912 and 1913, and a successful revival of it took place in the same theatre in 1920. Other noteworthy plays by Arnold Bennett are the comedy *The Title* (Royalty, 1918), and *Sacred and Profane Love* (Aldwych, 1919).

St. John Hankin [1869–1909] was one of the more enlightened dramatists of his age, and it is generally considered that his works are shamefully neglected. The best was perhaps *The Cassilis Engagement*. A contemporary of his, Allan Monkhouse [1858–1936] will be remembered for *The Conquering Hero* (Aldwych, 1924).

One does not of course judge the dramatic works of the present Poet Laureate, John Masefield [born 1875], by the frequency of their performance. They include *The Campden Wonder*, a domestic tragedy [1907]; *The Tragedy of Nan*, a romantic drama [1908]; his Japanese tragedy *The Faithful* [1915]; *Melloney Hotspur* [1923]; *Tristan and Isolt*, a Cornish play [1927]; and *The Empress of Rome*, from the French miracle play [1937]. His most successful play was

L

The Witch (from the Norwegian) which was originally performed at the Court Theatre in 1911. The Stage Society presented his tragedy *Pompey the Great* at the Aldwych in 1910, and a notable performance of *The Trial of Jesus* was given by the R.A.D.A. Players in their own theatre in 1926.

Ireland comes into the story again with J. M. Synge [1871–1909], a dramatist of marked ability who perhaps did not receive the recognition due to him. His finest work is to be found in the highly controversial comedy *The Playboy of the Western World*, first produced at Great Queen Street in 1907, and revived at the Mercury in 1939. *In the Shadow of the Glen* and *Riders to the Sea* were both staged at the Royalty in 1904. Unfortunately, his amusing farcical comedy *The Tinker's Wedding* does not appear to have been presented anywhere in London, though I should imagine that some of the more enterprising " little people " have played it sometime.

Another Irishman, Monckton Hoffe (born at Connemara in 1880), should be mentioned here for his *Many Waters*, originally produced as "The Unnamed Play" by the Repertory Players at the Strand in 1926. I also like *The Faithful Heart* (Comedy Theatre, 1921).

What a pity it is that one of the most brilliant writers in the world to-day has done nothing for the theatre in recent years. I refer of course to our illustrious friend W. Somerset Maugham, who was born in Paris in 1874, the son of the solicitor to the British Embassy.[1] *A Man of Honour* (Avenue, 1904) brought him an unjustified and unwanted reputation for pessimism and cynicism, so he concentrated upon a witty portrayal of more pleasant subjects with the result that his comedy *Lady Frederick* ran to over four hundred performances at the Court in 1907–8. The large number of theatrical managers who had assured him that his work was " uncommercial " had something to think about when in 1908 he broke all theatrical records by having four plays running concurrently in London. These were the comedy to which I have just referred, *Jack Straw* (Vaudeville), *Mrs. Dot* (Comedy), and *The Explorer* (Lyric). His next success was *Penelope* at the Comedy Theatre in January, 1909, with *Smith* to follow it at the same house.

Our Betters, a superb comedy, was first seen in New York in 1917. When it was put on in London at the Globe, in 1923, it ran for nearly two years. One of Somerset Maugham's most brilliant plays, *The Circle*, ran for about six months at the Haymarket in 1921, and has been recently revived.

[1] A biography will be found in my book *Writers' Gallery*.

Over two hundred performances were given of *Cæsar's Wife* (Royalty, 1919), *Home and Beauty* (Playhouse, 1919), *East of Suez* (His Majesty's, 1922), *The Letter* (Playhouse, 1927–8), and *The Secret Flame* (Playhouse, 1929), yet the reception given to his profoundly moving play about a middle-class family in the post-war period (*For Services Rendered*, at the Globe in 1932) was most inadequate, and even more disappointing was the public's appreciation of *Sheppey* at Wyndham's in 1933. Maugham remarked: " I am conscious that I am no longer in touch with the public that patronizes the theatre," and wrote all his later works in novel-form.

That excellent play *The Grain of Mustard Seed* brings to mind the name of Dr. H. M. Harwood, a physician born at Eccles, Lancashire, in 1874, who found that drama and medicine go quite well together ! His comedy *The Man in Possession* (Ambassadors', 1930) would stand revival.

The eminent actor-dramatist Harley Granville-Barker was born in London on November 25th, 1877, and went to the company at the Theatre Royal, Margate, as a pupil when he was barely fourteen. Within a year had secured an engagement in London under Charles Hawtrey at the Comedy, and when he was eighteen he was acting Shakespeare with Ben Greet.

His first play, written when he was sixteen, was performed by a company of amateurs, and he was only twenty-two when *The Weather-hen* (written in collaboration with Herbert Thomas) was produced in London at Terry's Theatre. In 1904 he joined J. E. Vedrenne in the management of the Court Theatre and produced a fine range of modern plays, including several by Bernard Shaw, which were staged with great skill and understanding.

Granville-Barker's most popular play, *The Voysey Inheritance*, was first produced at the Court in 1905, and has been revived several times in other theatres with considerable success. His tragedy *Waste* was originally banned by the Censor, and its first production was a private one by the Stage Society, of which he was a keen member, in 1907 at the Imperial. A revised version of it was played at the Westminster in 1936. I might also mention his comedy *The Madras House*, first seen at the Duke of York's in 1910 and revived at the Ambassadors' in 1925.

The theatre has seen little of the work of Rudolf Besier (born in 1878) apart from his great success *The Barretts of Wimpole Street* which was produced at the Queen's in 1930, and ran for nearly two years, giving Gwen Ffrangcon-Davies a wonderful opportunity to make a great hit as Elizabeth Moulton-Barrett. Similarly,

Ashley Dukes, who opened the little Mercury Theatre in Ladbroke Grove, London, in 1933, is known chiefly for *The Man with a Load of Mischief*, which ran for eight or nine months at the Haymarket in 1925. The name of Clemence Dane (Winifred Ashton) brings to mind *A Bill of Divorcement* which ran for over a year at the St. Martin's in 1921–2, and *Will Shakespeare*, another success at about the same time.

As far as the theatre is concerned, John Drinkwater [1882–1937] will be remembered for his famous play *Abraham Lincoln*, one of the triumphs of the Lyric, Hammersmith, where it ran to over four hundred and fifty performances, commencing in 1919. Rather less successful was his *Oliver Cromwell* (His Majesty's, 1923) and *Robert E. Lee* (The Regent, 1923); but his comedy *Bird in Hand* ran for over a year at the Royalty [1928–9] and was a tremendous success in America. *Mary Stuart* was put on twice at the Everyman Theatre, Hampstead, and was revived at the Old Vic in 1933, but like most of Drinkwater's plays (with the possible exception of *Abraham Lincoln*) it can be appreciated more easily when it is read. He worked in an insurance office for some years after leaving school, but met Barry Jackson in Birmingham in 1907 and formed an amateur society known as the Pilgrim Players, whose success with *Abraham Lincoln* enabled him to abandon his commercial career.

A. A. Milne[1] (born in 1882) has provided us with such plays as *Mr. Pim Passes By* [1919], *The Truth About Blayds* [1921], *The Dover Road* [1922], *The Ivory Door* [1927], *Michael and Mary* [1929], and *Sarah Simple* [1937]; all with splendid dialogue.

Now we come to two more Irishmen. St. John Ervine was born in Belfast on December 28th, 1883, and although his early works have a strong Irish piquancy, he acquired quite an English style as he developed, no doubt because he often had the London audiences in mind as he wrote. His best play is probably *John Ferguson* (Lyric, Hammersmith, 1920), though Dame Marie Tempest excelled in *The First Mrs. Fraser*, which ran for nearly two years at the Haymarket, in 1929, and no less successful were *Anthony and Anna* (Whitehall, 1935) and *Robert's Wife*, that highly entertaining story of clerical life, which ran to over six hundred performances at the Globe in 1937–8.

Sean O'Casey was born in Dublin in 1884 and claims that he was educated in the streets of that city while selling newspapers. He did not even learn to read until he was twelve, and as soon as he left school he became a builder's labourer. By re-soling his own

[1] See *Writers' Gallery*.

boots with cardboard he was able to go regularly to the Abbey
Theatre, Dublin, and through careful study of the excellent plays
produced there he learnt the way to earn a living as a playwright.
Eight laboriously-written plays were rejected before *The Shadow of
the Gunman* was accepted and staged at that same theatre in 1923.
For three weeks it played to packed audiences, and many hundreds
of people were turned away. His scenes of life in Dublin's slums,
Juno and the Paycock ran to over two hundred performances at the
Royalty in 1925, and in the ensuing year brought him the Hawthorn-
den prize. The Easter Rebellion of 1916 inspired *The Plough and
the Stars* (Fortune, 1926). Although Bernard Shaw praised *The
Silver Tassie*, this brutally realistic play was not particularly successful
when it went on at the Apollo in 1929. *Within the Gates* was
produced at the Royalty in 1934, and in *The Star Turns Red* (written
in 1940) we have evidence of O'Casey's interest in Communism.
One of his latest works is the spirited comedy *The Purple Dust*,
published in 1942.

J. E. Flecker [1884–1915] died a disappointed man. He never
saw his masterpiece *Hassan* produced. This superb play was a
great success at His Majesty's in 1923, when it ran for nearly
three hundred performances.

We must not overlook two authors of light comedy whose
work has delighted millions without doing the slightest harm to
English drama : Eden Phillpotts and Ian Hay. The former was
born in India in 1862 and worked as an insurance clerk for ten years
before he began studying for the stage. His greatest success was
The Farmer's Wife which ran for over thirteen hundred performances
at the Court Theatre in the nineteen-twenties. Ian Hay (John
Hay Beith), born in 1876, gave us that most amusing play adapted
from his novel *The Housemaster* (over six hundred performances
at the Apollo, 1936–7), *Tilly of Bloomsbury* [1919], *A Safety Match*
[1921] and suchlike, besides collaborating with P. G. Wodehouse,
Stephen King-Hall and Anthony Armstrong in the writing of other
comedies.

Graham Moffat (born in Glasgow in 1866) will be remembered
for the sugary *Bunty Pulls the Strings* (Haymarket, 1911) ; Harold
Brighouse (born at Eccles in 1882) for the amusing Lancashire
comedy *Hobson's Choice* (Apollo, 1916), and Frederick Lonsdale
(born at Jersey in 1881) for the ever-popular musical play *The Maid
of the Mountains* (Daly's, 1917 ; music by Harold Fraser-Simson and
J. W. Tate). His best work was the play *The Last of Mrs. Cheyney*
(over five hundred performances at the St. James's in 1925), but

I might also mention the popular farce *On Approval* (Fortune, 1927), and perhaps the comedy *The High Road* (Shaftesbury, 1927).

A former director and manager of the Abbey Theatre, Dublin, Lennox Robinson, who was born in Cork in 1886, has given us such brilliant plays as the jolly comedy *The Whiteheaded Boy*, which had nearly three hundred performances at the Ambassadors' in 1920 and was subsequently revived on several occasions. Other Irish dramatists of modern times include Edward Martyn [1859–1923], Lady Gregory [1859–1932], William Boyle [1853–1923], T. C. Murray (born in 1873), Lord Dunsany (born in 1878), Seumas O'Kelly [1881–1918], Brinsley MacNamara (born in 1890), George Shiels (born in 1886), Teresa Deevey, and Paul Vincent Carroll (born in 1900), and it is interesting to note that several of them were connected in some way with the Abbey Theatre.

If the thrilling crime plays of Edgar Wallace [1875–1932] are of no great literary value, their usefulness in the theatre cannot be denied. The best, perhaps, was *On the Spot*, in which a notorious brothel-owner gets away with every crime imaginable, but eventually is convicted for one he did *not* commit!

The farces and other plays of Ben Travers (born at Hendon in 1886) have always been very popular, particularly with the repertory companies, who can generally make up their losses on the classics with such plays as *A Cuckoo in the Nest*, *Plunder*, *Thark* and *Rookery Nook*.

Next, I must mention Clifford Bax (born in London in 1886), one of the founders of the Phoenix Society, whose masterpiece *Socrates* I have not yet been able to see on the stage. He re-wrote John Gay's famous opera *Polly* for the Kingsway in 1922, and gave us the romantic play *The Rose Without a Thorn*, which delighted many discriminating playgoers at the Duchess Theatre in the spring of 1932, and again in the following year at the Duke of York's.

One of the greatest playwrights of the day is undoubtedly James Bridie, who was born in Glasgow in 1888, educated in that city at the High School and the University, and achieved his first success in London with *The Anatomist*, which opened the Westminster Theatre in 1931. Other notable productions of his were *Tobias and the Angel* at the same theatre in the following year, *A Sleeping Clergyman* at the Piccadilly in 1933, and *The Black Eye* at the Shaftesbury in 1935. He collaborated with Claud Gurney for *Mary Read*, which was put on at His Majesty's in 1934. His latest successes include *Mr. Bolfry* at the Westminster [1943], and *It Depends What You Mean* at the same theatre in 1944.

T. S. Eliot, who was born in America in 1888 but who has lived the greater part of his life in this country, gave us *Murder in the Cathedral* (Mercury, 1935) and *The Family Reunion* (Westminster 1939); and R. C. Sherriff must be mentioned for *Journey's End* which ran for nearly two years at the Savoy in 1929–30 before it was played all over the world.

The great popularity of Ivor Novello cannot be overlooked. He was born in Cardiff in 1893, educated at Magdalen College School, Oxford, and made his début on the stage in 1921. His rise to fame was considerably accelerated by several successes in filmland, but even if he had not become such a favourite as an actor, his musical shows and plays would not have failed to attract the public. One recalls without difficulty *Fresh Fields* (Criterion, 1933–4), *Full House* (Haymarket, 1935), *Comedienne* (Haymarket, 1938), *Glamorous Night* (Drury Lane, 1935), *Careless Rapture* (Drury Lane, 1936), and *Crest of the Wave* at the same theatre in 1937. In London and on its provincial tours *The Dancing Years* has done much to brighten up dismal wartime evenings.

No book dealing with the theatre in modern times would be complete without a reference to Noel Coward,[1] who was born at Teddington in 1899, and was a polished little actor before he knew his multiplication tables. He started writing plays when he was in that rather awkward state of being too good for minor parts and insufficiently experienced for major ones. *The Vortex*, one of his earliest, was given a trial at the Everyman Theatre, Hampstead, before it went on at the Royalty, and started his meteoric rise to fame. By describing his *Fallen Angels* as " disgusting, vile and obscene " the critics sent thousands of people to see it, and a year's run at the Ambassador's was assured for his best work, *Hay Fever*. His famous musical show *Bitter Sweet*, originally staged in Manchester, was a modest success at His Majesty's, London, but caused a furore in America : special cordons of police had to be called out to control the crowds, seats were sold by speculators for as much as two hundred and fifty dollars a pair, and Noel Coward's private box was stacked every night with flowers, caviare and champagne by obsessed admirers.

His *Private Lives* had a three months' run at the Phoenix in 1930, with himself, Gertrude Lawrence, Adrianne Allen and Laurence Olivier in the cast, before it went to earn its author new glory in America. The spectacular *Cavalcade* brought him an ovation at Drury Lane, but his greatest success in recent years has

[1] A biography will be found in *Writers' Gallery*.

been *Blithe Spirit*, which has broken the record for a non-musical play held for more than fifty years by *Charley's Aunt* with a run of about fifteen hundred performances. His famous film about the Royal Navy, *In Which We Serve*, has enhanced his reputation in other directions.

J. B. Priestley,[1] born in Bradford in 1894, remains a giant among contemporary dramatists, and a reasonable review of his work would occupy far more space than I am permitted in this book, but it is interesting to compare his early successes, *Dangerous Corner*, *Laburnum Grove* and *Eden End*, for instance, with his experiments related to the " Time " problem, *Time and the Conways* and *I have Been Here Before*, and again with his more recent plays, such as *They Came to a City* and *Desert Highway*. There are critics who deplore his departure from the rôle of a mere entertainer, but these gentlemen seem to forget that British drama would never make progress if our best writers concentrated only upon amusing comedies and other " commercial successes." Surely no one could complain that such a play as *How are They at Home ?* taxes too highly the mentalities of our " tired business men " ? His *Johnson over Jordan* was a highly interesting experiment.

There is of course a place in the modern theatre for such comedies as John Van Druten's *Young Woodley*, which ran to nearly five hundred performances at the Savoy in 1928, and there must be few who would fail to be entertained by the Edinburgh medical students in *The Wind and the Rain* (Merton Hodge) which was given over a thousand performances at the St. Martin's theatre about ten years ago.

Looking back over the successes of the last twenty years we find Anthony Armstrong's *Ten-minute Alibi*, which enjoyed a run of over eight hundred performances ; *Whiteoaks*, by Mazo de la Roche ; *While Parents Sleep*, by Anthony Kimmins, which ran for over two years at the Royalty from 1932 to 1934 ; Leon Gordon's *White Cargo*, which played to packed houses at the Playhouse twenty years ago, and which is still a favourite with some of our repertory companies ; Arnold Ridley's popular *Ghost Train* ; Michael Egan's *Dominant Sex* ; *Tons of Money*, the farce by Will Evans and Valentine, which ran for two years at the Shaftesbury in 1922-23 ; and Walter Greenwood's *Love on the Dole*.

Denis Johnston, who for a couple of years before the Second World War was the television producer at the BBC, must be mentioned for his brilliant study of idealism and modern problems,

1 See *Writers' Gallery*.

Laurence Olivier as Richard III in the "Old Vic" production at the
New Theatre

Ralph Richardson and Dame Sybil Thorndike in *Peer Gynt* at the
New Theatre

The Moon in the Yellow River.   Here is another clever Irishman—
he was born in Dublin in 1901—who is likely to play an important
part in the future of British drama.   The late Reginald Berkeley
should also be mentioned for *The Lady With a Lamp.*

One of the most brilliant of our younger dramatists is Emlyn
Williams.   Born at Mostyn, Flintshire, in 1905 and educated at
Holywell County School, in Switzerland and at Christ Church,
Oxford, he intended to make a career in the teaching profession,
but the Oxford University Dramatic Society whetted his appetite
for the stage, and in 1927 he appeared at the Savoy Theatre as
Pelling's 'Prentice in *And so to Bed.*   This led to many other engagements in London and New York.   One of his greatest successes
as a playwright was his thriller *Night Must Fall,* which was given
well over four hundred performances at the Duchess Theatre in
1935–6.   At the same theatre a long run of *The Corn is Green*
was interrupted by the declaration of war in 1939.   Since then
we have had from his pen such excellent plays as *The Light of Heart,*
The Morning Star, *A Month in the Country* (adaptation of Turgenev's
play), *The Druid's Rest* and *The Wind of Heaven.*

Charles Morgan, the novelist, scored a notable success as a
dramatist with *The Flashing Stream,* which ran for over six months
at the Lyric in 1938, with Godfrey Tearle and Margaret Rawlings
in the leads.   It is to be hoped that this talented writer will do more
for the theatre now that the playgoer has shown such interest in
his work.

All the early plays of Dodie Smith were written under the
pseudonym of C. L. Anthony.   Her early success *Autumn Crocus*
(Lyric, 1931) was soon followed by such plays as *Service*
(Wyndham's, 1932), *Touch Wood* (Haymarket, 1934), and *Call it a*
Day, which monopolized the Globe for over a year from 1935 to
1936.   With Dame Marie Tempest as Dora Randolph and John
Gielgud as Nicholas Randolph, her brilliant comedy *Dear Octopus*
began a magnificent run at the Queen's in 1938.   Hitler's invasion
of Poland terminated it in September, 1939.

A motor accident in 1932 killed one of our most penetrating
young playwrights, Ronald Mackenzie (born in 1903), whose
Musical Chairs was such a great success at The Criterion.

The tremendous success of his light comedy *French Without*
Tears, which was given over a thousand performances at the
Criterion seven or eight years ago, did not spoil Terence Rattigan,
one of our youngest and most promising playwrights of to-day.
He was born in 1911 and educated at Harrow and Trinity College,

Oxford. The declaration of war upset the run of his *After the Dance* at the St. James's in 1939, and air-raids did nothing to help his *Follow My Leader* at the Apollo in 1940, but his *Flare Path*, *Love in Idleness* and *While the Sun Shines* may be numbered among the more successful plays produced during the Second World War.

If we were considering American plays in this book, much could be said about Joseph Kesselring's *Arsenic and Old Lace*, one of the greatest hits of the war years, and now in its second year at the Strand Theatre.

Well over a thousand performances have recently been given of Esther McCracken's *Quiet Week-end* at Wyndham's. Her other plays include *Quiet Wedding* (Wyndham's, 1938), *Living Room* (Garrick, 1943) and *No Medals* (Vaudeville, 1944), all of which have helped to make her one of our most prosperous playwrights of to-day. In much the same class fall Gerald Savory's amusing comedies : *George and Margaret*, for instance, was a two-year success at Wyndham's.

Although light comedies such as these serve a useful purpose, their exploitation for purely financial reasons is to be deplored when they keep serious drama out of the theatre. Referring to the recent productions at the Bradford Civic Playhouse, Mr. J. B. Priestley said recently : " This list of productions contains more plays of fine quality than can be discovered in the *sum total of all the plays produced during the last five years in London's forty theatres.*" This alarming statement from a distinguished dramatist who knows what he is talking about should be taken to heart by all lovers of the theatre in the London area. We need not despair, because during the past year or two there have been signs of a steady— but very slow—improvement, but we must see that the thousands of young people who are just beginning to take an interest in the theatre do not acquire the " snappy light comedy " habit. Unless they are led to appreciate other things, thousands of playgoers will become quite content to patronize only the sort of show that con-sists of nothing but smart, sophisticated small-talk prattled in the inevitable lounge-hall of the ubiquitous country house by a handful of players in a state of extreme boredom. There is generally the long-suffering father, the mother who is pathetically trying to re-capture some of her lost youth, a couple of luscious daughters, a rebel son who turns out to be a Jolly Decent Fellow after all, and the youngsters' idiotic friends. All very amusing—in small doses, but not likely to be of much use in the development of an art that must play an important part in the cultural life of a progressive nation.

Chapter XI

THE MODERN THEATRE

DURING the first few decades of the twentieth century there has apparently been no shortage of people willing to invest their money in the building of theatres in London and the provinces. We have witnessed the erection of dozens of new playhouses of various types, but as soon as the cinema became a serious rival to living drama, a substantial number of these theatres were converted for the new form of entertainment. To make matters worse, several of the remaining theatres have now been put out of use by enemy action, so at the time of writing there is something of a housing shortage in London's " theatreland " : it is almost impossible to get a stage for a play unless you are associated with one of the syndicates that own the capital's principal theatres. It is not very much better in the provincial towns.

The history of these twentieth-century theatres is not of any great interest or importance, because commercial exploitation has robbed most of them of their individual character, in fact the average West End house has now become merely a commodity in the financial negotiations of syndicates and wealthy backers. A theatre in which the works of Shakespeare are staged one week will be given over to a run of a silly farce immediately afterwards, and this might be followed by anything from Ibsen to musical comedy, or even one of those shows in which the only attraction is a series of poses by a bunch of nude glamour girls. Such a theatre has no " policy " and therefore it can scarcely acquire a " personality." There are of course some exceptions. The New Theatre, for instance, has in recent years distinguished itself as a centre of culture by housing the Old Vic and Sadlers' Wells productions (though it is quite unsuitable as an opera house), the Haymarket has renewed its fame with Shakespeare, and the Prince's has made a reputation for ballet, but generally speaking, the average London theatre of today has little character of its own. However, the reader might perhaps like to know when some of them were built.

The London Hippodrome was erected as a variety theatre in

1900, and the same year saw the building of the Great Queen Street Theatre, which afterwards became the Kingsway. The Apollo and the New Century (renamed the Adelphi in 1930) followed in 1901, the New in 1903, and the London Coliseum in 1904. The Aldwych, Scala and the Waldorf (now the Strand) were all built in 1905. Hicks's Theatre, now the Globe, was erected in the following year; the Queen's and the Playhouse in 1907, the Little in 1910, and the Prince's and the London Opera House (the Stoll) in 1911. The little Ambassadors' Theatre opened in 1913, the St. Martin's in 1916, and the Winter Garden in 1919. The year 1922 saw the remodelling of the Drury Lane Theatre. Among our more modern theatres we find the Embassy [1928], Piccadilly [1928], Duchess [1929], Phoenix [1930], Cambridge [1930], Whitehall [1930], Westminster [1931], and the Saville [1931]. This is not, of course, a complete list, and does not include certain playhouses that have been transformed by ingenious remodelling—the Savoy, for instance, with which a clever architect has worked wonders. One of the best theatres we now possess is the Prince of Wales's, which was rebuilt in 1937.

The fan-shaped auditorium is now superseding the traditional circular and horse-shoe types of theatre, and the familiar old galleries have given way to one spacious steeply-inclined balcony in many of the modern playhouses. The historic old pit is rapidly disappearing and being replaced by a curved ground floor of stalls. Boxes are not likely to exist much longer.

All these changes have come as the result of experiments to decide the ideal design for a theatre in which every seat in the house provides its occupant with an uninterrupted view of the stage—and at a reasonable angle. But there is also another modern tendency in theatre design : to reduce the division between the actors and the audience by breaking away from the picture-frame type of proscenium. The idea behind this is to make the audience feel that they are in the same room as the players instead of looking on from a completely detached environment.

In criticizing the modern theatre, we must always bear in mind that the ever-soaring price of land in central positions in our great cities severely restricts the architect : he is generally compelled to fit his theatre into an oddly-shaped site encumbered in dozens of ways. Furthermore, he must comply most scrupulously with the innumerable regulations imposed to safeguard the general public in the event of fire. These latter restrictions are very often the cause of bad acoustics. A proscenium of anything but wood, for

JOHN GALSWORTHY

Two views of the interior of the Savoy Theatre, London

The Shakespeare Memorial Theatre at Stratford-upon-Avon, interior
and exterior

[From the painting by W. R. Sickert, by courtesy of the Leicester Galleries
Leslie Banks and Edith Evans in *The Taming of the Shrew*

instance, is detrimental to the sound of the actors' voices. I mention this because there has been very harsh criticism of some of our most modern theatres by people who insist that the architects knew nothing whatever about acoustics. In one or two cases this might be true, but on the whole, the designers of our modern theatres have taken great care to make the actors' voices audible under reasonable conditions.

It must be admitted that British theatre design compares unfavourably with that of America, Germany and one or two other European countries, but the above reason accounts for most of the deficiency. Perhaps the great revival of interest in drama and music will encourage one or two of our leading architects to specialize more in the design of theatres and concert halls in the future.

One more word about acoustics : we are likely to see a considerable advance in the use of discreet amplifiers in the future. I say " discreet," because I am not suggesting that we should allow loud-speakers to boom at us from the walls of our theatres. Cleverly concealed microphones will probably play an important part in the theatre of to-morrow.

Questions concerning comfortable seating need scarcely be mentioned here, because most of our more progressive theatre-owners have learned their lesson from the cinemas. Nevertheless, one cannot help expressing the wish that one could get in and out of one's seat without disturbing other people.

There is still plenty of scope for the improvement of ventilation, and it is to be hoped that our post-war engineers will not be too proud to learn from their American cousins. One can scarcely exaggerate the value of a good circulation of purified air, warm in winter and cool in summer, without a draught being felt by the audience *or the players*.

TECHNICAL DEVELOPMENT

At the beginning of the twentieth century there were still a few theatres with gas lighting, but it must not be imagined that these were unprogressive houses, because good gas lighting was at that time preferable to the early forms of electric illumination. At the Lyceum, for instance, electricity was not installed until Daly took over. In her *Memoirs*, Ellen Terry wrote, " When I saw the effect on the faces of the electric footlights, I entreated Henry (Irving) to have gas restored, and he did. We used gas footlights and gas limes there until we left the theatre for good in 1902. To this I attribute much of the beauty of our lighting." Needless to say, vast improvements in electric stage lighting were made in the following twenty years, particularly in America and Germany.

The mechanics of the theatre have been striving to perfect their devices to improve the illusion of reality, and unless the cinema kills the more spectacular type of show we are likely to see great developments in technical equipment after the war. A greater use of electricity will enable us to scrap all the old-fashioned mechanical devices, and the rambling switchboards we know to-day will probably in time be replaced by a neat console, something like the type used by the builders of cinema organs, at which the operator will be able to work wonders in blending and contrasting lights, and conduct all the mechanical operations by the touch of convenient little " knife-handle " switches.

The revolving stage, which at one time looked as if it would revolutionize the theatre, has not been used to any great extent in this country, chiefly because few of our theatres have sufficient space to permit the installation of it. As far as I am aware there are three in London, but only one is in use at the time of writing. This fascinating device originated in Japan, but fired the imagination of the German stage mechanics, and a successful revolving stage was introduced in Germany as early as 1896 by Karl Lautenschlager of Munich. It consisted of a large turntable upon which three or four sets could be arranged in advance, so that a complete change of scenery necessitated only a third or quarter turn of the disc.

Experiments have also been made in sliding stages, which allow the complete set to be withdrawn on one side while another is moved into position from the other side, and sinking stages. The latter convey the entire set down into an underground chamber, where the stage hands remove it bodily from the lift and replace it with the next, which is in due course elevated to the view of the audience. All very ingenious ; but as we shall see shortly, the modern tendency (as far as drama is concerned) is towards a great simplification of stage settings, and therefore the tremendous expense of these elaborate devices would be difficult to justify.

Drury Lane, by the way, which alas ! has lost its lead in the story of the English theatre, was for many years noted for the excellence of its mechanical effects previous to the Second World War. At the present time it is being used by E.N.S.A.

In recent years there has been a steady increase in the use of the cyclorama in place of the old drop-cloth. It is a large, elliptical, concave structure of plasterboard placed at the back of the stage, upon which lights can be directed to produce ingenious background effects. Quite plain, it is of neutral colour to take all hues, and it also helps by serving as a sounding board, unless, of course, it is only a flimsy affair of canvas. By skilful use, many wonderful and beautiful effects can be obtained.

MODERN TRENDS

The twentieth century has brought radical changes in the theatre and many " movements " to promote its art. To trace the beginning of the " modern " theatre we have to go back to 1889 when Pinero produced *The Profligate*, and to 1891 when a young Dutchman named J. T. Grein started the Independent Theatre with a performance of Ibsen's play *The Doll's House*, and then proceeded to stage Shaw's *Widowers' Houses*, Zola's *Thérèse Raquin* and Ibsen's *Ghosts* in an attempt to keep the theatre abreast with contemporary culture.

This venture horrified the general public and bewildered the critics. The newspapers declared that a man who had the audacity to produce such a vile foreign play as *Ghosts*, of which the theme is the hereditary effect of venereal disease, should be prosecuted or hounded out of the country. The great social value of plays of this type was completely overlooked, and it seemed impossible that anybody could improve upon the plays of the old conventional school of dramatists who politely and conveniently avoided all problems of economics, metaphysics and politics. The desire of Ibsen and Shaw to dispel all the shams that concealed the struggle between society and the individual was deliberately misunderstood, particularly by the type of bigot who fulminated against any reference to sex on the stage but who was glad to patronize the prostitute when business took him a safe distance from home.

Grein's Independent Theatre started the revolt, and this in its turn promoted the rebellion against the old ranting style of acting and the fripperies of mid-Victorian presentation of plays. Out of this arose the Stage Society, founded in 1900 to produce on Sunday evenings plays of outstanding merit and experimental works which could not be performed in the ordinary theatres for financial or other reasons. The great value of the Society's activities was not adequately appreciated at the time, yet it discovered Granville Barker, helped struggling dramatists, and paved the way for several other similar organisations.

Out of the revolt against the reactionary theatre sprang also the Repertory movement, and the Arts Theatre Club at which groups of members present worthy plays before their fellow members and friends. Finally came the wonderful growth of amateur societies, the British Drama League, and so forth.

In passing, let me give just one instance of the social value of significant drama. When he was Home Secretary, Winston Churchill went to see a performance of Galsworthy's *Justice*. It made such a profound impression upon him that he immediately reformed the system of solitary confinement in our prisons.

The revolt also brought to an end the apotheosis of the actor. Until late in the nineteenth century, the actor was the star, and nobody else—not even the dramatist—was of the slightest importance; in fact, one or two of the public idols surrounded themselves with mediocre players so that their own brilliance would be all the more dazzling. But Pinero, Ibsen and Shaw brought the dramatist into the limelight, as it were, and " Going to see Irving " became " Going to see Shaw's new play." In more recent times, the producer has tried to snatch the honour, and powerful producer-managers, if not imbued with profound artistry, tend to become a menace.

Of the utmost importance was the part played by the Court Theatre during the Vedrenne-Barker partnership from 1904 to 1907. J. E. Vedrenne was manager of the Court in 1904 when he sought Granville Barker's help in staging *Two Gentlemen of Verona*. Barker agreed to assist on condition that Vedrenne helped him with six matinée performances of Shaw's *Candida*. These were successful, and brought about the famous partnership which did so much for the younger dramatist and became a fine school for actors. It produced several of Shaw's plays : *You Never Can Tell*, *Man and Superman*, *John Bull's Other Island*, *Major Barbara* and *The Doctor's Dilemma*, and led to the Repertory movement. The Management transferred to the Savoy in September, 1907.

Bernard Shaw took the greatest interest in the Court Theatre at that time, and attended rehearsals personally to explain to the players exactly what he expected of them. At these rehearsals he frequently demonstrated by playing parts himself—even feminine rôles !

THE INFLUENCE OF GORDON CRAIG

As I have already said, the modern tendency is all towards a simplification of stage settings. This does not necessarily mean a simplification of stage devices, although it makes elaborate mechanism less essential in the modern theatre. For this trend, Gordon Craig (son of Ellen Terry) and his followers are partly responsible.

J. B. PRIESTLEY

DAME SYBIL THORNDIKE [*Bass*

When Craig began his career as a scenic designer he was profoundly dissatisfied with all the stage settings he found in general use, and reacted to Irving's great love of realism and lavishness by advocating a fundamental change in the use of scenery. He prepared a series of revolutionary designs for stage settings and exhibited them in London, Vienna, Berlin and other capitals, and also designed a complete series of sets consisting entirely of simple screens for a production of *Hamlet* at Stanislavsky's Art Theatre in Moscow, but these were not really satisfactory.

Craig made little impression in England, and his ideas have been beneficial here by their influence rather than their adoption. This influence has brought about a wholesome desire for a simplification of scenery, and there is every reason for believing that the future of stage art will lie in something severe and dignified rather than the elaborate and spectacular. This is a controversial matter which cannot be discussed in detail here, but there are several books on the subject for those who are interested. Something of Craig's ideas came out in Granville Barker's famous Shakespearean productions : he dispensed with a great deal of the Victorian rubbish that for years had encumbered players on the stage ; and a similar trend marked the productions of the Stage and the Phœnix Societies.

The basic idea of this school of thought lies in the artist's rejection of the realistic. It is maintained that the art of the theatre is not merely the art of *naturalistic* illusion, but of *imaginative* illusion employing colour and symbols as in other forms of art. " By means of suggestion," Gordon Craig declares,[1] " you may bring on the stage a sense of all things—the rain, the sun, the wind, the snow, the hail, the intense heat—but you will never bring them there by attempting to wrestle and close with Nature, in order so that you may seize some of her treasure and lay it before the eyes of the multitude. By means of suggestion in movement you may translate all the passions and the thoughts of vast numbers of people, or by means of the same you can assist your actor to convey the thoughts and the emotions of the particular character he impersonates."

This is reasonable enough, but this school has its more advanced sections in which we find individuals who advocate futuristic effects that would be quite unintelligible to the average playgoer, just as surrealist pictures are to the ordinary man and woman. In this there is a grave danger ; for if expressionism is to be carried to extremes, the theatre will lose millions of its patrons to the

[1] *On the Art of the Theatre.*

M

cinema. There are highbrow freaks in the theatre as in every other sphere of artistic activity.

Craig's influence did much to make people realize that the author, actor, producer and scenic artist must unite and co-operate closely to produce their work of art, but as soon as he tried to reduce the actor to the status of a marionette he lost a great deal of sympathy.

The Swiss Dr. Appia was also a great pioneer of stagecraft. He roundly condemned the use of two-dimensional scenery with three-dimensional actors, and experimented with plastics for special units which could be grouped in the composition of scenery. He also did great work in exploring new uses for lighting. By his many experiments he showed that spotlights could be used not merely for illumination, but to produce special effects that gave a sense of solidarity to everything on the stage.

Briefly, the modern scenic artist does a great deal more than merely provide a setting according to direction : he strives to build up an effective background or environment that is absolutely in sympathy with the *mood* of the play. The setting plays a highly important part in the drama, yet it must never be obtrusive. A room, for example, can be made to seem quite real without possessing features that distract the attention of the audience.

Simplification is the keynote of good stagecraft. A single arch can be made to suggest the interior or environment of a great cathedral more effectively than a dozen attempts at elaborate reproduction by the old-fashioned means. As Dr. Appia says in his excellent book *Die Musik und die Inscenierung* when making suggestions for the forest of *Siegfried* : " We must no longer try to create the illusion of a forest ; but instead the illusion of a man in the *atmosphere* of a forest. . . . When the forest trees, stirred by the breeze, attract the attention of Siegfried, the audience should see Siegfried bathed in the moving lights and shadows, and not the movement of rags of canvas agitated by stage tricks. The scenic illusion lies in the living presence of the actor."

The setting must form the perfect environment, and " set off " the actor. The two primary conditions for the artistic display of the human body on the stage, according to Dr. Appia are : " a light which gives it plastic value, and a plastic arrangement of the setting which gives value to its attitudes and movements. The movement of the human body must have obstacles in order to express itself. All artists know that beauty of movement depends upon the variety of points of support offered to it by the ground and by natural objects. The movements of the actor can be made artistic only through the appropriate shape and arrangement of the surfaces of the setting."

The art of the modern stage is a perfect but complex fusion of the play, the actors, the setting and the lighting. As I have already said, they must all blend perfectly into a single work of art : if one does not harmonize with the rest, the whole thing is spoilt. " The art of the theatre," says Gordon Craig,[1] " is neither acting nor the play, it is not scene nor dance, but it consists of all the elements of which these things are composed : action, which is the very spirit of acting ; words, which are the body of the play ; line and colour, which are the very heart of the scene ; rhythm, which is the very essence of dance." Where Mr. Craig and I part company is when he goes on to insist : "*One is no more important than the other*, no more than one colour is more important to a painter than another, or one note more important than another to a musician." This is a false analogy, and has produced a lot of foolish notions prattled by irresponsible people to the intense irritation of the dramatists —the creators of the drama. Nevertheless, however much we dislike the eccentricities of Gordon Craig, let us never forget that his initial revolt was to a great extent responsible for the *décor* of such enlightened designers as Albert Rutherston, Oliver Messel, George Sheringham, Norman Wilkinson and Paul Shelving—to mention only a few in England alone.

THE REPERTORY MOVEMENT

The Repertory movement was really a revival of the old " stock companies " which had sunk to an appallingly low level, chiefly because they had persisted in presenting the same old Victorian plays and had perpetuated the worn-out unimaginative style of acting in the belief that anything was good enough for the provinces. Most of them finally broke up on the rocks of the theatre-owners' greed, for rising rents in London encouraged provincial proprietors to increase their charges out of all reason.

Grein's Independent Theatre was a strong incentive to Miss Annie Horniman, who had been private secretary to W. B. Yeats and had found confidence in herself at the Abbey Theatre, Dublin. In 1908 she bought the derelict old Gaiety Theatre in Manchester, transformed it into a modern repertory theatre, and opened it with a company of her own. There were difficulties, of course, but the degree of her success and the value of its contribution to the English

[1] *On the Art of the Theatre* (1905).

theatre may be appreciated from the fact that in the ensuing four-teen years she staged *over a hundred new plays*, and at the same time presented a remarkable range of other worthy specimens of en-lightened drama. Her right-hand man for years was Iden Payne. One of the most important branches of Miss Horniman's work was the discovery and production of plays that reflected north-country life and problems.

Then in 1909 Alfred Wareing founded the Glasgow Repertory Theatre with the idea of establishing a Citizens' Theatre, and two years later Basil Dean took over the Liverpool Repertory Theatre (now called The Playhouse). In 1913 Barry Jackson and John Drinkwater founded the famous Birmingham Repertory Theatre, which has performed a wonderful service to British drama by encouraging new playwrights and training some of the finest young actors in the country. It was the first theatre to stage Shaw's *Back to Methuselah*.

After the Great War the number of " reps " grew rapidly, despite the opposition from the cinemas. In 1921 Nugent Monck reconstructed the Maddermarket Theatre, Norwich, as an Eliza-bethan playhouse for the Norwich Players. It was formerly a church, by the way. Then it was but a few years before every provincial town of any size had a repertory company of its own. At the present time there are nearly a hundred ; most of them resident in their own theatres or attached permanently to leased accommoda-tion : we find them at Bath, Birmingham, Blackburn, Bolton, Bournemouth, Bradford, Bristol, Burnley, Buxton, Cambridge, Colchester, Crewe, Darlington, Dewsbury, Dundee, Edinburgh, Farnham, Glasgow, Halifax, Harrogate, Hastings, Kew, Leaming-ton, Leeds, Leicester, Letchworth, Lewes, Liverpool, Llandudno, Loughborough, Lytham, Macclesfield, Malvern, Morecambe, Newcastle, Northampton, Norwich, Nottingham, Oldham, Oxford, Penge, Perth, Peterborough, Richmond, Rhyl, Rochdale, Rother-hithe, Rugby, Rusholme, Sheffield, Southampton, Southport, Stockport, Swansea, Swindon, Tunbridge Wells, Wakefield, Walham Green, Watford, Westcliffe, Wigan, Windsor, Wolver-hampton and York, for instance, but this is not a complete list. Even the small Buckinghamshire town of Amersham can maintain its own " rep " with their own little Playhouse. Then there are the many travelling repertory companies, among whom we find the Arts Repertory Players, the Bankside Players, Sir Barry Jackson's company, the Pilgrim Players, and Donald Wolfit's excellent company.

VIVIEN LEIGH in The Mask of Virtue (from the painting by D. Edzard in the possession of H. L. Holman, Esq.)

Mary Jerrold and Lilian Braithwaite in *Arsenic and Old Lace* (Joseph Kesselring)

Scene from *The Beggar's Opera* (Sadler's Wells Opera Co.) Below: Scene
from *The Swan Lake* (Sadler's Wells Ballet)

Margot Fonteyn and Robert Helpmann in *The Swan Lake* (Sadler's
Wells Ballet)

The Repertory companies are undoubtedly doing much to promote the cultural work of the theatre, and few people realize the enormous amount of hard work entailed in their modest productions. The members of the smaller professional companies that produce a different play every week work under an almost intolerable strain, and although the experience is of great value to the younger players, the sheer drudgery is apt to tell in their work unless they possess excellent physique and faultless memories. Apart from the perpetual financial worries, this is the greatest problem the " reps " have to face.

A wonderful example of what *can* be accomplished in a small way was set by Ronald Adam who took over the Embassy Theatre, Swiss Cottage, in 1932 with a capital of less than a hundred pounds, and produced a hundred plays in four years. Quite a number of them were transferred to the West End. London playgoers should also be proud of the good work that for years has been done at the Q Theatre at Kew.

THE GREAT WAR AND AFTER

The Great War caused a boom in the theatre that almost killed British drama. The fighting men on leave flocked to the theatres with their womenfolk ready to accept absolutely anything in their craze for sheer amusement. Unlike the servicemen of the present war, among whom we find substantial numbers who are genuinely interested in drama, music and other cultural activities, they seemed perfectly satisfied with anything amusing or spectacular. *Chu Chin Chow*, an oriental musical show that began as a pantomime, ran for two thousand two hundred and thirty-eight performances at His Majesty's from August, 1916. *A Little Bit of Fluff*, a silly farce, ran for three years at the Criterion.

The speculators of Big Business were quick to see their opportunity and swooped upon the theatres to exploit them in the scramble for huge profits. Rents soared to the most unheard-of heights. Syndicates were formed overnight in an attempt to secure a monopoly in leases, and the pernicious system of sub-letting was carried on to scandalous extremes. *A* would lease a theatre to *B* for £200 a week, *B* would sub-let it to *C* for £300 a week, *C* to *D* for £350 a week, and so on. One producer was compelled to pay £600 a week for a theatre that had been let at £100 a week in 1914.

The result of this was simply that in most cases good drama was abandoned in favour of vulgar, trivial stuff that would attract the masses of uneducated people. Sir Barry Jackson had to withdraw one of Shaw's plays because he was losing money on it, despite the fact that it was bringing in a thousand pounds a week!

In his book *The Theatre in My Time* St. John Ervine says that when the backer of several revues was asked to invest his money in a play he retorted: " Eh, laad, I doan't want nowt to do wi' no 'igh-brow mook."

One of the bright spots of the war was at the Old Vic, where Lilian Baylis, acting against the advice of every manager consulted, persisted in presenting the plays of Shakespeare. She also started a fine repertory company and established a permanent company for ballet.

After the armistice most of the cultural and experimental work was done by the " little " or repertory theatres in the suburbs and certain provincial towns. With the support of Arnold Bennett, Nigel Playfair reopened the Lyric, Hammersmith, and caused a minor sensation with his year's run of Drinkwater's *Abraham Lincoln*, and with a remarkable revival of *The Beggar's Opera* in 1920, which ran for over eighteen months.

In September, 1920, Norman Macdermott opened the Everyman Theatre, Hampstead, and produced many intellectual plays, including Masefield's *Tragedy of Nan*, Galsworthy's *The Foundations* and *The Little Man*, Zangwill's *The Melting Pot*, and Arnold Bennett's *The Honeymoon* in the first season alone. These heralded the fine range of plays that included many works of Ibsen and Eugene O'Neill, the famous American dramatist. Macdermott's seasons of Shaw plays also deserve mention.

During the following summer the Old Vic Company received an invitation from the Belgian Government to appear at the Parc Théâtre, Brussels. They presented six plays of Shakespeare with outstanding success. It should be recorded here that Miss Lilian Baylis's excellent work with the Old Vic Company was officially recognized in 1929, when she was created a Companion of Honour.

Noteworthy in post-war years was Mr. Robert Atkins's production at the Old Vic in 1922 for the first time in England of Ibsen's dramatic poem *Peer Gynt*, translated by William and Charles Archer. Since that time, by the way, the Old Vic has given all the works of the First Folio of Shakespeare, as well as *Pericles;* a splendid enterprise never before undertaken in any English theatre.

The British Drama League has also played an important part in the revival of our national drama. It was founded on modest lines in 1919 by Lena Ashwell, Edith Craig, the late J. Fisher White,

Elsie Fogerty, Penelope Wheeler, Norman Wilkinson, W. J. Turner and Charles Tennyson, with the object of encouraging the art of the theatre both for its own sake and as a means of intelligent recreation among all classes of the community. It would be impossible to review the work of all its various committees in this book, but those who are interested can get plenty of information from the League's Honorary Secretary, Mr. Geoffrey Whitworth, at 9 Fitzroy Square, W.1.

It is partly due to Mr. Whitworth's untiring activities that the National Theatre movement made such substantial progress in the years immediately before the outbreak of the Second World War. For the present, of course, the whole scheme is shelved, but the movement is now sufficiently strong financially to give us every confidence that a National Theatre will figure prominently in the plans for the rebuilding of London. There is now a possibility that the original site, on which Bernard Shaw received the Theatre's deeds in 1938, will not be used. How convenient and appropriate it would be if the new temples of drama and music, the National Theatre and the Wood Memorial Hall, could stand together in London and form the major buildings of a new cultural centre for the nation! For the erection and maintenance of these two meritorious institutions, private individuals are subscribing liberally out of the little that is left of their ruthlessly taxed resources. Is it too much to ask that a State which has spent untold millions in fighting a war to preserve the freedom and ideals of western civilization should spend just a little when it is over to provide a home for our national culture?

The first aim of the National Theatre movement must be the achievement of fine dramatic art for its own sake. The building will be erected in Shakespeare's name " To provide in the Capital of the Empire a theatre where the people may have continual opportunities of seeing the best drama, past and present, produced with the utmost distinction and played by actors of the highest merit; to maintain the efficiency and dignity of the art of acting by providing opportunities for its exercise in its highest classical departments; to keep the plays of Shakespeare in its repertory; to prevent recent plays of merit from falling into oblivion; to produce new plays and to further the development of modern drama; to produce translations of representative works of foreign drama, ancient and modern; to stimulate the art of the theatre through every possible and suitable means; to organise National Theatre Tours throughout this country and Overseas."

The story unfolded in this book will have proved to the reader that the ordinary commercial theatre alone cannot safeguard our dramatic heritage, because being dependent upon its box-office returns it cannot keep in being good plays that did well in their day but which have ceased to produce large profits out of revivals, and it cannot encourage the genius of contemporary dramatists while their works are unknown and untried. Freedom from the tyranny of the box-office and from the necessity of paying large profits to the investor will enable the National Theatre to undertake this important work, and at the same time become a university of drama. It will employ a permanent company of some twenty or thirty players on yearly contracts, and its management will be in the hands of a Director who will be responsible to the Governing Body.

THE SHAKESPEARE MEMORIAL THEATRE

This chapter would not be complete without a reference to the Shakespeare Memorial Theatre at Stratford-upon-Avon and its Festivals, for the fame of this institution has spread all over the world.

For the original theatre, which was opened in 1879 with *Much Ado About Nothing*, we are indebted to a Stratford citizen, Charles Flower [1830–1892] who struggled for years against the apathy of the general public, undismayed by the jeers and spiteful attacks of the London critics. He gave the site, headed the first subscription list with a gift of a thousand pounds, and issued a public appeal for funds. Confident that all cultured men of means and goodwill would give financial support to the project, he built a modern Gothic theatre at a cost of twenty thousand pounds, but to his amazement the Queen's loyal subjects remained blandly indifferent. The general attitude in London may be summed up in the words of a writer in one of our national newspapers at the time : " To my mind, the whole business of the Memorial Theatre at Stratford-upon-Avon is a solemn farce calculated to puff up a few local nobodies with a mistaken idea of their own importance."

The greater part of the twenty thousand pounds was therefore paid by Charles Flower out of his own pocket, and it is worth noting that this public benefactor whose munificence and tireless efforts established one of the greatest traditions in modern theatrical history, went to his grave unhonoured by any official recognition.

The first theatre was a small rococo affair seating about eight hundred. It was described by Bernard Shaw (many years later, of

G. BERNARD SHAW

EMLYN WILLIAMS

course), as "an admirable building adapted for every conceivable purpose other than that of a theatre." Nevertheless, it housed some of the finest performances of Shakespeare ever seen in this country, and received a Royal Charter of Incorporation in 1925.

In the following year it was destroyed by fire, though the treasures of its library and art gallery were saved, and a local cinema was taken over and adapted as a temporary house for the Festivals. An appeal to the entire English-speaking world for funds to build and endow a new theatre was made immediately, with the support of Thomas Hardy and the leaders of the three political parties, Stanley Baldwin, Lord Oxford and Asquith, and Ramsay McDonald.

The Governors arranged an open competition among the architects of Great Britain, Canada and the United States to design a building "simple, beautiful, convenient; a monument worthy of its purpose." All the entries were submitted anonymously to a tribunal of eminent architects. Their final decision was unanimous, but even then they did not know the name of the architect whose design they had chosen. The successful competitor was a woman of twenty-nine!—Elisabeth Scott, daughter of a Bournemouth doctor. Her great-uncle was Sir Gilbert Scott. Bernard Shaw declared "Miss Scott's plan is the only one that shows any theatre sense." The foundation stone was laid on 2nd July, 1929.

This splendid, dignified theatre, with its fan-shaped auditorium, spacious stage and excellent equipment was opened on Shakespeare's birthday, April 23rd, 1932, by H.R.H. The Prince of Wales, and the first Festival in it commenced with *King Henry IV* (parts I and II).

OPERA AND BALLET IN THE TWENTIETH CENTURY

From the beginning of the century to the outbreak of the Great War, the Grand Opera Syndicate maintained Covent Garden's tradition with German, Italian and French operas, but from 1914 to 1918 the opera house was rarely used. Sir Thomas Beecham ran two summer seasons of opera there in 1919 and 1920, and then for five years it was used only for short seasons given by the British National Opera Company and the Carl Rosa Opera Company.

From 1925 to 1927 the London Opera Syndicate presented some good "international" seasons under the musical direction of the illustrious Bruno Walter, but in 1928 the Covent Garden Opera Syndicate was formed to continue the work and successfully introduced Diaghilev's Russian Ballet as well.

After a year as principal conductor Sir Thomas Beecham became the Artistic Director in 1933, and under his able baton the opera flourished until the Second World War brought the work to a standstill. When the nation regained its confidence in 1941 and demanded the resumption of cultural activity, Covent Garden was not ready to meet the people's requirements, and to our national humiliation, the famous opera house was converted into a dance hall! In recent years this has pricked many consciences, and it is hoped that by the time this book appears in print Covent Garden will again have been put to its proper use.

During Sir Thomas Beecham's regime in the "thirties" the house offered not only the familiar works but many special attractions to the opera-lover, including *Koanga* (Delius) in 1935, a memorable visit of the Dresden Opera in 1936, and in the following year a visit of the Paris Opéra company, who gave a remarkable performance of *Ariane et Barbe-Bleue* (Dukas).

The present century has also seen a wonderful revival at Sadler's Wells. In March, 1925, the Duke of Devonshire and a strong committee issued an appeal for funds to reopen this theatre as a centre for operatic and dramatic productions. It had been closed for years, after having sunk to the level of a music hall.

Over seventy thousand pounds was raised, and on January 6th, 1931, it was reopened with Shakespeare's *Twelfth Night* under the management of Lilian Baylis of the Old Vic. The first opera in the new theatre, *Carmen*, was given shortly afterwards.

In time, Miss Baylis, who had continued to manage the Old Vic, arranged that only opera and ballet should be performed at Sadler's Wells, and that only drama should be produced at the other theatre, so "the Wells" became a permanent opera house, with Laurance Collingwood and Charles Corri as joint conductors. It encountered many difficulties during the years of economic depression, but with the help of generous patrons, the Carnegie Trust and the BBC, it was able to survive. Later conductors, guest or otherwise, included Warwick Braithwaite, Sir Thomas Beecham, Albert Coates, John Barbirolli and Herbert Menges.

The reopening of Sadler's Wells encouraged Miss Baylis to establish the Vic-Wells Ballet under Ninette de Valois, with Constant Lambert as Director of Music. The company included several members of Diaghilev's company, which by then had been disbanded. Alicia Markova and Dolin were the first principal dancers, but in 1935 they left to form a company of their own. The Vic-Wells Ballet soon distinguished themselves with complete performances of Tschaikovsky's *Swan Lake* and *The Sleeping Princess*, besides such enterprising attractions as *Checkmate*, *The Rake's Progress*, *Facade*, *Le Baiser de la Fée*, *Horoscope* and *Miracle in the Gorbals*.

THE SECOND WORLD WAR

The declaration of war early in September, 1939, was followed immediately by an order which closed every theatre in the land because of the danger of air-raids. Within a few weeks, however, public feeling against this measure was so strong that all places of entertainment were allowed to reopen. No huge aerial armadas were sent against this country during the first winter, and many of the theatre managers thought they would be able to settle down for another lucrative boom. One or two of the London companies that had planned extensive provincial tours in anticipation of the bombing of London found that even the extremely irksome black-out did not deter the playgoer. John Gielgud, who had revived Oscar Wilde's brilliant play *The Importance of Being Earnest* with great success in London during the summer of 1939, took it on tour and found a wonderful reception waiting for him in the larger cities of Britain.

Thunder Rock by an American dramatist, Charles Ardrey, and *The Light of Heart* (Emlyn Williams) were the first of the wartime successes. The general confidence in the spring of 1940 induced the British Council to send the Vic-Wells Ballet to Holland, and they were busy establishing their reputation in that country when the Germans swarmed in and they were compelled to fly for their lives back to England.

The autumn of the same year brought heavy air-raids on London, and almost all of the theatres in the capital were compelled to close. A few matinées were given, and I believe one variety theatre kept its doors open, but the companies concerned with drama kept alive only by tours in the provinces, and as the air-raids spread, even these became difficult. If my space were not so limited, a few stories of the courage of players during air-raids would not be amiss at this juncture. The pessimists began saying that drama, like music, was " done for."

Then the amazing thing happened. Out of the horror, misery and turmoil sprang a craving for beauty, inspiration, and—yes ! education. The people demanded music, art, literature, and not the least, drama. The orchestras that had for years been struggling to pay their way found themselves overwhelmed with demands for concerts, bookshops were besieged, and even the directors of our repertory companies got an occasional smile from their bank managers. As soon as the air-raids became less severe, London regained its confidence and the theatre boom began, but those who had anticipated a hundred-per-cent demand for Susan Saccharin and Bertie Butterdrop, seductive leg-shows and hours of " swing music " were mildly surprised to find a substantial proportion of the public demanding Shakespeare, Shaw, Bridie, Priestley, Ibsen, ballet and even opera ! The lighter forms of entertainment continued to boom, of course, particularly when London's population was swelled by millions of refugees and American servicemen, but the theatre was to some extent saved the humiliation it experienced during the Great War. Alas ! one or two of the best playhouses were reduced to smouldering heaps of rubble by German bombs, but the destruction has not been upon a sufficiently large scale to cause any great difficulties. As I write, London is still being attacked by the fiery darts of the wicked,[1] but although we could do with half-a-dozen more theatres, the shortage of play-houses is nothing like so acute as the appalling scarcity of concert halls.

Curious, too, is the eagerness of the public to see plays that reflect people's feelings and trials in wartime, but it should be noted that the demand has been only for war-plays of quality, and not for spy stories and other thrillers. *The Morning Star* (Emlyn Williams) and Terence Rattigan's *Flare Path* are typical of popular war-plays.

In addition to the wonderful work of the Old Vic touring companies since their theatre was damaged by enemy action, there has been the significant emergence of the recently-formed Old Vic Theatre Company administered by Tryone Guthrie under the direction of Laurence Olivier, Ralph Richardson and John Burrell. Ralph Richardson, Laurence Olivier, Dame Sybil Thorndike and Nicholas Hannen made quite a sensation in their first repertory season at the New Theatre with *Richard III*, *Peer Gynt*, *Arms and the Man* and *Uncle Vanya*.

This new movement towards repertory in the West End was also joined by John Gielgud's company at the Haymarket, which included Leslie Banks, Peggy Ashcroft and Yvonne Arnaud. Gielgud, who rose to fame in a spectacular fashion during the early years of the war with *Dear Brutus* and *Macbeth*, has now won new

[1] The flying bombs closed several theatres for a couple of months during the summer of 1944.

Stage Lighting Equipment at Covent Garden: (Top) Bank of lanterns
for illuminating the cyclorama. (Bottom) The Dimmer Banks

Control Board for the Remote Dimmers at Covent Garden. (Below): Control-console for stage lighting in the style of a cinema-organ console. (As used at the London Palladium)

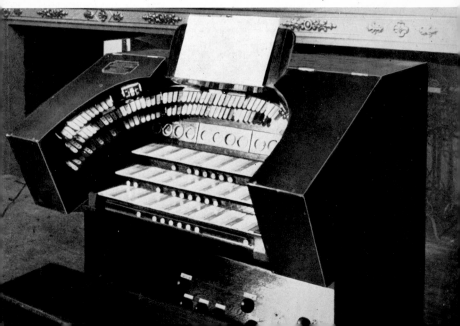

laurels with such plays as *Love for Love*, *Hamlet*, *The Circle*, *A Midsummer Night's Dream* and *The Duchess of Malfi*. This brilliant young actor's masterly Shakespearean productions will undoubtedly take their place in the history of the theatre.

Turning to opera, we find that during the war years the Sadler's Wells Company have been enjoying plenty of support both in London and in the provinces. They have been working under considerable difficulties, mounting the majority of their London productions in temporary accommodation at the New Theatre.

The tremendous interest in ballet at the present time augurs well for the future of this highly important branch of theatrical art. There are at least six companies in existence at the time of writing, all touring the provinces and giving more or less regular seasons in London. Apart from the Sadler's Wells Company we have the Anglo-Polish Ballet, Ballets Jooss, Ballet Rambert, the International Ballet, and Lydia Kyasht's company.

Perhaps one of the most significant developments in the theatre in wartime has been the extension of drama by C.E.M.A. (The Council for the Encouragement of Music and the Arts). The Council was formed in January, 1940, as a result of a suggestion made by Lord De La Warr, then President of the Board of Education, to the Pilgrim Trust. Three months later the Treasury made a " pound-for-pound " grant, and in March, 1942, the Pilgrim Trust was able to retire, leaving a thoroughly efficient organisation administering a Government grant. There are three panels of specialists to advise the Council on music, art and drama respectively. Mr. Ivor Brown is the Vice-Chairman of the Drama panel, on which we find J. B. Priestley, Miss Athene Seyler and Emlyn Williams ; and Mr. Lewis Casson is the Director of Drama.

Briefly, the Council associates itself with the work of non-profit-making theatre companies, making grants or loans as required, or acting as guarantor against loss, with the object of promoting the knowledge and appreciation of all that is of cultural value in the theatre. By this means such companies as the Adelphi Players, the Bankside Players, Dundee Repertory Company, the Glasgow Citizens' Theatre, Ballets Jooss, the Market Theatre, the Mercury Players, the Norman Marshall Company, the Old Vic Company, the Old Vic (Liverpool) Playhouse Company, Perth Repertory Theatre, the Pilgrim Players, Sadler's Wells Opera Company, Sadler's Wells Ballet Company, Tennent Plays Ltd., and the Travelling Repertory Theatre—have all been able to take drama (or ballet or opera, as the case may be) to remote parts of the country.

There are also six companies under the direct management of C.E.M.A. who are engaged primarily in performing at hostels for war workers. They are the Mary Newcomb Players, Ballet Rambert, West Regional Players, and the Stanford Holme, Walter Hudd and Patrick Ludlow companies.

Thus the people living in small towns and villages who in peacetime found it difficult to see even third-rate drama have now been visited by really competent artists playing anything from Shakespeare to Shaw. The work is continually extending, and there is little doubt that C.E.M.A. will continue to operate after the war. If the people of Britain demand a Ministry of Fine Arts in later years, C.E.M.A. might well be made the basis of it.

It is perhaps significant that the historic old Theatre Royal, Bristol, has through the efforts of C.E.M.A. become the first State-aided playhouse in Britain. In 1942 it was threatened with demolition, but loyal Bristol playgoers rose up in indignation, formed a Trust to buy it, and then leased it to C.E.M.A. It was redecorated, re-seated, and then reopened on May 11th, 1943, with Goldsmith's *She Stoops to Conquer*, preceded by a prologue specially written by Herbert Farjeon and spoken by Dame Sybil Thorndike.

C.E.M.A. is at present receiving a grant of a hundred and fifteen thousand pounds from the Exchequer. Here we have proof that the Government is willing to help the people if the people are prepared to help themselves. There is no reason why every town of any size should not possess its own Citizens' Theatre where good drama could thrive untrammelled by finance. This could easily be done through the existing repertory companies if they were backed by sound regional organization which would bring each theatre financial support from the villages in its area. (I am not in favour of making a charge upon the local rates for this purpose, because there would then be a danger of the Citizens' Theatre becoming merely a department of the local council under the control of a philistine committee). The people would in time regard their theatre as an essential instrument in their cultural life, and would be quite willing to pay for it by making an annual subscription which could entitle them to certain privileges not usually extended to the more casual play-goer.

The provinces have little or nothing to learn from London, and would do well to work out their own salvation in theatrical matters quite independently. They have nothing to fear. Efficient organization could make them quite independent of Government or municipal support, and it would be well to bear this in mind because the economic problems of the post-war period might seriously restrict or even terminate the activities of C.E.M.A.

The problems of the London theatres are rather different. The London manager caters for a cosmopolitan audience of anybody and everybody; unlike his provincial counterpart, he rarely "knows" his patrons, and looks upon everything as a speculation. If he decides to put on an intellectual play—not necessarily an "experimental" one—he knows that with an average amount of publicity and reasonably enthusiastic notices from the more enlightened critics he can "sell" the play to rather less than fifty thousand people. Yes, less than fifty-thousand out of the many millions who reside in the greater London area. His problem then is to get them all to come in the shortest possible time, and the money he makes, or loses, depends entirely upon the number of weeks' rent and other expenses he has to pay while they are making their attendances. But Shakespeare, you say, is booming at the Haymarket! Surely this means that there is quite a big demand for intellectual plays? Surely the people who are now demanding Shaw, Bridie, Priestley and Ibsen would flock to the London theatres if more good plays were put on? Surely they would continue to do so after the war?

Let me get this quite straight. I have said that those who expected a hundred-per-cent demand for light stuff were mildly surprised to find a substantial proportion of the public demanding Shaw, Shakespeare, Bridie and so forth. That is true, but of this number, only about one-tenth live in the greater London area at present, and of that tenth the majority are middle-class intellectuals who, if they are not in the services, are impoverished by taxation and cannot afford to pay West-end prices with any degree of regularity. They patronize the little suburban repertory theatres, and then if they are still unsatisfied, resort to play-reading. Out of the small amount of money they allow themselves for luxuries, they have to make allocations for symphony concerts and the purchase of books, and it must always be remembered that nothing short of sheer destitution would stop such people building up their own little libraries of treasured volumes. The poverty of the majority of the intellectuals in this country explains why most of London's forty-odd theatres are serving up revues, light comedies and whatnot. When there are plenty of people willing to pay fifteen shillings a head to see rubbish, why bother about the man with frayed cuffs who tenders half-a-crown for Ibsen?

Well, never mind, you say, we still have Shakespeare at the Haymarket. Yes, we have—just as long as Mr. John Gielgud and a couple of other people of his calibre lend their big names to it. Take Gielgud and one or two other brilliant people out of the cast and replace them with a few almost unknown but equally competent players and see what happens. When Gielgud fills a theatre for a Shakespearean production there are always plenty of people who go merely because they want to be able to talk to the Vicar about it. All the " best people " appreciate Gielgud.

It is chiefly in the more progressive Repertory Theatres that dramatic art is really thriving. There, the intelligent playgoer pays a few shillings, makes allowances for the innumerable difficulties under which the players are working and for the complete absence of springs in his seat, and finds satisfaction without being compelled to smoke dried cabbage leaves for a fortnight in order to pay for it. As the right sort of education prevails, the ranks of serious play-goers will continue to swell ; the majority of them will probably never be able to pay West-end prices, but why worry ?

Our story concludes, therefore, with the English theatre in a fairly healthy condition. It would be foolish to pretend that everything is just as it should be, but for the past two years there has been a steady improvement in all the conditions that affect the growth and well-being of dramatic art. Players and audiences alike have been stimulated with infusions of new blood, and the enthusiasm of youth is sweeping away the old prejudices and other stupidities that for years have retarded progress. Such enthusiasm, properly directed by enlightened people " wise and eloquent in their instruction," can and will secure the culture of our people in the difficult years that lie ahead of us.

INDICES

This book is indexed in two parts. Index I, (General) includes names of personalities, companies, theatres, places and subjects generally. Under Index II will be found titles of plays, opera, ballets, books and other literary and artistic works referred to in the text.

INDEX (1, General)

ABBEY Theatre, Dublin, 160, 165, 166, 179
Achurch, Janet, 159
Adam, Ronald, 180
Addison, Joseph, 53, 64, 65
Adelphi Players, 189
Adelphi Theatre (New Century), 106, 111–113, 125, 130
Admiral's Men, The Lord, 14, 19, 26, 32–34, 36
Ainley, Henry, 149
Albery, J., 128, 135, 137
Aldwych Theatre, 161, 162, 172
Alexander, Sir George, 149, 160
Alhambra, The, 133, 137
Allen, Adrianne, 167
Alleyn, Edward, 26, 32
Ambassadors', The, 161, 163, 166, 167, 172
Anglo-Polish Ballet, 189
Anthony, C. L., 169 (*see* Dodie Smith)
Angell Inn, Norwich, 85
Antoine, Mlle., 155
Apollo Theatre, 165, 170, 172
Appia, Dr., 178, 179
Archer, William & Charles, 182
Ardrey, Charles, 187
Armstrong, Anthony, 165, 168
Arnaud, Yvonne, 188
Arnold, Samuel, 99
Arts Repertory Players, 180
Arts Theatre Club, 175
Ashcroft, Peggy, 153, 156, 188
Ashwell, Lena, 182
Astley, Philip, 95, 107
Astley's Middlesex Ampitheatre (Olympic), 107
Atkins, Robert, 182
Austin, Esther, 133
Avenue Theatre, 138, 159, 162

BAKER, Joseph, 86
Ballet, 104, 137, 139, 171, 182, 185, 187, 188
Ballet Rambert, 189, 190
Ballets Jooss, 189
Bancroft, Lady (Marie Wilton), 119, 123–127, 130, 143–145
Bancroft, Sir Squire, 119, 124–126, 143–145
Banks' Cockpit, York, 86
Banks, Leslie, 156, 188
Bankside Players, The, 180, 189
Barker, H. Granville, 159, 160, 163, 175–177
Barrett, Wilson, 133, 152
Barrie, Sir James, 138, 148

Barry, Edward, 121
Barry, Mrs. Elizabeth, 44, 46, 47, 55
Barry, Spranger, 72–75
Bateman, H. L., 128
Bath, 59, 84, 85, 88, 91, 93, 109, 112, 147, 180
Bax, Clifford, 166
Baxter, Robert, 27
Baylis, Lilian, 182, 186
Beaumont & Fletcher, 40, 45, 54
Beaumont, Francis, 35
Becket, Mrs. G. A., 114
Beecham, Sir Thomas, 185, 186
Belgravia Theatre, 136 (*see* Court Theatre)
Bellamy, Mrs. George Anne, 72, 75
Belle Sauvage, La, 14
Bennett, Arnold, 161, 182
Benson, Sir Frank, 151, 160
Berkeley, Reginald, 169
Bernhardt, Sarah, 123, 135, 141, 158
Besier, Rudolf, 163
Betterton, Thomas, 43–46, 51, 52, 54, 55
Bijou Theatre, 158
Birmingham, 83, 92, 101, 112, 132, 164, 180
Birmingham Repertory Company, 154, 155
Birmingham Repertory Theatre, 180
Blackfriars Theatre, The, 17, 20–22, 32
Boar's Head, The, 14
Booth, Barton, 53–55, 57
Booth, Edwin, 152
Boucicault, D. L., 107, 124, 127, 130
Bowman, Mrs., 44
Boyle, William, 166
Bracegirdle, Mrs. Ann, 44, 46, 49, 55
Bradford, 143, 155, 180
Bradford Civic Playhouse, 170, 180
Braham, Augustus, 131
Braham, John, 114
Braithwaite, Dame Lilian, 156
Bridie, James, 154, 156, 166, 188, 191
Brighouse, Harold, 165
Bristol, 25, 88–90, 93, 109, 112, 147, 180, 190
British National Opera Company, 185
Brooke, Gustavus, 108
Brough, Lionel, 152
Browning, Robert, 116
Bruce, Edgar, 125, 139
Brunswick Theatre, The, 96
Buckstone, J. B., 116, 125, 126, 132, 147
Bull The, 14
Bunn, Alfred, 102, 112
Burbage, James, 16, 17, 20–22, 27
Burbage, Richard, 17, 18, 27, 32, 35
Burke, Edmund, 78